# Wealth and the Demand for Art in Italy
## 1300–1600

# Wealth and the Demand for Art in Italy

## 1300–1600

RICHARD A. GOLDTHWAITE

The Johns Hopkins University Press
Baltimore and London

28830

Originally published, 1993
Johns Hopkins Paperbacks edition, 1995
04 03 02 01 00 99 98 97 96 95     5 4 3 2 1

The Johns Hopkins University Press
2715 North Charles Street
Baltimore, Maryland 21218-4319
The Johns Hopkins Press Ltd., London

Library of Congress Cataloging-in-Publication Data

Goldthwaite, Richard A.
Wealth and the demand for art in Italy, 1300-1600 / Richard A.
Goldthwaite.
p.     cm.
Includes bibliographical references and index.
ISBN 0-8018-4612-9 (hc : alk. paper)
ISBN 0-8018-5235-8 (pbk. : acid-free paper)
1. Wealth—Italy—History.  2. Art patronage—Italy—
History.  3. Art, Renaissance—Italy.  4. Consumption
(Economics)—Italy—History.  I. Title.
HC310.W4G65   1993
339.4'7'0945—dc20     92-38328


A catalog record for this book is available from the British
Library.

# Contents

# Contents

# Acknowledgments

THE FOLLOWING FRIENDS READ PARTS of this manuscript at one moment or another in its evolution and generously and frankly offered helpful comments: James Banker, Karen-edis Barzman, Alison Brown, Patrick Chorley, Samuel Cohn, Dale Kent, Kent Lydecker, Kathleen Much, Reinhold Mueller, Alessandro Nova, Duane Osheim, Marco Spallanzani, Phoebe Stanton, William Tronzo.

I am deeply indebted also to the institutions that have provided financial support for this project: the John Simon Guggenheim Memorial Foundation, for a fellowship to study in Italy; All Souls College, for an invitation to spend two terms in Oxford; the Center for Advanced Study in the Behavioral Sciences, Stanford, for a visiting fellowship (with financial support provided by the National Endowment for the Humanities and the Andrew Mellon Foundation); and, above all, the Johns Hopkins University, for sabbatical leave in all the above instances.

# Wealth and the
# Demand for Art in Italy
## 1300–1600

# Introduction

WHY DID ITALY PRODUCE SO MUCH ART in the Renaissance? We are so conditioned to regard these products as art that a question about mere quantity seems somehow irrelevant if not irreverent. Yet, with respect to the level of demand as well as to taste, patronage in Renaissance Italy represented something new in the history of art, for people not only redirected their spending habits according to new canons of style, but they demanded substantially more art and a greater variety of it. Acquisition of art was in fact a notable economic activity. Had palaces and churches, villas and gardens, sculpture and painting, and the variety of ecclesiastical and domestic furnishings all been produced in the traditional medieval style, we would still be confronted with a major change in material culture. Italians not only enlarged their world of goods: they invented a seemingly infinite variety of new forms, they refined the skills with which these things were produced, they introduced fashion as a dynamic for the continual renewal of demand, and, finally, they initiated the quest for the very definition of art that elevated some of these goods into a higher spiritual realm. All this productive enterprise gave rise to the tradition of skills and the social diffusion of taste that are today deeply embedded in the culture of Italy and that have strongly colored foreigners' image of the country. The material culture resulting from this production, therefore, deserves to be brought into our picture of the Italian Renaissance on its own terms. Consumption itself is a cultural phenomenon of which art is only one manifestation.

The central task of this study is to view art in the larger context of the world of goods of which it is a part and to consider the demand for art as therefore subject to some of those forces that generate material culture by changing the quantity and nature of goods in general. Seen in this perspective, the things we today call art have characteristics not fully comprehended in the term—namely, functions within the material culture of a society; and these functions set the parameters in which the demand for art operates. In a certain sense, the thrust of the evolution of the very definition of art from the Italian Renaissance onward has been to obscure its relation with ordinary things, an effort that has culminated in the isolation and exaltation of art objects in today's museums. To show how wealth and material culture affect the demand for art is not to denigrate one of the greatest achievements of our own civilization but, on the contrary, to enhance the fascination of art by putting it in its most essential context, one that in fact only further excites our wonderment at the power of art to go beyond the very terms of its existence as a physical object.

Art, including the demand for it, is traditionally studied on its own terms. Indeed, it is possible to select any distinct kind of object out of the universe of goods for research into the variables that impinge on the demand that brings it into its existence. The demand for panel painting, for instance, has been studied within the cluster of considerations that constitute the standard agenda of art-historical research—form, content, style, painters, and patrons. In this framework demand arises from the intentions of the patron; and although these are often difficult to sort out for any one person, the range of possible motivations—piety, retribution, commemoration, conspicuous consumption, pride, pleasure— is set within a system of values and attitudes specific to a particular culture. Traditional patronage studies operate within this context for demand and tend to focus on individual patrons, artists, and works.

Whatever the motivation for demand, however, choice is confined to the larger world of goods in which the patron lives out his or her life. A fifteenth-century Florentine who commissioned Botticelli to paint an altar picture could have had a variety of motivations for doing so; but prior to selecting the artist, that patron probably had already arrived at the decision to do something about the physical arrangements of an altar. This prior decision occasioned—though not necessarily so—the demand for a picture along with a variety of other things for the altar. That Botticelli got the commission is a matter of the patron's taste, but that so much of Botticelli's output consisted of altar pictures is a matter of society's needs. The demand for art, then, depends on changing needs for certain kinds of things; and although these needs operate as variables that do not necessarily prompt a demand for art, material culture conditions an essential component of this demand.

THE TRADITIONAL HISTORIOGRAPHY OF RENAISSANCE ITALY has little to say about these new consumption habits. What explanations have been proffered are general and tend to emphasize the precocious development in Italy of a capitalist economy complete with the accumulation of wealth and the emergence of a bourgeois mentality. Yet, to say Italians consumed more in the Renaissance because they were wealthier is to overlook the extraordinary wealth of the Bardi, Peruzzi, and other early fourteenth-century merchant-bankers, not to mention the great landed aristocrats of northern Europe, just as to attribute the new consumer behavior to the spirit of bourgeois accumulation requires us to regard sixteenth-century Italians as more bourgeois than the Bardi and Peruzzi—a notion that raises more than a little perplexity.

Another aspect of bourgeois behavior that has been seen as imping-ing on Italian consumption habits is social emulation. Historians have taken it as virtually a law of social behavior throughout the history of medieval and early modern Europe that wealthy non-nobles imitate the ways of the nobility and seek to enter into its ranks. Georges Duby regards this behavior as the explanation for the downward diffusion of aristocratic values that gave vitality to the development of medieval culture in general; and historians who have discovered the roots of modern consumerism in the eighteenth century take it for granted that once people in the lower ranks of society had more disposable wealth and greater access to markets with cheaper goods, they instinctively directed their consumption to social emulation. This law is widely held as operative also in the behavior of Italian urban elites during the Re-naissance: scholars from Alfred von Martin to Robert Lopez have built major interpretative schemes about the Renaissance on the transforma-tion of the bourgeoisie into an aristocracy. Social emulation, however, no more than greater wealth or bourgeois mentality explains why Ital-ians wanted new kinds of objects that were not part of the material culture of the traditional nobility. Moreover, to characterize this con-sumption as the absurd and wasteful spending that Thorstein Veblen, looking at modern society in the light of the law of social emulation, encapsulated in his popular concept of "conspicuous consumption" begs the question of just what is the prestige that makes something conspicuous—the craftsmanship of a relatively inexpensive maiolica vase or a panel painting, for instance, as against the much greater intrin-sic material value of jewels, silver plate, and other traditional luxury goods.

The anthropologist Daniel Miller concluded his recent book on con-sumption by observing that it has been a "surprisingly elusive compo-nent of modern culture, which, although apparently highly conspicu-ous, has consistently managed to evade the focus of academic gaze, and remains the least understood of all the central phenomena of the mod-ern age, that is material culture."[1] Very likely consumption has so

1. Daniel Miller, *Material Culture and Mass Consumption* (Oxford, 1987).

eluded anthropologists and historians alike because, ironically, it is so conspicuous. In our supply-sided economic world, with its culture of consumerism, consumption is viewed from the side of the producer, not the consumer; it is exalted primarily as the main engine of economic activity, fueled by the insatiable appetite of consumers, lubricated by advertisers, and driven by capitalist producers to keep the entire system going. Not surprisingly, perhaps, the vulgarity and triviality of contemporary consumer culture have so appalled moralists and intellectuals that they have refused to consider the possibility of making some cultural sense of consumption on its own terms as a willful act of the consumer. In any case, to consider consumption in Renaissance Italy as the greed and individualistic self-gratification characteristic of *homo oeconomicus* is to undervalue the extraordinarily expansive nature of the Renaissance world of goods and to overlook the common objectives and shared values of individual behavior, just as to condemn consumption as the alienating materialism of an exploitative economic system is to ignore the cultural values Italians generated through the goods they bought.

We would do well to heed John Ruskin's challenge to traditional economic analysis, still valid after a century: Ruskin "fearlessly" condemned economics as no science at all, because it "omitted the study of exactly the most important branch of the business—the study of *spending.* . . . The vital question, for individual and nation, is never 'how much do they make?' but 'to what purpose do they spend?'" This study has thus arisen out of the curiosity of an economic historian about the demand that stimulated the arts sector of the Italian economy to extraordinary performance from the fourteenth through the sixteenth centuries, when it underwent growth with respect to innovation and variation of products and to refinement of processes as well as to total output. The task was to search for the wellhead of the demand for durable goods that nourished this artistic vitality, and much of the burden of the discussion is to put into relief the conditions that were peculiar to Italy in contrast to the rest of Europe. The study, in short, tries to say something about the new consumption habits of Italians that produced a major change in their material culture.

THE TRADITIONAL ANTHROPOLOGICAL APPROACH to consumption rests on the assumption that people buy intentionally as the result of a deliberate decision informed by the values of their culture. Rather than buying goods merely for private enjoyment, inspired by individual tastes, people fill up their environment to give order to their world and endow it with a meaning that justifies their very existence. Moreover, within this cultural context the goods people surround themselves with help establish, and maintain, relations with other people, so that consumption involves them in a sort of ritual activity. Even if certain kinds of consumption seem only to satisfy personal pleasure rather than to make a social statement, it is nevertheless likely that those pleasures themselves are socially conditioned. In short, any particular historical configuration of consumption habits appears as a function of the culture of that moment in a way that blurs distinctions between luxury goods and necessities, between taste and needs, between, even, art and other kinds of objects.

This approach fails, however, to deal with one of the most notable aspects of the history of consumption in modern times: the internal dynamic of change. The new consumption habits Italians developed in the Renaissance differed from traditional behavior not only in substance with reference both to material goods and to cultural values: demand also acquired an inner dynamic for growth and change of a kind it had never had before. The Italians worked out and defined values, attitudes, and pleasures in their possession of goods so that these things became the active instruments for the creation of culture, not just the embodiment of culture. The act of consumption, therefore, became an interactive process between consumer and goods by which culture itself was generated; and in this sense it will not be an anachronistic exaggeration to talk about something we can rightfully call consumerism. The new consumer habits introduced into economic life a creative and dynamic process for growth and change that was fundamental to the development of the West, becoming eventually, in our own times, the most characteristic feature of our economic system; it also opened up an expansive world of goods in which people came to have a new kind of relation to their possessions.

In a sense, the result of this enquiry is an enlargement of Jacob Burckhardt's classic—and much debated—vision of Renaissance Italy as the birthplace of the modern world; to his formulation about the Italians' discovery of antiquity, nature, man, and the individual is here added their discovery also of things. As much as anything else, these habits of spending marked what is new about the Renaissance and what set Italy off, economically as well as culturally, from the rest of Europe at the time. Moreover, the venture of Italians into the world of goods may be said to have inaugurated modern times, for the new attitude about goods that arose in Italy marked the first stirring of what today is called consumerism.

Art, too, belongs in this context. It was in this heady atmosphere of an expanding and changing world of goods that Italians discovered art, and the history of how they did this has yet to be written. In the Middle Ages art did not exist as a primary category by which objects were identified; but if, in the course of the Renaissance, art created consciously as such emerged as a specific kind of object, this new realm of art did not have an altogether autonomous existence. For all the exaltation of art in our own times, art still is an integral part of material culture. Art is an index to culture not only for the style in which it is made and for the scholarly, literary, and religious ideas that make up its content but also for its mere existence as a consumer object. Whereas we know something about how art eventually achieved its intellectual status in the Renaissance, with the separation of the higher "fine" arts from the "minor" ones, we do not know very much about why many kinds of art objects came into existence in the first place. In any case, the eventual emergence of an attitude about art as a particular kind of object, consciously endowed with style and with content, is one of the most notable features of the Renaissance; by the same token, the emergence of self-conscious patronage of the arts, in practice and as an ideal, marks one distinctive way consumption habits changed in the Renaissance. In fact, by enshrining these objects in museums we pay homage to the luxury consumption of the past and thereby reverently celebrate the passion for spending for things that keeps the capitalist system of the West going.

THIS BOOK, THEN, IS NOT A HISTORY of Renaissance art as that subject is traditionally understood. It is in a certain sense not about art at all. It makes no attempt to interpret works of art, to explain changes in style or the emergence of various regional and stylistic schools of artists, to deal with taste and preferences, or indeed to say anything at all about why art looks the way it does. In fact, this study is largely indifferent to the quality of art, and it has nothing to say about individual artists. Moreover, the discussion is not directed to putting art in its usual social context. The reader will encounter as few individual patrons as individual artists, and he or she will learn little about patronage in general as that subject is currently understood. Nor will the reader be led into the social content of Renaissance art by way of a study of its subject matter or its ideological assumptions. Finally, there is no discussion of the art market understood as the mechanism for the artist-patron nexus. Instead, this study of demand shifts the focus from all these considerations about art in particular to the overall material culture of which it was a part.

The discussion is divided into three parts. The first part presents the economic background for demand, and the second and third parts deal with the demand that generated the material culture—religious and secular—out of which art emerged. The first part assumes that greater wealth was a permissive cause for the rise in consumption, and the discussion therefore involves in part an assessment of the general performance of the Italian economy, although the objective is not a comprehensive economic history of Italy. Rather, the argument is directed, first, to demonstrating the continual accumulation of wealth in Italy throughout the Renaissance that was the necessary precondition for consumption and, second, to analyzing the structure of this wealth to show how its distribution and fluidity conditioned demand.[2]

The point of departure for the discussion of the demand for religious art in the second part is the consideration of what is called a consumption model, by which is meant not a historian's construct of a configuration of variables that explain behavior but a collectivity of goods that constitute the objective of consumption. Within the world of religious goods this model was defined by liturgical functions. The material culture of religion throughout this period underwent change not so much in its essential nature as in its sheer quantity and extent, and therefore the rise in the production of religious art is attributed to the increase in the number of consumers and the rise in the level of their consumption. This discussion involves an analysis of both the demand from within the church for enlarging its physical plant and the demand by the lay public for the kind of clerical services that entailed consumption of liturgical goods. The concern is less with the spiritual forces behind demand than with the identification of the agents of demand, or consumers—less, in other words, with the content of religious art than with the magnitude of its production.

In the third part the demand for secular art is related to altogether new consumption habits that arose out of the unique conditions of urban society in Italy. The burden of the discussion is to show how a new secular consumption model arose, how it represented a departure from traditional consumption habits of medieval Europe, and how it accounts for a vast expansion of the material world of goods, including for the first time the elevation of many kinds of goods to the realm of art. The model as defined here consists only of durables associated with housing—buildings and domestic furnishings—and not food or clothing, since architecture and the decorative arts comprehend most of the things we associate with the Renaissance world of art—palaces, villas, and gardens on the one hand; the pictures, sculptures, and other kinds of furnishings filling up these spaces on the other. It is argued that

2. An earlier version of Part I appeared in *I Tatti Studies*, 2 (1987), 15–39.

this material culture represented the first stirring of the urge to consume that was to break out in what is now called the consumer revolution in the eighteenth century and culminate in the consumerism of our own times.

To recapitulate in somewhat different terms, each of these three parts constitutes a discrete study of demand: the first, demand as a function of wealth and therefore of the performance of the economy; the second, demand as a function of the number and identity of consumers; and the third, demand as a function of the goods consumed. The demand factor has been much neglected—or rather, taken for granted—in the economic history of the West; demand has been regarded as arising from needs and taste, both of which have roots deep in generalized culture— if not the human psyche—much beyond the pale of the economic historian's scholarly expertise. One of the ultimate objectives of this investigation is to inspire more methodological exploration of ways to get a grip on a historical understanding of this essential dynamic of any economic system.

What is missing in the scheme presented here for the study of demand is a consideration of demand as also a function of the producer, a notable absence inasmuch as the argument can be made—as will be adumbrated in more than one place in the ensuing discussion—that it was in Italy during the Renaissance that artists became the first producers in the history of the economic development of the West consciously to refine the techniques for taking control of demand, manipulating and arousing it yet further in order to attract it to their own output. This aspect of demand is an essential—if not, indeed, the defining—dynamic of modern consumerism; but a discussion following this path would take us to the supply side of the marketplace and therefore beyond the confines drawn for the present discussion. I hope to deal with the subject in a second volume dedicated, in fact, to the production of art in Italy from the fourteenth to seventeenth centuries.

Some may consider it a highly suspicious enterprise to talk about Italy as a whole in this early period, protesting that at the time the place was little more than a geographical expression and that in any case no one can ever hope to master the scholarship of such a fragmented historiographical tradition; to them I can only respond that this book does not pretend to be either a comprehensive survey that follows a precise chronological and geographical scheme or a monographic study that rests solidly on new research and a thorough review of all the secondary literature. Instead, what follow are discursive and very general essays that range widely over a diverse variety of historical themes in the history of Renaissance Italy; but overarching the entire enterprise is a concern for the uniqueness of Italy and its artistic traditions in European history, for the relation of wealth to patronage, for the work of art as artifact in the context of material culture, for the background for the very discovery of art, and, more generally, for the origins of modern consumer culture.

# The Economic
# Background

THE LEVEL OF WEALTH
Economic Performance
Political Transfers
Accumulation of Wealth

THE STRUCTURE OF WEALTH
Urban Concentration
Social Distribution and Redistribution
The Rich Get Richer

DECLINE AND CONCLUSION

THE RISE OF DEMAND in Renaissance and Baroque Italy for churches and palaces and for their furnishings brought about a massive transfer of resources from savings and investment to consumption. The extent of spending is self-evident in the extraordinary abundance, variety, and quality of goods that still survive; in fact, the very enormity of Italy's artistic patrimony has inspired this investigation into the material conditions of its creation. Another measure of this consumption can be taken in the widespread view of economic historians that the appropriation of so much wealth for consumption rather than for investment must account for the eventual economic decline of Italy from the sixteenth century onward. This spending, according to Ruggiero Romano, summing up the received wisdom in a recent survey of the period, put at least a "veritable brake" on the economy.[1] If consumption reached a level at which it had such a negative effect on the performance of the economy, presumably because it drew resources away from more productive uses, then one might wonder about the basic economic conditions that provided Italians with so much disposable wealth and about the extent to which wealth alone accounted for the rise in demand for consumer durables.

Economic conditions do not explain why people want the things they buy. Yet, whatever its wellhead, demand has somehow to get to the marketplace: its path there follows the course made possible by the economic system, and once there, it is conditioned by the realities of the marketplace. Wealth fixes the limits for spending: it is a permissive, not an effective, cause of consumption. Moreover, the distribution of wealth determines the number of consumers and the level of their consumption; and its redistribution or fluidity, putting wealth in new hands, determines one process by which demand is renewed and thereby sustained. The vigor of demand, therefore, depends, first, on the amount of wealth available for spending and, second, on the social structure through which wealth is distributed. In both respects Italy enjoyed extraordinarily favorable conditions for the development of a

1. Ruggiero Romano, "La storia economica. Dal secolo XIV al Settecento," in the Einaudi *Storia d'Italia*, Vol. 2, pt. 2 (Turin, 1974), p. 1865. The more recent survey by Maurice Amyard, "La fragilità di un'economia avanzata: L'Italia e le trasformazioni dell'economia," in the Einaudi *Storia dell'economia italiana*, Vol. 2 (Turin, 1991), pp. 5–137, does not discuss consumption and luxury production.

luxury market, and the elucidation of these conditions is tantamount to an economic "explanation" of the Renaissance considered not as a new period in the history of taste but as a consumption phenomenon. The level and structure of wealth, in other words, help explain why demand was so vigorous and why, therefore, production of consumer durables became a highly conspicuous, if still relatively small, sector of the Italian economy.

## THE LEVEL OF WEALTH

### Economic Performance

The extraordinary consumption that resulted in the material culture of the Italian Renaissance was sustained by the immense wealth of Europe's most developed economic area. Economic growth in Italy was historically founded on the geographical position of the peninsula in the Mediterranean, between the Near East on the one hand and western Europe beyond the Alps on the other. The older urban economies of the Near East were relatively developed with respect to the production and commerce of luxury goods, and from the eleventh century onward markets for these same luxury goods opened up in the developing rural economies of western Europe. Growth and development within Italy resulted from the enterprise of Italian merchants in various towns as protagonists in the trade between these two economic areas.

In the commercial sector Italians monopolized the trade of luxury items imported from the Near East and distributed throughout northern Europe; going abroad into both areas as merchant-colonizers, they dominated the maritime transport of these goods, created the network for their distribution, and promoted trade in other goods to balance payments. With the possibility of transferring credit throughout this vast commercial system, stretching across the Mediterranean and western Europe, the Italians also created a financial infrastructure, becoming Europe's preeminent international bankers; and they extended this activity into princely finance, including the vast international operations of the papacy. Finally, within Italy itself productive forces arose in the agricultural and manufacturing sectors directed, on the one hand, to balancing payments for luxury goods from the Near East and, on the other, to meeting the growing demand in the luxury markets of the West. In short, Italians aggressively took the initiative in exploiting the relation between the developed economy of the eastern Mediterranean and the undeveloped economy of western Europe. They were the leaders in the economic growth of the West from the eleventh century onward, and their own economic development outpaced that of the rest of Europe. The Italian system, being oriented toward the export of goods and services, had built into it a favorable balance of payments with western Europe, and therefore Italy enjoyed a continuing accumulation of wealth.

The clear leadership Italians exerted in the economic growth of the West is well understood for the medieval phase. It is widely thought, however, that with the demographic crisis brought on by the plagues of the mid-fourteenth century the Italian economy began its secular decline. Indeed, most older economic interpretations of the Renaissance explain the release of resources for consumption as the very mark of decline. According to one thesis, the Black Death and successive devastating plagues of the fourteenth century produced an "inheritance effect" of hedonistic spending as a result of the greater wealth enjoyed by the survivors. A more widely cited explanation, however, is the so-called Lopez thesis: economic "hard times" after the Black Death discouraged entrepreneurs from further ventures and thereby released more wealth for consumption, which was in effect a kind of "investment in culture" to achieve social status by men who saw their business prospects threatened. This notion, suggested by Robert Lopez in a public lecture a generation ago, has taken on the status of a "thesis" not because he or anyone else has elaborated on specific aspects of the proposition but rather because, given the logic of its own terms, it has provided a convenient and congenial explanation for a major change in economic behavior. Thus the notion has appealed to those historians who seek in the economic and social world confirmation of the political decline Italy clearly underwent as communal governments were transformed into oligarchical and despotic regimes and the entire peninsula fell victim to the international balance-of-power struggle among the great European monarchs. The historiographical phenomenon of the extraordinary success of such a disembodied thesis is itself an indictment of historians for our failure to come to grips with a central problem in Italian Renaissance studies.[2]

The view that the Italian economy was contracting in the Renaissance through the sixteenth century has for the most part been conducted from the vantage point of knowing how things came out in the

2. See bibliographical note in Richard A. Goldthwaite, "The Economy of Renaissance Italy: The Preconditions for Luxury Consumption," *I Tatti Studies* 2 (1987), 17. More recently Ruggiero Romano, in his conclusion—"Linee di sintesi"—to *Storia dell'economia italiana*, 2: 338–44, rejects the notion of any significant change in the Italian economy from the thirteenth through the eighteenth centuries, labeling the entire period as one of "stagnazione plurisecolare." Some of the contributions to this recent volume, however, contradict such an interpretation.

end. The economic development of Italy arose as a result of the initiative Italians took in the Middle Ages to exploit its intermediary geographical position between two distinct economic areas—the Near East, with its well-established urban markets in luxury goods, and Europe, with its slowly developing rural economy. By the fifteenth century Italian economic development had left the Near East behind, and Italians were fully exploiting the new markets that opened up in the region with the expansion of the Ottoman Empire. In the other arena of their operations, however, the Italians faced serious challenges that eventually they could not meet. In northern Europe the situation was the reverse of what it was in the East: from the sixteenth century onward northern Europe began to catch up and do for itself what the Italians had been doing for it, so that Italians were slowly forced to relinquish their role as protagonists of economic development. Except for the Genoese, they lost out completely in the shift of international trade away from the Mediterranean to northwestern Europe as the European economy expanded into the Atlantic and subsequently around the entire globe; and the Genoese, who had tied their fortunes to Spain, eventually lost out as that power went into decline in the seventeenth century.

With the rise of the new world system of trade, the Near East was circumvented as a major international entrepôt for goods from the Far East. Hence, the Mediterranean lost its central position in the traditional spice trade; moreover, the entire region came into the orbit of the English and Dutch maritime empires. By 1600 the wool staple was collapsing in the face of competition, even in its home markets, from the cheaper new draperies of the English; and except for silk, exports declined to a trickle of specialized luxury products—increasingly including the accumulated artistic patrimony of past production. In short, the Italians lost the eastern prop of their economic position, while in the expanding western markets they were preempted by northern Europeans; and so Italy was eventually isolated in a backwater of the rapidly expanding global economy of modern Europe. "Let us face it," admitted a Florentine in the eighteenth century, looking back on better times, "our economy rested on a monopoly. We waxed rich thanks to the barbarous ignorance and indolence of others."[3]

Hence, by the seventeenth century, worldwide expansion of the European economy had left Italy behind, and demographic stagnation within the peninsula would seem to indicate that the economy had reached the upper limits of its ability to sustain the population. In the

---

3. Quoted in Domenico Sella, *Crisis and Continuity: The Economy of Spanish Lombardy in the Seventeenth Century* (Cambridge, Mass., 1979), p. 104.

traditional view, however, several important aspects of the economic situation in Italy have been overlooked, and they are the major themes in the following discussion. First, certain structural features of the operations of Italians within the international system as a whole remained intact well into the seventeenth century if not beyond, assuring a continuing favorable balance of payments and hence the further accumulation of wealth, albeit at an ever slower rate. Second, further development within the internal economies of Italy continued throughout the sixteenth century even while markets abroad were contracting. Backward linkages from the cloth staple (wool and silk) were forged within Italy itself to assure the supply of raw materials; and a consumer linkage released altogether new productive forces, including those that created the material culture of the Renaissance. Finally, much wealth poured into Italy through political and ecclesiastical channels completely outside the economic sphere of normal business operations.

Whatever the nature and extent of decline in the later Renaissance, therefore, Italy did not lose the immense wealth it had accumulated during the earlier era of vigorous economic expansion. On the contrary, internal economic development generating new wealth continued into the seventeenth century, by which time the Italians had clearly lost any role whatsoever in the expanding economy of early modern Europe. In the view sustained here, in short, Italy developed internally into what Carlo Cipolla has called a fully mature economy by the standards of the preindustrial capitalist world; and this economy had sufficient momentum to keep going, at least for a while, even as its export sectors closed down. The objective of the following discussion is not to present a comprehensive view of the performance of the Italian economy but to put into relief the continuing accumulation of wealth, however that performance is to be judged, through the Renaissance and into the seventeenth century.

THE LEADING SECTORS OF ITALIAN SERVICE OPERATIONS abroad—the "invisible" exports—continued to show many positive signs of further development throughout the later Middle Ages and into the sixteenth century. Improvement in the efficiency of shipping resulted in the greater regularity and frequency of voyages and in lower insurance rates and transportation costs. Banking profited from a rise in the demand for financial services from the great monarchical states of northern Europe at a time when their fiscal systems were not yet well enough developed to handle all the problems arising from their growth as political and military organizations at the end of the Middle Ages. This market expanded too rapidly for the Italians to maintain a monopoly, and by the sixteenth century they faced competitors from Germany and elsewhere who often were in a better position than the Italians to use political leverage to advance their financial interests. Nevertheless, the Genoese were the first to take advantage of the financial opportunities that opened up with the worldwide expansion of Spain at the beginning of the sixteenth century; and before the rise of Amsterdam in the seventeenth century, they dominated the great international financial fairs that moved from Lyon to Besançon in 1535 and finally, in 1579, to Piacenza in Italy itself.[4]

The staple in international trade was luxury cloth, and in the historiography of decline much has been made of the contraction of the northern European markets for Italian woolens at the end of the Middle Ages in the face of rising production in the Low Countries and in England. Nevertheless, the Italian industry continued to flourish even though its market became more confined within the Mediterranean area. Cheaper sources for wool were found in Spain and in central and southern Italy itself; as a result of this latter development, the agricultural sector in the region was strengthened, and the wool industry in Italy as a whole enjoyed increased self-sufficiency. Moreover, new markets opened within Italy. The two largest markets were Naples and Rome, both of which became boom cities as capitals of revitalized states that attracted much wealth from abroad—Naples as the capital of the trans-Tyrrhenian kingdom of the Aragonese, and the papacy as the seat of the international ecclesiastical system. In response largely to the growing internal market, the industry in Florence, Venice, and other northern cities greatly expanded production and improved quality in the fifteenth and sixteenth centuries. Moreover, with the establishment of the Ottoman Empire, important new markets opened in the eastern Mediterranean; and by the end of the fifteenth century the most important centers for the production of wool cloths for export were probably selling enough cloth there to balance payments for raw silk and other luxuries from the region. It was not until the beginning of the seventeenth century that the Dutch and English invaded the Mediterranean and captured its markets—including those in Italy itself—with their lighter and cheaper woolens.[5]

The reversal in the silk market came close to being complete. With

4. H. Kellenbenz, "Lo stato, la società, e il denaro," in Kellenbenz and A. De Maddalena, *La repubblica internazionale del denaro tra XV e XVII secolo* (Bologna, 1986), esp. pp. 340–68.

5. Hidetoshi Hoshino and Maureen Fennell Mazzaoui, "Ottoman Markets for Florentine Woolen Cloth in the Late Fifteenth Century," *International Journal of Turkish Studies* 3 (1985–86), 20–21.

the commercial growth of the great maritime cities in the eleventh century, silk became a principal item of international trade. Both Venice and Genoa encouraged production in their eastern colonies, but Lucca succeeded in establishing itself as the first major center of production in Italy itself, although there had been some production in Sicily and Calabria in the Byzantine period. Evidence has been found for production in other places in the thirteenth century, following the immigration of silk workers from Lucca; and from the early fifteenth century onward the industry flourished in Florence, Bologna, Genoa, Milan, Venice, and subsequently in other smaller towns across northern Italy. Italian silk came to dominate markets in northern Europe, and, like wool cloth, it eventually moved into markets that opened up in the Near East after the establishment of the Ottoman Empire. Concurrently, with the promotion of silkworm culture throughout Italy, in both the north and the south, backward linkages were developed to the supply of the raw material; and by the mid-sixteenth century the industry, like wool, was largely supplied from the home territory. In the seventeenth century new markets opened up in central and eastern Europe and in Spanish America. The historiography of early modern Italy has taken slight account of the extent to which the vigor of this industry alone probably assured Italy a favorable balance of payments well into the eighteenth century.[6]

The less familiar history of cotton is only slightly less a success story.[7] This new industry appeared in the towns of northern Italy from the twelfth century onward; and if Italy was never able to supply this industry with raw materials (except the small quantities that came from Venetian imperial possessions), cotton cloths nevertheless became a major export to northern Europe. Although, beginning in the fourteenth century, German competition cut seriously into these markets, Italians continued to dominate the trade in the best-grade raw materials, which came from the Near East, and the Lombard cities maintained a monopoly in the higher-quality products. Finally, all these textile industries—wool, silk, and cotton—were further strengthened at the end of the Middle Ages by the cultivation of woad in Lombardy, the opening of the alum mines at Tolfa, and the increased domestic produc-

6. Bruni Dini surveyed the history of this industry in Italy in the later Middle Ages at the XXIV Settimana di Studi of the Istituto Internazionale di Storia Economica "Francesco Datini" at Prato in May 1992, dedicated to the history of the silk industry in Europe; his paper will be published with the proceedings. See also notes 21 and 22 below.

7. Maureen Mazzaoui, *The Italian Cotton Industry in the Later Middle Ages, 1100–1600* (Cambridge, 1981).

tion of other dyestuffs, so that the entire sector of the cloth staple largely freed itself from dependence on foreign sources for these secondary raw materials.

From the thirteenth century onward the manufacturing sector expanded into a great variety of luxury crafts whose development followed a pattern of increased variation and innovation of products, steady improvement of competitive advantage in local markets against imports from abroad, and expansion into foreign markets. Liturgical utensils, accessories, and furnishings constituted a distinct category of these goods that satisfied a steady demand generated by religious needs, and Italian products enjoyed great success in markets abroad—at Avignon, for instance, where Francesco Datini, the merchant of Prato, imported liturgical vestments, silver and gold utensils, and paintings produced in Florence at the end of the fourteenth century.[8] Other products were cheaper substitutes for imports and were produced in great quantities and distributed widely abroad. Already in the thirteenth century the Venetians complemented their maritime economy with the production of glass, saddles, soap, metalwork, items made out of rock crystal, and other luxury goods.[9] The history of maiolica, albeit a minor industry, encapsulates this development within the manufacturing sector oriented to the production of consumer durables. By the fourteenth century, Italians in various places were learning how to produce high-quality tin-glazed pottery of the kind that heretofore had been imported from the Islamic world; and by the sixteenth century, the industry had expanded the variety of its products, both in style and form, much beyond anything known in the Near East, hence stimulating demand and finding new markets both at home and abroad. The same development characterizes the history of panel painting, from the importation of Byzantine icons in the thirteenth century to the growth of numerous and distinctive local industries (or "schools"), culminating in the highly individualized production by artists in the sixteenth century who worked on personal commissions from all over Europe.

Some of these industries, like wool and silk, expanded their markets abroad not only into northern Europe but eventually, by the fifteenth century, into the Near East itself. Such was the general economic decline of the Near East at the end of the Middle Ages that Italians found

8. R. Piattoli, "Un inventario di oreficeria del Trecento," *Rivista d'arte* 13 (1931), 246–47.

9. Angeliki E. Laiou, "Venice as a Centre of Trade and of Artistic Production in the Thirteenth Century," in *Il medio oriente e l'occidente nell'arte del XIII secolo*, ed. Hans Belting (Bologna, 1982), pp. 11–26.

markets there for agricultural products such as oil, sugar, honey, and saffron;[10] and they were able to capture the new markets that opened up with the conquest of the eastern Mediterranean by the Ottomans in the later fifteenth century. Besides cloths—silk and wool but also less expensive cotton and linen—Italians exported many other luxury and nonluxury items produced in Italy to the Ottoman world. Glass and soap, for instance, were supplied by Venice;[11] and maiolica from various places has been found in archaeological excavations in Egypt. The economic growth of Italy thus reached the point where the relation between developed and underdeveloped areas that provided the dynamic for so much of the luxury trade in the Mediterranean earlier in the Middle Ages was completely reversed. When in 1489 the Florentine government sent an embassy to the Egyptian sovereign, the accompanying gifts included silk cloths, gold brocades, and furniture in wood worked with ivory and bone—luxury items produced in Florence and requiring the kind of craftsmanship that had been the pride of Islam a century earlier.[12]

ARGUMENTS FOR THE ECONOMIC DECLINE of Italy have largely been based on performance of those sectors oriented to foreign markets. Seen in this international perspective, the economy certainly underwent a relative decline at the least; but contraction of markets abroad did not necessarily mean loss of a favorable trade balance, however much it was reduced. A favorable balance of payments in foreign trade from exports both visible and invisible, however, was not the only source for the accumulation of wealth. Throughout the fifteenth and sixteenth centuries the internal economy underwent considerable development. First, the infrastructure of the economy was strengthened as regional economies improved on the utilization of local resources; second, as increased wealth got channeled into consumption, rising internal demand stimulated growth in the manufacturing sector outside the cloth staple that went well beyond product substitution for luxury goods formerly imported from the Near East.

Development in medieval Italy was highly uneven throughout the peninsula: being politically fragmented into a large number of city-

10. Eliyahu Ashtor, "Il commercio italiano col Levante e il suo impatto sull'economia tardomedioevale," in *Aspetti della vita economica medievale* (Atti del Convegno di Studi nel X Anniversario della morte di Federigo Melis, 1984; Florence, 1985), pp. 15–63.

11. Michael Rogers, "Glass in Ottoman Turkey," *Deutsches Archäologisches Institut, Abteilung Istanbul: Istanbuler Mitteilungen* 33 (1983), 239–66.

12. M. Spallanzani, "Fonti archivistiche per lo studio dei rapporti fra l'Italia e l'Islam: Le arti minori nei secoli XIV–XV," in *Venezia e l'oriente vicino* (Venice, 1989), pp. 85–86.

states and a few territorial principalities, Italy was, in a certain sense, only a geographical expression for a variable collection of urban and regional economies. Nevertheless, the polynuclear urban structure of the economy of Italy underwent a process of tighter integration in the course of the later Middle Ages. The port cities of Venice and Genoa built extensive internal trade networks oriented toward international markets, and the international merchants and financiers of Genoa and Florence found increasing opportunities in new luxury markets and government finance within Italy itself. The regional infrastructure was also strengthened. Venice, Milan, and Florence developed as centers of extensive regional economies that by the fifteenth century were being reinforced by political domination of the capital city. The incorporation of central Italy into the papal states resulted in the emergence of Rome as a capital city integrating the entire region in a single fiscal and economic system by the sixteenth century. By this time, too, Naples as the capital of the Aragonese trans-Tyrrhenian kingdom dominated the south. The increasing reliance of the cloth staple in the north on sources in the south for the supply of both wool and especially silk, the exploitation of both the papal states and the kingdom of Naples by northern financiers, and the rapid growth of Rome and Naples as luxury markets for northern merchants were all major factors in the further integration of much of the peninsula into a veritable economic system. In the mid-sixteenth century Piedmont, too, was brought into this system by Genoese and Milanese merchants who found the court at Turin a new market for luxury goods and the countryside an important source of supply for raw silk.

The development that followed from this greater economic integration of Italy in the fifteenth and sixteenth centuries has been put into a new perspective by recent scholarship directed to studying specific local economies. These studies have shown how the continuing development in both the manufacturing and agricultural sectors increased productivity and generated additional wealth within the overall Italian system at a time when foreign sources of wealth were drying up; and the growing consensus about the continuing vigor of various regional economies of Italy through the sixteenth century has superceded the older view of general decline based chiefly on the increasing difficulty Italians had in selling goods and services abroad and on notions about the so-called retreat of investment to the land and the wasteful expenditure for luxury goods.[13]

---

13. For a recent historiographical discussion, see Judith Brown, "Prosperity or Hard Times in Renaissance Italy?" *Renaissance Quarterly* 42 (1989), 761–80.

The economies of the three major cities that had promoted much of the earlier expansion still showed considerable strength in the fifteenth and sixteenth centuries. The case for Genoa is by far the clearest. After having lost their eastern Mediterranean empire and suffered prolonged political instability in the later Middle Ages, Genoese merchants, speculators, and financiers nonetheless moved into the expanding Spanish empire in the sixteenth century. With their hands deep in the Spanish till, into which flowed the immense treasure found in the New World, they rapidly ascended to the highest rung of international banking and finance, where they exercised extensive control over the great financial fairs. This expansive phase in the history of international finance, in fact, has been called "the century of the Genoese," and it lasted well into the seventeenth century. In Florence both the wool and silk industries remained strong through the sixteenth century; and some Florentine bankers, though now increasingly concentrating their activities in Italy itself, enlarged the scale of their operations much beyond the level of their better-known predecessors of the Quattrocento. The strongest case for decline has been made about Venice, which in the course of the sixteenth century saw the loss of its traditional maritime power in both shipping and commerce. At the same time, however, growth of the industrial sector, including luxury textiles, glass, and a variety of metallurgical and chemical products, allowed Venice to maintain a favorable balance of payments, though bullion continued to flow eastward in the spice trade; and with the stabilization of the population in the seventeenth century, the level of employment remained high and real income did not fall. Moreover, the city's territorial expansion on the mainland in the later fifteenth century carried with it considerable development in the agricultural sector, including land reclamation, introduction of rice and maize, and more rational estate management.[14]

It is of some historiographical significance, given traditional notions about the negative effects of the Spanish domination of much of Italy in the later Renaissance, that our view of the economies of the two regions directly ruled by Spain has been subject to the greatest revision. In Lombardy, metallurgical industries in Milan remained strong; manufacturers of arms and armor found new markets by successfully retool-

---

14. G. Cozzi and M. Knapton, *La repubblica di Venezia nell'età moderna dalla guerra di Chioggia al 1517* (Turin, 1986), p. 172; Richard T. Rapp, *Industry and Economic Decline in Seventeenth-Century Venice* (Cambridge, Mass., 1976), pp. 165–66; Ugo Tucci, "Venezia nel Cinquecento: Una città industriale?" in *Crisi e rinnovamenti nell'autunno del Rinascimento a Venezia*, ed. V. Branca and C. Ossola (Florence, 1991), pp. 61–83. The literature on the agricultural sector is reviewed in Paola Lanaro Sartori, *Un'oligarchia urbana nel Cinquecento veneto: Istituzioni, economia, società* (Turin, 1992), pt. 7.

ing to meet technological innovations in firepower as well as to enhance artistic quality of traditional hand arms. Both silk and wool industries expanded in provincial cities as well as in the capital, and Cremona enjoyed considerable prosperity as a major producer of cottons. Milan had a heavy concentration of industries of various kinds, most of whose production (according to a commentator in 1631) was exported to other states; and the city was noted for its artisans. A large number of manufacturers also sprang up throughout the countryside, and Domenico Sella has emphasized the importance of the development of rural industries as the foundation for the later leadership of the region in the industrialization of modern Italy. Moreover, the "move to the land" by urban investors is now seen not as a flight of capital from the city but as a conscious business decision. As a consequence of heavy investment in irrigation systems, land reclamation, farm buildings, mills, and habitations, the rural economy was reinvigorated with improvements that increased productivity. Investment in both rural industry and agriculture was partly a consequence of the territorial policy of the Spanish to break the hold cities traditionally had on the rural economy.[15]

The Kingdom of Naples, too, experienced vigorous economic development under the Spanish—at least initially, before it eventually fell into the torpor that has been its fate ever since. The capital city attracted the nobility to settle permanently in it; and the astounding growth of its population, increasing by four to five times from the beginning of the sixteenth century to the middle of the seventeenth to become Europe's largest city, outpaced the population growth of the rest of the kingdom to the point where the city may have accounted for a sixth of the total population. This growth in itself generated an expanding urban market that stimulated agricultural enterprise throughout the kingdom. Merchants from other Italian cities—above all, the Genoese but also Florentines—ever mindful of new markets and ready to take advantage of the vacuum left behind by absentee barons now living in Naples, invaded the countryside and moved into the position of intermediary between owners and peasants. With the countryside thus exposed to entrepreneurs and speculators, traditional feudal exploitation became

---

15. Carlo M. Cipolla, "The Decline of Italy: The Case of a Fully Matured Economy," *Economic History Review* 5 (1952), 181; Giovanni Vigo, *Fisco e società nella Lombardia del Cinquecento* (Bologna, 1979), pp. 9–20; Sella, *Crisis and Continuity*; Aldo De Maddalena, *Dalla città al borgo: Avvio di una metamorfosi economica e sociale nella Lombardia spagnola* (collected articles; Milan, 1982); Luciana Frangioni, "Aspetti della produzione delle armi milanesi nel XV secolo," in *Milano nell'età di Ludovico il Moro* (Milan, 1983), 1: 195–200; idem, "La politica economica del dominio di Milano nei secoli XV–XVI," *Nuova rivista storica* 71 (1987), 253–68.

endowed with a genuine capitalistic flavor that generated considerable economic development. In response to demand for raw materials from cloth manufacturers in northern Italian towns, silkworm culture was introduced, especially in Calabria, and wool production virtually doubled. Exports from the kingdom in fact exceeded imports well into the seventeenth century. The city of Naples grew as the commercial center of the growing rural economy, and its port profited from being tied into the vast Spanish commercial and military system. It had no fewer than seven deposit banks by 1600, with holdings in the millions of ducats—more than Venice at the end of the fifteenth century. The newly prosperous nobility now in permanent residence there assured a booming market for luxury goods, including art. This economic vitality eventually gave out in the early seventeenth century, the tragic victim of both the oppressive tax policies of the Spanish and the rigid structure of land ownership; but in the meantime, a temporary spurt of economic development had produced new wealth, much of it ending up as profits in the hands of north Italian entrepreneurs and as tax revenues directed to the Spanish military machine in Lombardy.[16]

One general development in the transformation of regional economies throughout the fifteenth and sixteenth centuries was the growth of smaller towns that exploited locally available raw materials to manufacture highly specialized products. New industries stimulated diversification and growth of the rural economy as they extended their markets throughout Italy. Pescia, near Lucca in Tuscany, was not much more than a local market village in the fourteenth century, but over the next two centuries it grew into a prosperous center for the production of paper and the supply of raw silk to the growing Florentine industry. Carpi, transformed from a mere fortified rural village before the Black Death into a minor princely capital, specialized in the production of a kind of straw hat (*cappelli di truciolo*, made with raw materials from poplar and other trees in the countryside) that was exported all over central Italy. The new maiolica industry sprang up in numerous small places scattered all over the peninsula, from Castelli in the southeast to Abisola in the northwest, each producing wares of a distinctive kind.

16. Giuseppe Galasso, *Economia e società nella Calabria del Cinquecento* (Naples, 1967); idem, "Society in Naples in the Seicento," in *Painting in Naples 1606–1705: From Caravaggio to Giordano*, ed. D. Whitfield and J. Martineau (London, 1982), pp. 24–30; Luigi De Rosa, *Il Mezzogiorno spagnolo tra crescita e decadenza* (Milan, 1987); John A. Marino, *Pastoral Economics in the Kingdom of Naples* (Baltimore, 1988); Antonio Calabria, "Finanzieri genovesi nel Regno di Napoli nel Cinquecento," *Rivista storica italiana*, 101 (1989), 578–613; idem, *The Cost of Empire: The Finances of the Kingdom of Naples in the Time of Spanish Rule* (Cambridge, 1991), ch. 1.

Faenza developed into the most important center for this industry, and its products gained such international renown that foreigners adopted the town's name itself as the generic term for the product. Fabriano and Colle Valdelsa, like Pescia, became major producers of paper, another new product. Many of these new specialty products that circulated well beyond local markets were catalogued as the "most notable and spectacular things" of Italy in a curious publication described as a traveler's commentary, translated from Aramaic and edited by Anonymo d'Utopia, that went through several editions at the middle of the sixteenth century.[17]

Growth in those arts and crafts within the manufacturing sector oriented to the market for consumer goods is manifest in the surviving artifacts that have inspired this study into the demand for them. Through product and process innovation, producers demonstrated a capability for expanding the variety and quantity of products and improving their quality; they drew almost entirely on the resources—both material and human—of Italy itself, and they had some success in extending their markets abroad. As a result, there were more skilled laborers and a larger variety of skills, ranging from carpentry, pottery, and metalworking to what today are called the fine arts. At the time of Dante, Florence had a population organized around the wool industry with its large component of unskilled and low-skilled labor; two centuries later, it had a richly textured society of artisans famous for the variety and quality of their skills. Over the same period Venice, too, developed an industrial complex that has been described as much more advanced than that of England in the late sixteenth century.[18] The richness of the Italian world of goods was one of the attractions that drew Charles VIII to Italy in 1494; and he took back to France numerous

17. Ortensio Lando, "Commentario delle più notabili & mostruose cose d'Italia & altri luoghi, di lingua aramea in italiana tradotto, nel quale s'impara & prendesi istremo piacere. Vi e poi aggiunto un breve Catalogo delli inventori delle cose che si mangiano & si bevono, nuovamente ritrovate & da M. Anonymo d'Utopia composto" (1st ed. Venice, n.d.; rst. Venice, 1550, 1553, 1554, 1569). See Giovanni Sforza, "Ortensio Lando e gli usi ed i costumi d'Italia nella prima metà del Cinquecento," *Memorie della R. Accademia delle Scienze di Torino*, 2d ser., 64 (1914), 16–29.

For the places mentioned in this paragraph, see Judith Brown, *In the Shadow of Florence: Provincial Society in Renaissance Pescia* (Oxford, 1982; hereafter cited as *Pescia*); Antonio Ivan Pini, "Commercio, artigianato, e credito nella Carpi di Alberto III Pio e l'istituzione del Monte di Pietà" (1492), in *Società, politica e cultura a Carpi ai tempi di Alberto III Pio* (Atti del Convegno Internazionale; Padua, 1981), 2:561–636; Richard A. Goldthwaite, "The Economic and Social World of Italian Renaissance Maiolica," *Renaissance Quarterly* 42 (1989), 5 and passim.

18. Rapp, *Industry and Economic Decline*, pp. 9–10.

artisans—painters, ebonists, furniture makers, alabaster workers, gold-smiths, organ makers, embroiderers—as well as 87,000 pounds of goods, including rugs, books, pictures, statues, and furniture.[19] This conspicuous material culture worked its charms on his successors as well as the other monarchs of Europe who fought one another to con-trol the peninsula in the early sixteenth century and competed also for the attraction of Italian artisans to their kingdoms.

Many of these new skills required highly individual talents; and to meet competition, artisans also learned how to manipulate taste by improving their skills, introducing new products, and changing design to create fashion—all of which is reflected in the quality, variety, and rapidly changing style of the arts in Renaissance and Baroque Italy. Some—painters, sculptors, architects—achieved the ultimate goal of selling themselves as, by definition, elite producers of unique products. Their elevation to the new emerging realm of the fine arts marked the greatest success of this sector of the economy. The economy thus saw the appearance of a sector that, however small, came to have built into it the capacity for renewing demand for its own production (and it will take a second volume to round out this study of demand to explain how, on the supply side, producers themselves stimulated and shaped de-mand). The world of consumer goods the Italians created—the material culture of the Renaissance—was thus much richer in variety and more open to dynamic and rapid change than that of any of the earlier Medi-terranean civilizations.

Although this was the most rapidly developing sector of the econ-omy, its output was nevertheless a minuscule part of the total produc-tion of goods and services. Most of the consumption of rich families, such as the Riccardi and Strozzi in seventeenth-century Florence (the two whose budgets have been studied), went for clothing, servants, and food; only a small part of the enormous expenditures for building ended up in the hands of highly skilled craftsmen; and what was left for furnishings represented a relatively small investment—for all their fame as patrons, the great Borghese family spent only one-half of 1 percent for painting and sculpture over twenty-nine years. Neverthe-less, this sector generated a tradition of craftsmanship that represented an extraordinary development of human capital, and it also generated a tradition of taste that itself became a cultural value impinging directly on demand. It was, above all, in this area of "social" or "cultural" capital that the economy of Renaissance Italy experienced substantial develop-ment. Ex post it may be regretted that Italy did not participate in the

19. M. E. Levasseur, *Histoire des classes ouvrières en France* (Paris, 1859), 2:6–7.

worldwide expansion of the European economy in the sixteenth century, or, worse, that it did not undergo an industrial revolution; but regrets should not obscure the development of the sector that gave the Italian economy a highly distinctive character at the time as well as traditions—cultural and economic—that are still very much alive today, more so perhaps than in any other place, and that constitute strong components of Italy's current prosperity—for to the extent that the historical reservoir of both skills and taste still fuels its economy, Italy in a very real sense still lives off the development of human capital achieved in the Renaissance.

THE DEVELOPMENT OF THE ITALIAN ECONOMY down to the later sixteenth century can be recapitulated by distinguishing three phases in the secular trend: first, beginning with the Commercial Revolution from the eleventh century onward, growth of an international commercial sector oriented to the luxury market and dependent on foreign sources for supply, chiefly the Near East; second, development of an industrial staple with growth in the domestic production of luxury cloths directed to markets abroad in the rest of Europe and eventually in the Near East itself; third, increased production of durable goods, including what today would be called product, process, and style innovation directed to arousing and maintaining new demand. The balance of payments steadily improved as the economy continued to develop, especially as it moved into the second phase in the thirteenth century. As one looks over the international scene of Italian operations at the beginning of the sixteenth century, it is not easy to find manufactured products of value that were imported into Italy in notable quantity. Timber, furs, pewter, tin, fish, and other raw materials from the north could hardly have added up to very much value, and imports of manufactured luxury products were virtually nonexistent. From the east came the raw products needed for industrial production—such as raw silk, cotton, dyestuffs for textile production, and soda for glass and soap—and the exotic raw materials that had always been staples in the international luxury market as they passed through Italy on their way to the north—above all pepper but also other spices, as well as perfumes and precious and semiprecious stones; but by the sixteenth century, the chief item manufactured in the area that Italians continued to buy was rugs—typically a product of an underdeveloped economy.

It is important to note that the expanding world of goods constituting the material embodiment of Italian Renaissance culture was not supplied by imports. Demand, directed by the desire for many new kinds of objects and increasingly conditioned by a highly self-conscious taste, stimulated productive forces within Italy itself; and still, in the sixteenth century, except for a few items such as tapestries from the north and carpets from the east, Italians wanted few luxury goods manufactured abroad. The development of the consumer linkage with the rise of demand for luxury goods did not affect the balance of payments; in other words, wealth was not lost from the economic system as a result. Rather, consumption was a stimulus to further internal development and to the production of new kinds of wealth—and this is no place more apparent than in what has come to be called the art market.

Moreover, as the European economy outperformed Italy's and aggressively developed into a worldwide system, northern Europeans did not turn to the exploitation of Italy as Italy had turned on the Near East. They began doing for themselves what Italians had been doing for them, thereby pushing Italians out of their traditional medieval positions in the international economy, and they excluded them from the further expansion of Europe; but they left Italy itself alone. They made little effort to tap the enormous wealth of the place either by seeking to capture its domestic markets (except for English woolens) or by investing in its productive enterprises (in the way foreigners have exploited the American economy today); Dutch capital, for instance, flowed throughout Europe in the seventeenth century but hardly penetrated Italy.[20] Not even Spain, one of the most economically backward areas in Europe, exploited its political domination of Italy after the mid-sixteenth century to tap the sources of wealth in Italy itself; on the contrary, for reasons indicated above, the Italian economy can be said to have profited, at least in the short run, from Spanish domination.

Hence, while Italian entrepreneurs operating abroad saw a falling-off of business and a drop in profits in the sixteenth century, the secular movement of wealth into Italy may have slowed down but was not reversed; and the balance of international payments probably remained favorable throughout the entire period that is the concern of this study. France, in fact, suffered a trade imbalance with Italy well into the early modern era. Lyon, which grew rapidly as a center of international commerce under Italian auspices at the end of the fifteenth century, was almost exclusively an import market throughout the sixteenth century; and luxury imports there were perceived as coming largely from Italy. Not until the seventeenth century did the French challenge the secular imbalance with a royal mercantilist policy of massive state investment

20. Violet Barbour, *Capitalism in Amsterdam in the Seventeenth Century* (Ann Arbor, 1963), pp. 116–17.

to promote luxury industries, and even then the deficit continued into the eighteenth century.[21] Likewise with England, notwithstanding the invasion of English shipping into the Mediterranean at the end of the sixteenth century and the success of English new draperies in pushing Italian products out of Mediterranean markets, Italy continued to enjoy a favorable balance of payments for almost all of the seventeenth century, mostly owing to silk exports.[22] Whatever the performance of the economy with respect to specific sectors and regions, to total output and productivity, or to the general well-being of Italians themselves, wealth continued to flow into Italy, albeit at an ever-slower pace owing to the inexorable deterioration of its international position. Economic decline did not mean a loss of wealth, nor did it preclude the continuing accumulation of wealth.

## Political Transfers

International commerce and related business enterprise were not the only activities that brought wealth into Italy. So did war. Throughout the Middle Ages, Italy was a focus for the political ambitions of northern rulers, who drained off resources from their homeland to pay for their ventures. For some of the Holy Roman Emperors, from the Ottonians through the Hohenstaufens, Germany served as little more than a tax base to finance their ambitions in Italy. After final defeat of the imperial party, the Angevins moved in, using their considerable wealth in France to finance the conquest of the Kingdom of Naples in 1268; and once there, marriage into the Hungarian royal family enabled them to tap the most important source for gold in Europe so that they could pay for their further military exploits in the south. When, in turn, the Aragonese came, first into Sicily in 1282 and then to the mainland in 1435, they drew on the resources of their Iberian kingdoms, which included Barcelona, the only major European emporium of trade and banking in the Mediterranean outside of Italy; and wealth flowed into Naples once it became the capital of their new trans-Tyrrhenian empire.

Foreign ventures in southern Italy in one way or another involved the papacy, whose vital interests were at stake; and after the failure of imperial efforts in the mid-thirteenth century, the pope entered the fray

---

21. Salvatore Ciriacono, "Per una storia dell'industria di lusso in Francia. La concorrenza italiana nei secoli XVI e XVII," *Ricerche di storia sociale e religiosa* 14 (1978), 181–202. Jean Meuvret, "Circulation monétaire et utilisation économique de la monnaie dans la France du XVIe et du XVIIe siècle," in his *Etudes d'histoire économique* (Paris, 1971), p. 135 (on situation in Lyon).

22. Gigliola Pagano de Divitiis, *Mercanti inglesi nell'Italia del Seicento: Navi, traffici, egemonie* (Venice, 1990), esp. pp. 144–52.

more vigorously. He did not hesitate to tap the vast resources of the church all over Europe by declaring a new kind of crusade, now not in the Near East against infidels but in Italy itself against Christian enemies in the pope's backyard—against the imperial heirs Manfred and Conradin, against the Aragonese in Sicily and then in Naples, and against Ghibellines everywhere. Although during much of the fourteenth century the papacy was in exile in Avignon, where it took refuge from the tumultuous politics of Italy, its primary political objective during these years was nothing less than the return to Italy. To this end it tightened its bureaucratic grip on the church throughout Europe in order to improve its revenue-collecting mechanisms. Never before had the papal fiscal system been so successful in tapping the wealth of the universal church, and much of this wealth went to pay the cost of the long, protracted campaign to carve out an independent papal state in central Italy. Transfers came in the form of bullion, for the papacy did not at this time operate on deficit financing. If, after the papacy's return to Italy, it had to bow to conciliar pressures from strengthened monarchical churches to give up much of its income from procurations, common services, annates, and other traditional sources, it promoted other kinds of spiritual instruments such as indulgences, dispensations, and venalities to keep some income flowing in from abroad. And these ecclesiastical transfers were a one-way flow.[23]

With the French invasions in 1494, Italy became the international theater of operations in the first phase of the modern balance-of-power struggle among the major European kingdoms; and yet more resources were poured into the peninsula by the French, Spanish, and Hapsburg monarchies as they struggled for domination. The enormous amount of money that they spent to pay for the maintenance of troops during these ventures remained behind after they left, and it more than paid the cost of the loot carried away. Later in the century, preparations by the Spanish from their base in Italy for the campaign against the Turks in the East probably brought yet more money into Italy. The papal government made the most of this new crusade to wring as much tax revenues as it could out of its subjects, but it clearly exploited the situation to use the money for its political objectives at home.[24]

The full economic consequences of these wars can hardly be as-

23. Peter Partner, "Papal Financial Policy in the Renaissance and Counter-Reformation," *Past and Present*, no. 88 (1980), pp. 19–20; for an overall view of papal policy in Italy in the earlier period, see N. Housley, *The Italian Crusaders: The Papal-Angevin Alliance and the Crusades against Christian Lay Powers, 1254–1343* (Oxford, 1982).

24. Luciano Palermo, "Ricchezza privata e debito pubblico nello stato della chiesa durante il XVI secolo," *Studi romani* 22 (1974), 302.

sessed; it is a grim task to balance the destruction of life and property against the benefits to the economy brought on by the redistribution of wealth resulting from military spending. In his recent discussion of the impact of war on the economy in Renaissance Europe, John Hale strikes a generally positive balance—not, however, without feeling a bit uncomfortable about doing so.[25] Yet, in Italy, where professionals had largely taken over fighting by the fifteenth century, war was less destructive in its direct impact on the economy than in northern Europe; the devastations brought on by the invading French armies in northern Italy at the beginning of the sixteenth century have been called only an ugly interlude.[26] For over four hundred years, from the twelfth to the sixteenth century, wars in Italy were often international affairs; hence they produced one positive economic effect they hardly had elsewhere: for over four hundred years, from the twelfth century (and probably earlier) to the sixteenth century, the repeated military engagement of foreigners set off one-way flows of considerable wealth into the peninsula.

Like the ugly presence of war that often casts its dark shadow across the picture we have of Renaissance Italy, Spanish rule in Milan and Naples is regarded as a grim feature on the political scene, an incubus that dominates the historiography of late Renaissance and early modern Italy. Yet, as already observed, Spain, with a very backward economy as compared with Italy's, did not use its power for economic exploitation. On the contrary, Italy as a whole quite likely profited, in an economic sense, from the eventual Spanish domination of much of the peninsula, however oppressive the new political and fiscal regime was. The Spanish king poured resources into the peninsula not only to assure political dominance within Italy but also to build up a military base to support international operations both in the Mediterranean against Turkish expansion and in northern Europe against threats to the Hapsburg Empire and the Catholic church. In Lombardy, which was essential to the logistics of the European-wide military system of Spain, the government spent heavily for defense, both for construction of fortifications and for stationing of troops. Since local tax revenues were not sufficient to pay these expenses, let alone provide a surplus to be appropriated for uses abroad, the regime engaged in massive deficit spending, with balances made up by transfers from other Spanish lands.[27] Like-

25. J. R. Hale, *War and Society in Renaissance Europe, 1450–1620* (New York, 1985), ch. 8.

26. Vigo, *Fisco e società*, p. 11.

27. Sella, *Crisis and Continuity*; Franco Angiolini, "L'economia del milanese nel sistema imperiale spagnolo," *Società e storia* 5 (1982), 391–99.

wise, Spanish occupation of Naples brought the kingdom into the wider orbit of a world empire; and, along with the new opportunities for internal economic development already remarked, many northern Italian entrepreneurs made large fortunes there in military contracts and state finance. However oppressive the regime was in raising tax revenues to support Spanish wars in the rest of Europe, it imported enormous quantities of bullion in the late sixteenth and early seventeenth centuries; and much of this wealth left Naples for other Italian states as profits in the hands of entrepreneurs and as government transfers to Milan.[28]

A second economic consequence of the Spanish occupation of Lombardy and Naples was the opportunity for the sophisticated operators of the more developed Italian economy to exploit the access they now had to the undeveloped domestic economy of the dominating power. Italian bankers moved into the highest financial circles of the Spanish worldwide empire and therefore were able to tap directly the huge treasure that began to flow into Spain from the New World. In particular, the Genoese, who already had extensive commercial operations in Spain, profited directly from the new arrangements. They raked off profits from their financial services to the monarchy in facilitating the transfer of American bullion to the north, where it was needed to pay for Spanish military operations; and they streamed into Spain—and some ventured into the New World—to exploit commercial and financial opportunities opening up in a backward economy suddenly infused with new wealth. So extensive were the exchange operations alone with Spain that a new class of Genoese financiers came into existence who, according to the Venetian ambassador in 1593, disdained the normal commercial operations of buying, selling, and shipping merchandise as socially inferior activities.[29]

A third economic consequence of the Spanish presence in Italy was felt in the fiscal sphere of the various states that remained independent. The Spanish domination of Naples and Lombardy meant that the entire peninsula was brought into the Spanish sphere of influence to the exclusion of the other European monarchies; as a result, the Italian state system, after centuries of virtual anarchy, found itself frozen into a political stability of a kind that had never before been experienced. Already from the peace of Lodi in 1454 to the French invasions in 1494 Italy had enjoyed a precarious peace; but after 1529 peace was virtually

28. De Rosa, *Mezzogiorno spagnolo*, pp. 31, 96–97, 102.
29. Cited by Gino Barbieri, *Ideali economici degli italiani all'inizio dell'età moderna* (Milan, 1940), p. 70.

absolute. There was hardly a major war in Italy, except for the Florentine conquest of Siena in 1555, to the War of Castro in 1642 (the War of the Mantuan Succession in 1629 was fought between France and Spain). In this situation of indirect foreign domination, the Hapsburgs in effect bore a large part of true defense costs, so that the Italian states—with the notable exception of Venice, which had to defend its maritime interests abroad against Turkish threats—were able drastically to reduce military expenditures. Since defense is the largest item in the budget of a government in any epoch, ancient or modern, the relative peace Italy enjoyed after the general European settlement of the mid-sixteenth century that left Spanish dominance intact—at whatever political cost—had the effect of easing the tax burden on the rich and powerful, thereby increasing disposable income for consumption.

At the very time rich Italians were ironically reaping economic benefits from foreign domination, Europeans beyond the Alps, by way of contrast, were burdened with the heavy costs of civil wars, wars of religion, and the general conflagration of the international power struggle that lasted well into the seventeenth century. Hence, while the market for durable goods was booming in Italy, its expansion in northern Europe was stunted by the appropriation of much of the area's rapidly growing wealth for political and military purposes.

## The Accumulation of Wealth

The flow of wealth into Italy through business, political, and ecclesiastical channels slowed down in the sixteenth century but was not reversed. Moreover, the demographic trend over the entire period, from the fourteenth through the sixteenth centuries, had the effect of further accelerating the rate of the accumulation of wealth as measured on a per capita basis. The fourteenth-century plagues, for all their devastating effects, left in their wake many fewer people to enjoy the accumulated wealth of the past; and by the time the overall population again reached its preplague levels, almost two centuries later, the total wealth that had accumulated in the meantime was much greater than it had been before the plague years. Moreover, northern Italy, where much of the wealth was concentrated, had fewer people than the great European kingdoms to share the wealth of a much more developed economy. In 1500 the population of the region, which saw the greatest economic development, was about two-thirds that of Spain, less than one-half that of Germany, and much less than one-third that of France.[30] If these economic and demographic factors could somehow be statistically mea-

30. Jan de Vries, *European Urbanization, 1500–1800* (London, 1984), p. 36.

33

sured and graphically plotted, it might be concluded that per capita wealth in northern Italy increased exponentially over that of the rest of Europe in a relatively short period—precisely the time when it began to manifest itself in the demand for more durable goods.

The accumulation of bullion in Italy cannot be measured in precise terms. The eventual evaluation of the balance of payments will have to deal with what John Day, with reference to the unfavorable balance Europe as a whole had with the Near East, has called "the great bullion famine" at the end of the Middle Ages. European countries perennially had monetary problems related to the supply of gold and silver; but apart from the general direction of the bullion flow to the east, little is understood about exactly when shortages occurred, how serious they were, or how they fit into the general economic situation. The picture we currently have of the problem has been sketched by scholars who have concentrated on England, France, and the Low Countries; and seeing the bullion drain polarized between northwestern Europe and the Near East, they have not asked what happened to it in Italy, which obviously lay in the path of the flow as it passed through the hands of Italians trading in the luxury goods northern Europeans wanted in ever-greater quantities after the Black Death. Yet, it seems reasonable to suppose that, given the nature of their trade, the Italians skimmed off something of this wealth as it passed through their hands.[31]

Evidence from fifteenth-century Florence points to the plentiful supply of bullion in the city. In his study of the operations of the Medici bank in northern Europe, Raymond de Roover recognized the problem Italian entrepreneurs had in knowing what to do with profits accumulated in an area where there was little they wanted to buy; and although much of their financial operations in the north resulted from efforts to utilize credits by shifting them over the entire map of western Europe, in the end profits came back to Florence in the form of bullion. Fifteenth-century business accounts record the importation of gold not only from the north but also on occasion from the east in the hands of merchants who found nothing to buy there with profits from the sale of manufactured goods, and there is little evidence in these accounts of a

31. A recent survey of the problem of the bullion flow, with full bibliographical material, is J. Munro, "Bullion Flows and Monetary Contractions in Late-Medieval England and the Low Countries," in *Precious Metals in the Later Medieval World*, ed. J. F. Richards (Durham, 1983), pp. 97–158. For the earlier period in Italian history, see D. Abulafia, "Maometto e Carlo Magno: Le due aree monetarie italiane dell'oro e dell'argento," in the Einaudi *Storia d'Italia: Annali*, vol. 6 (Turin, 1983), pp. 223–70. There is much information on this subject in F. C. Lane and R. C. Mueller, *Money and Banking in Medieval and Renaissance Venice*, vol. 1: *Coins and Moneys of Account* (Baltimore, 1985).

reverse flow. From the later fourteenth century onward there was so much gold in the city that it commonly showed up also in the hands of ordinary working men, including unskilled laborers, who were frequently paid cash in florins.

In the later sixteenth century much of this gold must have left Florence in exchange for silver. Cipolla's study of the Florentine mint in the latter part of the century documents the vast quantities of Spanish silver from the New World that poured into Italy and the steady increase in the value of new issues of coin. In the last third of the century, for all the constriction of business operations abroad, Florence alone minted about 40 percent as much silver as was being minted in England. The value of issues in Milan in the 1580s actually equaled that of England, while between 1581 and 1610 the Venetian mint turned one-third more gold into coin than was unloaded in Seville. Not all of this output was destined for the Near East. That the major Italian cities continued to draw significant bullion flows from Europe into their mints would indicate that the basic structure of European commerce was still, through the sixteenth century, oriented around the Italian system. Far from suffering an unfavorable balance of payments, Italians apparently enjoyed an increase in the supply of hard currency throughout the latter third of the sixteenth century.[32]

The large quantities of bullion that flowed into Italy throughout the Renaissance did not end up as hoards or treasure in the hands of the rich and powerful. In the north great feudal lords probably kept as much wealth as they could in disposable form to be ready for military exigencies and loans in service to the king. On his death in 1376 the Earl of Arundel and Surrey had no less than £60,000 in gold and silver stored away, equal to over 360,000 florins, well over three times the wealth of the richest merchant recorded in the 1427 tax records of Florence. Although Arundel's treasure was exceptional in size, he being probably the richest person in England at the time, the practice was probably not unusual; in fact, hoarding has been cited as a cause for bullion shortages in the economy.[33] In Italy, however, various despots at the end of the fourteenth and in the early fifteenth century are documented as having deposited large amounts of money for safekeeping in the public treas-

---

32. Carlo M. Cipolla, *La moneta a Firenze nel Cinquecento* (Bologna, 1987), esp. pp. 101–2. Whatever one's estimate of Cipolla's analysis of the "crisis" at Florence during these years to explain this monetary phenomenon, he has documented the impressive flow of silver into the Florentine economy. See also Ugo Tucci, *Mercanti, navi, monete nel Cinquecento veneziano* (collected articles: Bologna, 1981), pp. 306–8.

33. C. Given-Wilson, "Wealth and Credit, Public and Private: The Earls of Arundel, 1306–1397," *English Historical Review* 418 (1991), 1, 23; see also below, p. 241.

uries of Venice and Florence, where it was put to work in communal finance. Nor did businesses make it a practice to keep large reserves in cash. In the extensive documentation of their business and private affairs, Florentine businessmen seldom indicate keeping much cash on hand. Once in his ledger, opened from 1462 to 1469, Francesco Sassetti recorded hiding 4,400 florins in a water closet, but within three months he had depleted almost all of it; and after the florins were all gone, he observed, "I no longer want to put myself to this trouble, because I don't know whether I could succeed in watching over them for a long time—in fact, I don't believe so." At the time of the death of Filippo Strozzi in 1491, his heirs found an extraordinary treasury of over 52,000 florins—over half the value of his estate—stored away in bags in the basement of his house, but this was undoubtedly savings in preparation for the expense of his great palace only recently begun. Rich Florentines were more likely to deposit even small amounts of excess cash in banks for short-term security rather than hide it away temporarily.[34]

Nor did Florentines, for all their incipient consumerism, convert large amounts of wealth into gold and silver treasures. They typically possessed modest amounts of silver tableware—mostly eating utensils. The famous inventory made at the death of Lorenzo de' Medici in 1492 lists some silver cutlery but hardly any plate or precious liturgical utensils, and what gold and silver was tied up in his great collection of rare and precious objects of all kinds was in the form of mountings. It was presumably a disposition against the uneconomic use of bullion that explains why the Venetian ambassador in England remarked the large amounts of silver put into plate in that country. The Italians put ever-greater quantities of gold and silver into liturgical utensils (as we shall see), but there is no way to measure how much bullion this syphoned out of circulation. Only as investment opportunities dried up did they tend to buy more silverware, and in the seventeenth century this becomes a notable category in the household accounts of the rich as it had not been earlier. Ugo Tucci cites the opinion of a Neapolitan in the eighteenth century that the silver there amounted to 7 million ducats in money, 9 million ducats in religious objects, and 11 million ducats in plate in private hands—almost three times more in treasure than in coin.[35]

---

34. Archivio di Stato di Firenze, Carte strozziane, ser. 2, no. 20 (Sassetti's ledger, 1462–69), fol. 71v; Richard A. Goldthwaite, *Private Wealth in Renaissance Florence: A Study of Four Families* (Princeton, 1968), p. 63 (on Strozzi). See also the general observation of Raymond de Roover, *The Rise and Decline of the Medici Bank* (Cambridge, Mass., 1963), p. 228.

35. Tucci, *Mercanti, navi, monete*, p. 279.

The large quantities of bullion that flowed into Italy during the Renaissance thus had an immediate impact in the market by inflating the supply of money; and that supply was further augmented—in Italy far more than in any other part of Europe—by the sophisticated financial techniques developed from the fourteenth century onward to reduce transaction costs that had the effect of generating credit, facilitating transfer, and increasing the velocity of circulation. Deposit banks operating on reserves and offering use of current accounts for transfer were well-developed institutions familiar to the merchant class of Venice, Genoa, and, to a lesser extent, Florence. Business practices widely diffused beyond the merchant ranks of urban society further facilitated the liquidity of wealth. The knowledge, practice, and discipline of keeping accounts were deeply instilled in the habits of entrepreneurs of all kinds, including also artisans and shopkeepers in provincial towns (to judge from their surviving account books in places such as fourteenth-century Prato and fifteenth-century Arezzo): they kept an array of standardized records, knew double entry, thought abstractly in terms of moneys of account, dealt in credit, and were familiar with sophisticated instruments of transfer.

Repercussions in the market of the growing supply of money, in both bullion and its more liquid forms, were manifest in a variety of ways in the course of the sixteenth century. In Florence and Lucca one outlet in the capital market in which some measure of this abundance of wealth can be taken was the limited-liability partnership contract (*in accomandita*), which allowed outsiders to invest in businesses without assuming the liability of a partner. Although this instrument had been made available to Florentines by legislation in 1408, it seems to have been used rarely in the fifteenth century, when investment capital was largely in the hands of the patrician class; but throughout the second half of the sixteenth century, more and more businessmen were induced to utilize this device to tap the growing supply of available capital in the hands of people outside their ranks. In the first quarter of the seventeenth century, investment in Florentine businesses through this instrument alone rose from 1 million to 3 million ducats, a figure whose enormity can be appreciated by noting that the total liquid capital in the city as registered in the Catasto of 1427 amounted to 4.5 million florins. Moreover, investors in this new instrument now included many people farther down on the economic scale than had ever before made passive investments in other men's businesses—presumably because they now had much more disposable wealth to invest.[36]

---

36. Maurice Carmona, "Aspects du capitalisme toscan aux XVIe et XVIIe siècles: Les

In general, however, investment opportunities in business did not keep pace with the growing supply of money. With contraction of economic horizons abroad, highly liquid wealth experienced something of a hemorrhage as outlets for it closed down. Entrepreneurs were not prepared or disposed to take advantage of the growing capital market by refining the instruments for attracting available wealth, and so neither the Florentines nor the Lucchesi took the next step beyond the limited-liability partnership to develop the joint-stock company. Instead, the scale of operations remained small. Since little investment was needed for plant and equipment in a preindustrial economy, there were virtually no capital-goods industries (hence, loss of foreign markets for the staple did not lead to serious unemployment problems and major dislocations). Moreover, since individual entrepreneurs in both the industrial and commercial sectors were not driven by ambitions to capture a monopoly position in the market, they did not need to devise ways to enlarge operating capital. Finally, with few exceptions the rich did not invest in the artisan enterprises that were fueling the growth of the consumer-durables sector of the economy.

A symptom of this situation in the capital market was the intensity with which investments flowed into the ever-fewer outlets at home it could find. One of the most important of these was land, and the flight of capital from the city is the basic motif in many of the social and cultural themes found in the traditional historiography of late Renaissance Italy. With demand far outstripping supply and strengthened by the liquidity of capital, the price of land skyrocketed: in Lombardy it went up three to four times in the later sixteenth century, more than twice the rate of inflation.

With other investment outlets shrinking, deposit institutions became increasingly important in accommodating the growing quantity of available capital. These included the Monti di Pietà, which had sprung up at the end of the fifteenth century under Franciscan auspices to offer an alternative to Jewish moneylenders as agents for distress loans; but success in attracting deposits did not come until well into the sixteenth century, as evidenced by the notable architectural presence these institutions assumed even in small towns at that time. Other charitable institutions, including orphanages and hospitals, also went into the business of accepting interest-bearing deposits; and following these examples, governments themselves finally took the initiative in

sociétés en commandite à Florence et à Lucques," *Revue d'histoire moderne et contemporaine* 11 (1964), 103 (graph). For the validity of the comparison of values two centuries apart, see note 58 below.

opening deposit banks as large-scale public institutions. Public banks were designed to accommodate the growing demand for the safekeeping of cash and for greater efficiency in effecting transfer through giro operations; they did not, it is important to note, activate private cash reserves by channeling savings into credit available for investment (most of these banks in fact were prohibited from doing so by statute). The first public bank opened in Palermo in 1552, and by 1600 others had opened in Naples (seven all together), Genoa, Venice, and Milan.

The availability of cash prompted some governments for the first time to consolidate their debt and organize it more rationally on credit operations with recourse to the capital market so they could reduce dependence on the traditional devices of forced loans and floating debts and still avoid direct taxation. In some places governments took over the operations of the Monti di Pietà, and the same objective of tapping the capital market lay behind the establishment of state deposit banks. The papal government, with its vast bureaucracy rapidly expanding in the late fifteenth century once it had established its territorial independence as a secular state, restructured its huge debt with long-term credit institutions. At first these were in the hands of a relatively few international bankers—notably the Genoese—but in the course of the sixteenth century, the papacy showed considerable imagination in creating other investment opportunities through permanent sinking funds derived from the sale of offices and knighthoods. The demand for these honors was high; and with a plentiful supply of capital, Italians from all over the peninsula invested in the church. Rome thus became a major capital market. At the beginning of the seventeenth century the papacy was paying out annually for debt service more than the total private income in the entire Florentine state in 1427 (as reported in the Catasto of that year).[37] By the seventeenth century the investment portfolio of moderately wealthy Italians typically included credits in various government funds not only at home but also in Rome (and perhaps elsewhere as well); and these holdings represented deliberate investment decisions, not the accumulated value of forced loans of the kind imposed in the fifteenth century. The Genoese also invested much of their immense wealth abroad in the debt of northern European governments and continued to do so well into the eighteenth century.

Yet another index of the growing glut in the capital market in the late sixteenth century is the falling interest rate. Interest rates paid by business had never been very high in a market as vigorous as that of

37. Partner, "Papal Financial Policy," p. 26; Sella, *Crisis and Continuity*, pp. 45–46; Palermo, "Ricchezza privata," p. 307.

fifteenth-century Florence: 8 percent was normal, and it rarely went as high as 10 percent for investment in time deposits with partnership firms. By the end of the sixteenth century, however, Lorenzo Strozzi, owner of the Strozzi palace, who had over half his estate invested in banks and the Monte, was earning only 2 to 5 percent on the former and 3 percent on the latter. At the beginning of the next century the papacy was paying less than 5 percent interest on the offices it sold, and its bonds usually sold at more than 4 percent above par. By this time in Genoa, where profits had been flowing in from financial operations in the Spanish world, the rates paid by the Casa di San Giorgio had fallen from around 4 percent in the mid-sixteenth century to less than 2 percent. The fall in interest rates through this period has so impressed Cipolla as an index of the level and liquidity of wealth in an economy with insufficient investment outlets that he has added a "credit revolution" to the various other revolutions with which economic historians have marked the successive transformations of the Western economy on its way to modernization.[38]

The accumulation of wealth found another outlet, finally, in spending; and it is the task of this book to examine the demand that forged the consumer linkage to the arts, the most vigorous and imaginative sector of the economy.

### THE STRUCTURE OF WEALTH

Greater wealth is only part of the explanation for the greater consumption of luxury goods. The vigor of demand depended also on the social structure of wealth—that is, first, its distribution, both geographical and social, and, second, a certain weakness or instability in ownership that resulted in the fluidity of wealth or its redistribution. A structural analysis of wealth in Italy during the fifteenth and sixteenth centuries along these lines reveals that: (1) wealth was distributed among relatively numerous consumers for the most part concentrated in many urban markets; (2) the ranks of these consumers were constantly changing so that demand was renewed and thereby sustained at a high level; and (3) the rich tended to become richer, which meant a rise in the level of individual spending. These social conditions taken all together go a long way toward explaining why Italy probably enjoyed the most fa-

---

38. Carlo Cipolla, "Note sulla storia del saggio d'interesse," *Economia internazionale* 5 (1952), 255–74. On Strozzi, see Adam Manikowski, "Elitist Consumption Society: Lorenzo Strozzi's Aristocratic Enterprise in the Seventeenth Century" (typescript of English translation of book published in Warsaw, 1987). On the papacy, see Partner, "Papal Financial Policy," p. 26.

vorable conditions in late medieval Europe for the eventual development of a vigorous luxury market.

## Urban Concentration

The fundamental facts about the distribution of wealth in Italy are the political fragmentation of the peninsula into states of widely varying economic development and the concentration of wealth in towns. No one capital city dominated as a governmental center that, like London and Paris, also tended to be the central market for the economic life of the country. When the city-states of Venice and Milan expanded to incorporate other formerly independent towns, they made little effort to integrate the larger regional economy under their control at the expense of subject towns; hence Verona, Brescia, Cremona, Pavia, and other subject cities retained a high degree of economic autonomy. The subordination of Pisa (along with the smaller Tuscan towns) by the Florentines was an exceptional case. Bologna, Cremona, and Verona, all subject cities, were among the few cities that grew to a larger size in the sixteenth century than they had ever been in the communal period. Milan, Venice, and Florence were centers of major regional urban networks that extended well beyond political boundaries, but no one city dominated the peninsular economy as a whole, nor did any have a monopoly over a single sector. Venice and Genoa always enjoyed pre-eminence as ports, although not without challenges—the former from Ragusa and to a much lesser extent Ancona, the latter from Livorno. Florence was a leading textile-manufacturing and banking center; but with the shifts in the international economy that came about in the fifteenth and sixteenth centuries, it could not dominate either sector. Although Genoa became a major center of banking and finance, Milanesi, Venetians, and Lucchesi played a role as well; and numerous cities began to produce luxury textiles for export.

Other towns had their particular economic activities of varying importance to the system as a whole. Some had specialized industries, ranging from armaments at Milan to maiolica at Faenza. Some were centers that performed particular services, like the university towns of Bologna, Padua, and Pavia. Rome had a unique economic position as the capital of an international ecclesiastical organization. A special group of towns peculiar to Italy were the seats of the independent condottieri. These men drained off the kind of wealth from the larger states that in the northern European kingdoms remained in the hands of the political-military establishment. War, in other words, was a professional economic activity in Italy that redistributed wealth from commercial and political centers to lesser places in a way that did not happen

elsewhere in Europe; and the profits of war paid for significant patronage in Ferrara, Mantua, Urbino, and a host of smaller court towns,
especially in Emilia and the Romagna. The economy of Italy, in short,
for all its international orientation, consisted of a polycentric system of
politically autonomous and diverse but complementary and interlock-
ing urban economies. With its division into port, staple, and capital
cities and its decentralized development of commercial, industrial, and
financial sectors, the Italian economic system never underwent the dislocations and shifts that created the crises suffered by the Flemish towns
at the end of the Middle Ages.

The geography and chronology of Italian art, with its division into
distinct schools and periods, were a result of the particularity and vari-
ability of these many urban markets. The production of consumer
durables was not dominated by a single market. Producers were distributed in a large number of places, and they had greater direct access to
local rural markets. The level of production that permitted the development of panel painting in Lucca, Siena, and Florence in the late thirteenth and early fourteenth centuries, for instance, owed more to demand from the immediate countryside than from markets elsewhere in
Italy. Local artisans in autonomous markets were more likely to develop distinctive ways of doing things, and the course of this development
varied from one place to another depending on the vicissitudes of each
particular town and its local economy. With its rapid emergence in the
sixteenth century as a center of patronage on a scale heretofore unknown, Rome attracted artists from all over Italy; but it never became a
national market strong enough to dominate Italy's polycentric urban
economy and to uproot local artisan traditions.

The absence of any one dominant economic center and the fragmentation of the economy into numerous political entities are obvious-
enough facts about the distribution of wealth in Italy. So too is the
concentration of wealth in cities. The urbanization of Italy, however,
has not always been understood in its fullest implications for the development of consumer markets. Wealth in Italy was urban not just in the
sense that it derived from those industrial, commercial, and financial
activities characteristic of the economic development of towns but in
the sense that rural wealth, too, was largely in the hands of people who
lived in towns—and even in Italy, for all its economic development,
agriculture remained, as in all preindustrial economies, the largest sector. Of the total wealth in the Florentine state as represented in the 1427
Catasto, almost two-thirds (including one-half of the land) was owned
by residents of the capital, who constituted only about one-sixth the
population; and in Lombardy a century later no less than four-fifths of

the land was in the hands of townspeople. In fifteenth-century England, by way of contrast, two-fifths of the land belonged to the rural aristocracy and gentry alone and another fifth to ecclesiastical foundations for the most part scattered throughout the countryside.[39]

The greater urban concentration of rural wealth in Italy resulted in part from the move by landowners into the towns during the early period of the commune. This process alone, in fact, accounts for the economic vitality of many provincial towns like Ferrara and Mantua that, remaining little more than local markets not fully integrated into international economic networks, never saw the evolution of a distinct capitalist elite. Later, in the sixteenth century, the opening up of some of the most important new markets for the arts occurred in those places where rural elites who had heretofore remained aloof from cities felt secure enough to make the move into them, thereby changing their way of life and injecting massive new wealth into the consumer market. Thus Rome became a major market for consumer spending in the early sixteenth century partly because the old feudal nobility, assured of the stability of papal government and the security of its own status vis-à-vis the pope, transferred its permanent residence into the city, where it supplemented the spending by the growing curial and financial elites in the local luxury market. Likewise, Naples took its turn on the stage of Italian art history at the end of the sixteenth century, by which time the prestige and security of the Spanish regime, dominated now by a viceroy and not a resident monarch, had induced the old feudal families to abandon their traditional strongholds in the countryside for residence in the capital. Genoa, too, underwent its great architectural transformation from the moment in the later sixteenth century when its old commercial nobility finally pulled up its rural roots and became once and for all fully integrated into urban life as it had never been previously, for all its involvement in international commerce.

Complementary to the urbanization of the landed classes in the communal period was the increasing acquisition of land by the rising class of urban entrepreneurs as they reinvested their earnings—a process that rarely led to the abandonment of the town for the country. The so-called refeudalization of urban elites in the sixteenth century was a notable stage in the concentration of rural wealth in the hands of townspeople (for, as we shall see, it certainly did not mean their literal "return to the land"), increasing the potential for consumer spending not only in the larger cities but in provincial markets as well, like those where

---

39. P. J. Cooper, *Land, Men, and Beliefs: Studies in Early Modern History* (London, 1983), p. 19 (hereafter cited as *Studies*).

Lorenzo Lotto, the Bassano, Palladio, and a host of other artists pros-
pered. In northern Europe, in contrast to Italy, land remained for the
most part in the hands of men who lived in the country, whether older
landlords who long resisted the move into the city or newer ones who
had abandoned the city for the country. Even in the highly urbanized
region of Germany, the wealth of towns did not include much of the
surrounding land. In vast areas of northern Europe, therefore, a much
higher percentage of wealth was immobilized in land owned by both
nobles and peasants, who often lived far from large urban centers; and
these conditions precluded the dynamic expansion of a market for durable goods. Nothing like a massive infusion of rural wealth into cities
occurred in northern Europe until the later seventeenth century. What
made Italy distinctively different from the rest of Europe, in short, was
not just the growth of towns, with all the economic developments
associated therewith, but the much greater concentration in towns of
the wealth of the whole economy, rural as well as urban.

As a result of its urban concentration, wealth in Italy was more
susceptible to the attractions of the market, including consumption;
and the sophisticated capitalist mechanism of the urban markets of Italy
facilitated expansion of the exchange economy, since wealth was more
liquid, or more easily convertible to liquid forms. Fluidity of wealth
increased the potential of access to the market for more people farther
down the economic ranks; and with so many towns densely scattered
throughout central and northern Italy, much of the rural population
also found itself drawn into a local urban market and a monetized
economy. Ready access to the market and liquidity increased the potential purchasing power of wealth, thereby inducing people to spend their
wealth and enticing producers to compete for that wealth. The market
thus had its own dynamic that stimulated consumption. The anthropologist Igor Kopytoff, wondering about the process of "commoditization" in history and following Braudel's notion that behind the rise of
capitalism in this period was the vast enlargement of material culture,
concluded that "the exchange function of every economy appears to
have a built-in force that drives the exchange system toward the greatest
degree of commoditization that the exchange technology permits. . . .
In large-scale, commercialized, and monetized societies, the existence
of a sophisticated exchange technology fully opens the economy to
swamping by commoditization. . . . The internal logic of exchange
itself pre-adapts all economies to seize upon the new opportunities."[40]
This drive to commoditization was well advanced in the numerous

40. Igor Kopytoff, "The Cultural Biography of Things: Commoditization as Process,"

urban markets of Italy by the later Middle Ages as compared with most other places in Europe.

The significance of the urban concentration of wealth also lies in the uses to which it was put as determined by the behavior of urban elites. Much of the thrust of the later discussion about secular consumption habits is directed to showing how the urban consumer behaved differently than the rural noble. The erosion of the traditional consumption model of the medieval rural aristocracy and the emergence of a different one—to use the terms in which the discussion will be cast—was a process inextricably tied up with the urbanization of wealth, not only because more wealth came into the city but also because this wealth was spent according to distinctly urban habits of consumption. Later something will be said about how these habits were induced by the emergence of a more positive attitude toward the spending of disposable wealth and by the creation of a favorable moral environment for certain kinds of private consumption, so that by the later sixteenth century Giovanni Botero, the first student of urban life, could take it for granted that the rich in cities spend more lavishly than their counterparts in the country.

When, in the seventeenth and eighteenth centuries, the great landed nobles in England and France were finally attracted into the city, if for no longer than the duration of the social season, their way of life there aroused demand for all those things associated with urban living that the Italians had long been enjoying. Since the market in both countries was largely concentrated in a single capital city, however, consumption there went much beyond anything Italy ever experienced. The development at that time, above all in London, of new commercial techniques by producers to get control of the highly concentrated demand in this one market so they could arouse it yet further and direct it into specific channels marks the revolutionary stage in the development of modern consumer society as we know it today.

## Social Distribution and Redistribution

The social structure of wealth within cities also impinged on demand. Little precise data exists for assessing the degree of concentration of wealth in the hands of urban elites. The best material comes from Florence; but the study of the 1427 Catasto by David Herlihy and Christiane Klapisch, which sacrificed economic for demographic crite-

in *The Social Life of Things: Commodities in Cultural Perspective*, ed. A. Appadurai (Cambridge, 1986), pp. 64–91.

ria, did not publish the data for their wealth-distribution curve in a way that facilitates comparisons. Nevertheless, according to their data, the richest 100 men (about one-sixth of 1 percent of the total households of the state) possessed one-sixth of the total wealth of the state; but just over one-half of the total wealth of the state was in the hands of no fewer than about 3,000 men, or almost one-third of all the households in the capital itself—an extraordinarily low concentration as compared with what we know about other places. In England at this time it has been estimated that a mere 250 men owned 20 percent of the country's total acreage, with no more than 51 barons owning 21 percent of all land with a yield of more than £5 a year; the great landowners and gentry together owned more than 40 percent of the land. By the eighteenth century the nobles of Europe (including by this time Italy as well) had a still greater concentration of wealth in their hands, with their share rising to well over one-half of total wealth. In the United States at the end of the nineteenth century, the richest 1 percent owned about one-half of all real and personal property; and currently (1992) they own 37 percent of total wealth, more than that owned by the lowest 90 percent of the population.[41] In this secular perspective the concentration of wealth in fifteenth-century Florence was not high. There is no reason to believe that the distribution of wealth was much different in Florence from that in Genoa, Venice, and other cities in a period when, with few exceptions, entrepreneurs did not operate through cartels, monopolies, and other large-scale business organizations that might have facilitated more massive concentrations of personal wealth. Many difficulties beset any attempt to compare wealth-distribution curves across time and space, however; and much more comparative data will be needed before a full picture emerges of the situation in any one place.

It was certainly not that rich Italians were wealthier than other rich Europeans. Indeed, it goes without saying that monarchs of the great northern European kingdoms had resources far beyond that of the greatest Italian despot. The three largest landowners in England during the reign of Henry VI had incomes estimated to have been at least

41. Giorgio Borelli, *Città e campagna in età preindustriale, XVI–XVIII secolo* (Verona, 1986), p. 16 (the Veneto in 1740); Cooper, *Studies*, pp. 17–19; S. J. Woolf, "Economic Problems of the Nobility in the Early Modern Period: The Example of Piedmont," *Economic History Review* 17 (1964), 273 n. (Lombardy, Papal State, Venice); John James, "Personal Wealth Distribution in Late Eighteenth-Century Britain," *Economic History Review* 41 (1988), 561; Marvin Schwartz, "Preliminary Estimates of Personal Wealth, 1982: Composition of Assets," *Statistics of Income Bulletin* 4, no. 3 (Winter 1984–85), 1; Nell Painter, *Standing at Armageddon: The United States, 1877–1919* (New York, 1987), p. xx.

£5,000 to £6,000, equivalent to around 35,000 florins, at a time when the full capital value of the estate of the richest merchant of Florence (based on capitalization of income, as reported in the Catasto of 1427) was just over 100,000 florins—and it goes without saying that the wealth of a great feudal landlord extended much beyond any monetary assessment. The northern European capitalist classes, too, included men whose wealth was substantial by Italian standards. Several royal financiers in France in the first half of the sixteenth century were worth over 1 million livres (about 400,000 florins); and German cities had their share of merchants—besides the Fuggers—whose wealth was not out of line with those from much larger Italian cities. On the eve of the Reformation one merchant in Strasbourg was reported to be worth 150,000 Rhenish florins, and at least 53 merchants in Augsburg and 37 in Nuremberg had more than 10,000 Rhenish florins in taxable wealth, high enough to have ranked them among the upper 1 percent of Florentines in 1427 (although they would have ranked somewhat lower than this in the early sixteenth century owing to the rise in the highest levels of wealth in Florence in the meantime).[42]

If wealth in Italy was not highly concentrated at the top rung of society, it was also distributed downward into the lower ranks. The considerable increase in real wages after 1348 put a larger share of wealth into the hands of workers, and they improved their earning power as they became more skilled with the transformation in the manufacturing sector brought about by the increased production of luxury goods. In the 1427 Catasto only 14 percent of households had no property at all to declare—a surprisingly low figure in view of the level of poverty in the wealthiest countries today notwithstanding (if not because of!) the further development of capitalism. Wealth in Florence was widely enough distributed that the middling class of artisans, shopkeepers, and others outside the ranks of the patriciate—perhaps for the first time in the history of the West—began to show up in the market for luxury goods. The fifteenth-century record book of the painter Neri di Bicci consists largely of his dealings with clients more or less of his own class, and a century later Vasari tells us that some clients of the major artists of his day were tradesmen and artisans. It was, after all, a modest broker in the bankers' guild who commissioned Botticelli's *Adoration of the Magi* in the Uffizi. Inventories across the fifteenth and sixteenth

---

42. Cooper, *Studies*, p. 19; Françoise Bayard, *Le monde des financiers au XVIIe siècle* (Paris, 1988), p. 416; Thomas Brady, *Ruling Class, Regime, and Reformation at Strasbourg* (Leiden, 1978), p. 103. The Rhenish florin was worth about one-fourth less than the Florentine florin in 1500; see note 58 below.

centuries document the growing quantity of furnishings, including artworks, in the homes of Florentines well below the level of the patriciate. Nevertheless, as has been already observed, by modern standards the downward penetration of wealth in society was utterly insufficient to release the kind of effective demand that produced the consumer revolution in eighteenth-century England and France.

Although the diffusion of wealth, then, was predominantly confined to the upper classes, mobility within their ranks assured its frequent redistribution at a rate much higher than that of any other place in Europe. Princely patronage, so much more variable and better financed in Italy than elsewhere in Europe, was largely conditioned by the inherent instability of the state system arising from what Burckhardt called the illegitimacy of power. The *signori* began appearing on the scene in large numbers in the fourteenth century as solutions to the problems of communal politics, both at home and abroad. Over the next century new men were forever showing up in their ranks, and the gradual emergence of the five major states and the establishment of the precarious balance of power in the mid-fifteenth century did not mean the immediate elimination of many lesser despots, who succeeded in surviving in the interstices of the greater states. The condottieri were a particularly fluid group. The system of mercenary warfare of which they were a part was founded on their activity as independent entrepreneurs operating in a peninsula-wide market, and they had greater possibilities for employment and therefore for upward mobility into the ranks of princes. The kaleidoscopic changes in the Marches, the Romagna, and Emilia reflected the fluidity of power and therefore of wealth among these men, many of whom—like Federico da Montefeltro, Sigismondo Malatesta, Alberto Pio, and a host of others— enjoyed their moment of glory in the annals of art patronage. There were, of course, many more independent princes in Germany, from the Electors to imperial knights; but their ranks were relatively frozen as a legal class, and neither they nor outsiders could improve their status by tapping the wealth of cities either as despots or mercenaries.

Political consolidation under a new regime, moreover, could temporarily set off new currents of social mobility within urban elites, and this happened frequently in the fluid political world of Renaissance Italy. When the Medici finally took over Florence as hereditary princes in 1537, they did not rely altogether on the older families in the patriciate to staff their government. Down to the beginning of the seventeenth century, more than two-fifths of their appointees to the Council of 200, the second most important body in the state, and almost two-thirds of the Florentines admitted into the new ducal Order of Santo Stefano came from outside the ranks of the older political elite.[43] In Naples, too, the rate of mobility within the aristocracy was higher than one might expect in Italy's most traditional feudal society. The sixteenth century saw much fluctuation in the fortunes of the aristocracy and a continual injection of new blood. Much mobility resulted from the establishment of a new government and the dislocation of the nobility from the countryside to the capital. Absentee barons were more dependent on the commercial market with all of its fluctuations, and land records show that estates were frequently divided and broken up and new ones assembled. At the same time, reforms of the new Spanish regime designed to weaken the nobility and to create new kinds of taxes included the issuance of new titles and the liberalization of the selling and transferral of fiefs, and this policy led to turnover in the ranks of the nobility and further fluidity of estates as they passed into different hands.[44] The loosening within the ranks of the nobility stimulated demand for land from outsiders, especially from Genoese financiers. The result was what has been called a virtual "explosion" in the land market from the mid-sixteenth to the mid-seventeenth century (although the rapid monetization of the economy did not lead to capitalism and the final erosion of feudalism).[45]

The principal institution that served as an instrument of upward mobility in Italian society in general was the church. Mobility was built into its very structure, given the nonhereditary nature of clerical status, and its ranks were therefore relatively accessible. Elites could exploit the church in order to preserve and advance their status; yet outsiders, too, could gain entry into it in order to pursue their fortunes. From top to bottom of the clerical hierarchy, frequency in turnover was high. In the sixteenth century there were 18 popes in contrast to 7 monarchs in France, 5 each in England and the Empire, and 4 in Spain—and almost all these popes represented a different family. On the average, 3 new cardinals were appointed each year in the half-century from 1471 to 1527; and the College of Cardinals grew from around 20 in the late fifteenth century to 50 in the second half of the following century, by which time almost all were Italian, 102 Italians alone taking their place within one generation, from 1512 to 1549.[46] No courtly aristocracy in

43. R. Burr Litchfield, *Emergence of a Bureaucracy: The Florentine Patricians, 1530–1790* (Princeton, 1986), pp. 25, 37.

44. Galasso, "Society in Naples," pp. 24–30.

45. Gérard Delille, *Famille et propriété dans le royaume de Naples (XVe–XIXe siècle)* (Rome and Paris, 1985), pp. 67–85.

46. D. S. Chambers, "The Economic Predicament of Renaissance Cardinals," *Studies in Medieval and Renaissance History* 3 (1960), 290.

feudal Europe experienced anything like this mobility.

Enlargement of the College of Cardinals was symptomatic of the growth of the papal bureaucracy in general during the Renaissance, and so yet another route of upward mobility opened up. The bureaucracy took shape at Avignon as the papacy sought to establish its authority over the entire church; and once the popes were back in Italy with a solid territorial foundation, they had to organize government to meet the exigencies of an anarchical political situation. With its center in Rome and its affairs increasingly directed to Italian concerns, the bureaucracy also became more Italian in its personnel. Moreover, the opening up of new career possibilities as bankers and tax farmers made Rome an enormous market that attracted fortune seekers from all over Italy to the increasing exclusion of foreigners; and a financial oligarchy emerged that rose rapidly to become in effect a new Roman papal nobility, largely supplanting the older baronage and controlling church offices and finances. Since clerics technically could not assert familial claims to their office, the immense wealth of the church was constantly plundered to benefit their families in the form of benefices, pensions, and outright gifts resulting from the alienation of church property. The rapid turnover in the holders of these offices and the lack of any dynastic continuity therefore meant the constant redistribution of the church's immense resources. The same dynamic of social fluidity also assured the rapid renewal of demand for luxury goods that is a major explanation for the mounting extravagance of patronage in the Holy City through the sixteenth and into the seventeenth century.[47]

The major dynamic in the mobility of wealth, however, was inherent in the economic system itself, largely based as it was on commerce, finance, and industry. As Guicciardini observed in one of his *ricordi*, "the natural vicissitudes of human affairs brings poverty where there once were riches," and he saw this as a short three-generation cycle— the same rhythm that in northern Europe marked the stereotypical move of the successful merchant family into the landed gentry. The

---

47. Barbara Hallman, *Italian Cardinals, Reform, and the Church as Property, 1492–1563* (Berkeley, 1985), pp. 6–8; Partner, "Papal Financial Policy," p. 61. On new wealth, see Paolo Prodi, "Il 'sovrano pontefice,'" the Einaudi *Storia d'Italia: Annali*, vol. 9 (Turin, 1986), pp. 210–11; and Adriano Prosperi, "La figura del vescovo fra Quattro e Cinquecento: Persistenze, disagi, e novità," in *Storia d'Italia: Annali*, vol. 9 (1986), p. 248. On the pattern of mobility of papal families, see Wolfgang Reinhard, "Papal Power and Family Strategy in the Sixteenth and Seventeenth Centuries," in *Princes, Patronage, and the Nobility: The Court at the Beginning of the Modern Age, c. 1450–1650*, ed. R. G. Asch and A. M. Birke (Oxford, 1991), pp. 329–56.

families that constituted the political elite of places like Florence, for instance, seem to have remained fairly constant in the fifteenth century; but curiously this political status did not provide the same kind of economic security for individual members who entered the business world. Their fortunes came and went, new men were always showing up on the scene, and establishment figures were forever exiting. Something of this fluidity is reflected in the number of palaces in Florence that were built by new fortunes (Rucellai, Strozzi, Gondi), or did not get finished for sudden lack of funds as a result of bankruptcy (Barbadori, Ilarioni) or inheritance (Rucellai, Gondi), or passed into new hands with a change in fortune (Boni-Antinori, Pazzi, Pitti). Some of the most familiar names in the annals of business history—Andrea Barbarigo, Francesco di Marco Datini, Giovanni di Bicci de' Medici, Giovanni Rucellai, Filippo Strozzi the elder—represented new wealth if not new families. So long as men kept their wealth in business, they could not assure the financial stability of their families, many of whose histories reveal how elusive permanent wealth could be in the early Renaissance; in any case, business dynasties operating the same business over generations during the fourteenth to the sixteenth centuries, like those found in the south German towns, are not easy to find—and in Italy this was not a result, as in England, of the social move of successful entrepreneurs into the rural gentry.

Economic developments of the sixteenth century opened up yet more opportunities for new and larger fortunes. The greatest of these were made in tax farming and government loans with the expansion of public finance in Italy and abroad, in the international exchange fairs, and in the many commercial and financial activities Italians took up throughout the Spanish realm, from Naples to Spain itself and also in the New World. Land also, both in the north and in Naples, yielded better returns for its owners as investment in it took on a more businesslike character. Moreover, whenever businessmen shifted investments to land, as they increasingly did in the sixteenth century, whether because (as tradition has it) they were losing their nerve and wanted to secure their patrimonies, or whether simply because (as recent scholarship is revealing) agriculture offered better prospects for profits, their "move to the land" left room for new men to take the vacated places in the business world and try their hand at making their own fortune. If many failed, so too many succeeded. The continual turnover of families and individuals in the business world has been observed in both Lombardy and Venice in the sixteenth century; and, given the nature of business and of economic conditions in general at this time, there is no reason to think the phenomenon was not widespread throughout Italy.

Upward mobility through new wealth was so much a fact of life in Italy that by the sixteenth century, churchmen who wrote about economics took cognizance of it, and their explicit justification of wealth has been called the most important new idea to be found in their otherwise traditionally scholastic thought.[48]

In short, Italian society was subject to a dynamic of change unlike that of any other in Europe. Elsewhere wealth was predominantly in land and therefore less subject to instability, it was largely in the hands of a closed caste that experienced less mobility, and it moved from one generation to another over well-charted and confined genealogical routes. Infusions of new blood occurred, and demographic and political forces took their toll in the genealogical fortunes of the landed aristocracy; but while the cast of characters might thus change, the basic solidity of the structure remained unaltered. In Italy the political, economic, and ecclesiastical elites were much more subject to turnover in their ranks, so that wealth flowed from one's hands to another's and kept getting spent over and over again.

In the later Renaissance countervailing forces had the effect of tightening up the social structure. The expansion of the papal state eliminated a host of lesser despots in the Marches, Umbria, and the Romagna; and the general pacification established by the presence of Spain in Naples and Lombardy rendered obsolete the class of condottieri. With the virtual freezing of the political order, elites, both oligarchical and courtly, consolidated their power by defining themselves legally and closing their ranks to outsiders as the Venetians had done over two centuries earlier; and they adopted inheritance practices—most notably the imposition of ties of inalienability on land and the limitation of marriage of younger sons to keep estates intact—designed to perpetuate the wealth and status of their families. At the same time, investment habits tended to immobilize wealth in land and state debt, removing fortunes from the vicissitudes of the business world, which in any case became increasingly circumscribed by the expanding capitalist economy of northwestern Europe.

No discussion of the distribution of wealth in Italy directed to understanding the demand for art could be complete without mention also of the church. Over a generation ago Cipolla posed the problem of what happened to the church's wealth in the later Middle Ages, but only

48. De Maddalena, *Dalla città al borgo*, p. 326; Sella, *Crisis and Continuity*, pp. 94–95, 219; Ugo Tucci, "The Psychology of the Venetian Merchant in the Sixteenth Century," in *Renaissance Venice*, ed. J. R. Hale (Totowa, N.J., 1973), p. 364; Barbieri, *Ideali economici*, pp. 12, 19–20, 51–52.

recently has the question begun to be investigated.[49] Yet, it is difficult to determine what ownership of property and economic power meant, since the church was not a monolithic structure. Wealth was fragmented among myriads of diverse institutions ranging from small parish churches to rich monasteries and convents. Although in the fifteenth century the Florentine church is thought to have possessed between one-fourth and one-third of the land in the state, no one institution was very wealthy. In the Catasto of 1427, which documents the private estates of eighty-six men worth between 10,000 to just over 100,000 florins, the two richest monastic houses (the Badia and the Certosa) registered property valued at only about 20,000 florins; no more than two others along with three or four hospitals and confraternities were worth over 10,000 florins; and many of the rest had minuscule holdings worth only several hundred florins.[50] Moreover, much of this institutional property—including income from spiritual services linked to properties—was for all practical purposes further divided up through perpetual tenancies in private hands, and privatization often meant exploitation for purposes of family policy. This situation prompted Giorgio Chittolini to observe that the figure of the great prelate of the northern European kind as energetic manager of his monastery appears anachronistic and almost unthinkable in fifteenth-century Italy.[51] In short, much of the wealth of the church in Italy was for all practical purposes incorporated in the same structures as private wealth and therefore subject to the same fluid conditions.

It is generally thought that the property of the church fell off at the end of the Middle Ages but then grew rapidly beginning in the sixteenth century. In 1645, religious institutions in Florence had 2,750,000 florins deposited in the Monte di Pietà alone. At the end of the sixteenth

---

49. For the problem in general, see Giorgio Chittolini, "Un problema aperto: La crisi della proprietà ecclesiastica fra Quattro e Cinquecento," *Rivista storica italiana* 85 (1973), 353–93; Giovanni Miccoli, "La storia religiosa," in *Storia d'Italia*, vol. 2 (1974), pp. 897–904; Enrico Stumpo, "Il consolidamento della grande proprietà ecclesiastica nell'età della Controriforma," in *Storia d'Italia: Annali*, vol. 9 (1986), pp. 265–89.

50. Gene Brucker, "Monasteries, Friaries, and Nunneries in Quattrocento Florence," in *Christianity and the Renaissance: Images and Religious Imagination in the Quattrocento*, ed. T. Verdon and J. Henderson (Syracuse, N.Y., 1990), pp. 42–62; John Henderson, "The Hospitals of Late-Medieval and Renaissance Florence: A Preliminary Survey," in *The Hospital in History*. ed. L. Granshaw and R. Porter (London and New York, 1989), p. 77.

51. Chittolini, "Un problema aperto," p. 388. See also P. J. Jones, "From Manor to Mezzadria: A Tuscan Case-Study in the Medieval Origins of Modern Agrarian Society," in *Florentine Studies: Politics and Society in Renaissance Florence*, ed. N. Rubinstein (London, 1968), pp. 238–39; Paolo Prodi, *Il Cardinal Gabriele Paleotti (1522–1597)* (Rome, 1967), 2:323–24, 353.

century about one-fourth of the real estate in Ravenna and Imola was in church hands; in Cremona, these institutions possessed one-fourth of all the property within the walls and, at the beginning of the seventeenth century, one-third of the land in the countryside; in Bologna, monasteries and churches occupied about one-sixth of the land within the city. In the early seventeenth century Venice repeatedly legislated—in vain—to limit further acquisitions. At the same time, however, the clerical population had also been growing, reaching 6 percent in Bologna and 10 percent in Cremona. Whether the structure of wealth changed within the church as it became wealthier in the later Renaissance, and how these conditions might have impinged on the demand for religious art, are subjects that have yet to be studied.[52]

Land holdings hardly represent the full ecclesiastical patrimony. The economic power of the church consisted less in the extent of the property belonging to ecclesiastical institutions than in its ability to influence private consumption habits. The church had an enormous capacity to generate income through various services; and given the ingenious efforts to market these with the growth of a monetary economy in the Middle Ages, offering an entire range of products from offices to indulgences, the church successfully tapped a large share of the wealth accumulating in Italy. Much of the immense physical plant of the church, which included its artistic patrimony, represented the power to channel private, communal, and princely consumption to its own ends. How it did this will be discussed in the second part of this book.

## The Rich Get Richer

If the tightening up of the upper classes in the later sixteenth century reduced the fluidity of wealth, it may also account for the marked tendency of the rich to get richer in the course of the century. Estates grew in size as the upper classes now abandoned the earlier practice of partible inheritance among sons and turned to primogeniture in practice if not in law. The demographic consequence of such behavior probably explains much of the increased concentration in ever-fewer hands of the collective wealth of a class that limited inheritance within families at the same time that it was politically closing itself off to outsiders. The

52. Giovanni Ricci, *Bologna* (Bari, 1980), pp. 117–19; B. Caizzi, "I tempi della decadenza economica di Cremona," in *Studi in onore di Armando Sapori* (Milan, 1957), 2: 1013, 1015; Aurora Scotti, "Architetti e cantieri: Una traccia per l'architettura cremonese del Cinquecento," in *I Campi e la cultura artistica cremonese del Cinquecento* (exhibition catalogue; Milan, 1985), p. 390; Chittolini, "Un problema aperto"; Giuseppe Pallanti, "La proprietà degli enti ecclesiastici in Firenze e contado dai primi del Cinquecento alla fine del Seicento," *Ricerche storiche* 13 (1983), 87.

Venetian nobility saw a 62 percent decline in its ranks from 1500 to 1797; and older families in the Sienese nobility experienced a decline of only slightly less (58 percent) from 1560 to 1760, with new admissions falling off at a yet higher rate. The trend in both cities led to problems of staffing offices for which only nobles were eligible. The wealth accumulating in these and other places undergoing a similar development must have been divided by fewer and fewer people as time went on. The extent to which a few grew richer at the expense of the many in this process of the rich getting richer is a question not addressed in the current historical literature.[53]

The greater wealth of the rich can also be explained by some of the new opportunities for a higher level of profits that accompanied the economic changes of the sixteenth century, although this is not a subject for which there is much information. Throughout the Middle Ages a few bankers had always managed to make great fortunes as occasional financiers for the princes of Europe; but once deficit financing became general policy for the growing papal bureaucratic apparatus and the vast Spanish empire, a veritable class of financiers arose who could count on a more or less permanent tap on the immense wealth of these governments. The self-consciousness of Genoese financiers as a class apart from ordinary bankers and merchants that emerged in the sixteenth century has already been remarked. Landowners, too, from the feudal nobility of Naples to the urban rich in the north who were increasingly shifting investments to land, benefited from economic change in the sixteenth century—the rise in population, the price inflation in foodstuffs, and the consequent lag in urban wages, not to mention the mounting evidence from both the north and the south for improved agricultural productivity during this period. As mentioned above, the "return to the land" that was so emphasized in older views of the sixteenth century as a social phenomenon is now increasingly regarded—at least in some areas, such as Lombardy and the Veneto—as the consequence of economic decisions to shift capital to a more lucrative investment outlet.

The shift of the cloth staple from wool to silk also increased the possibilities of much greater profits for the individual operator in the industrial sector. In Florence, the largest center for the production of cloth, wool manufacturers had traditionally accumulated substantial

53. James C. Davis, *The Decline of the Venetian Nobility as a Ruling Class* (Baltimore, 1962); R. Burr Litchfield, "Demographic Characteristics of Florentine Patrician Families, Sixteenth to Eighteenth Centuries," *Journal of Economic History* 29 (1969), 191–205; George R. F. Baker, "Nobiltà in declino: Il caso di Siena sotto i Medici e gli Asburgo-Lorena," *Rivista storica italiana* 84 (1972), 584–616.

wealth; but with shops numbering well over a hundred and a ceiling of around 5,000 florins in capital to the scale of operations of a single enterprise, no one firm had more than 2 or 3 percent of total output. Although the richest merchant-bankers invested also in cloth manufacturing, they were not likely to own more than two or three firms at the most. The industry—as distinct from the international marketing of the finished product—was a conservative investment offering relative security but limited possibilities for large profits, and no great fortunes were made in this sector alone. It was otherwise with silk, once the industry was well established by the end of the fifteenth century: there were many fewer producers, but profits and growth could be spectacular. For instance, in 1470 the sons of Antonio Serristori set up a firm with a capital of 5,333 florins, an investment equivalent to the top rank of wool companies; over the next twenty years they increased their capital to 21,644 florins and in the meantime withdrew profits that represented an average annual return of no less than 33 1/3 percent on their original investment. The production of a Salviati firm over six years at the beginning of the sixteenth century exceeded 100,000 florins, almost twice the value of the largest patrimony recorded on the tax roles a hundred years earlier. These are not isolated examples: by the sixteenth century, silk manufacturers in Florence were making fortunes on a scale that had never been possible in the wool industry, and the situation must have been the same in the other cities where the industry was also rapidly expanding.[54]

However changing economic conditions in the sixteenth century impinged on the level of private wealth, the rich profited from a much lighter tax burden that left them more money for consumption. On the one hand, governments needed less for military outlays, and, on the other, they found alternatives to taxation by borrowing in the more developed capital market. Already in the second half of the fifteenth century, the general balance of power established among the major states gave most of them some respite from military expenditures; and the situation became more or less permanent in the sixteenth century with the stabilization of the political situation by the dominant presence of Spanish power in Milan and Naples. In Florence, once the Medici had come to power in 1434, taxes never again struck the rich as they had earlier, leaving, for example, Francesco Datini, the great merchant of Prato (d. 1410), with an annual tax bill of just over 1,000 florins over the last dozen years of his life. Military expenditures fell off in the fifteenth

54. For the Serristori: Archivio di Stato di Firenze, Archivio Serristori 595 (*libro segreto* of the firm, 1470–92). Dini refers to the Salviati: see note 6 above.

century, and the patriciate was able to utilize accumulated credits from past forced loans to pay current taxes. In the long run, the nobles of Venice, in fact, received more in interest on the public debt than they paid in taxes.[55]

Sixteenth-century governments that wanted to tighten their grip on the reins of power throughout their territories were wary of taxing the upper class. The Spanish government in Lombardy never tried to wear down the resistance of the upper class to innovation in the fiscal system that might have left them harder hit with taxes both on their land and on commerce, and they contributed little to the state budget.[56] In Tuscany the only direct tax was on real estate, and private account books reveal how little the rich paid. The heirs of Giovanni di Jacopo Corsi, who died in 1571 leaving an estate of about 90,000 ducats, paid only 807 ducats for the *decima* (the principal direct tax) over the next ten years, although they continued to increase their wealth over the same period. Lorenzo Strozzi, the resident of the great Strozzi palace whose estate rose from 56,000 scudi in 1595 to 218,000 scudi in 1670, paid only about 7 percent of his gross income over this entire period in taxes of all kinds, including customs and charges on real estate sales and dowries.[57] Governments took advantage of the hemorrhage of the growing capital market to organize finances around efforts to attract wealth as an investment in the state rather than around direct taxation, and the system worked only because by this time the costs of government were low enough that direct impositions of either taxes or forced loans on the rich could be kept to a minimum.

It is a slightly observed phenomenon how much richer the rich actually became in the course of the Renaissance. The ascent can be precisely documented for Florence, where we have the fairly reliable tax assessments of the 1427 Catasto and subsequently a rich record of private accounts.[58] Whereas at the beginning of the fifteenth century the

55. Frederic C. Lane, "Public Debt and Private Wealth, Particularly in Sixteenth Century Venice," in *Mélanges en l'honneur de Fernand Braudel* (Toulouse, 1973), 1:317, 320ff.

56. Sella, *Crisis and Continuity*, p. 72; Vigo, *Fisco e società*, p. 315.

57. For Corsi: Archivio di Stato di Firenze, Archivio Corsi Guicciardini Salviati 19, fols. 74, 108. For Strozzi: Manikowski, "Elitist Consumption Society"; on the annual average he paid 385 scudi out of an income of 5,575 scudi; in the entire period he paid only 28,860 scudi in taxes. Presumably taxes paid by the Riccardi were not significant enough to be mentioned in the analysis of their wealth in the seventeenth century by Paolo Malanima, *I Riccardi di Firenze: Una famiglia e un patrimonio nella Toscana dei Medici* (Florence, 1977). In general, see Litchfield, *Emergence of a Bureaucracy*, p. 99.

58. The following estimates have been calculated on the basis of these considerations: first, an approximate doubling of the purchasing power of the florin across the fifteenth century and into the sixteenth due to debasement of local currency (the ratio of florin to

100,000-florin estate of Palla Strozzi made him by far the wealthiest man in the city, with only three other men more than half as wealthy, a century later many men were much richer. The estate nominally of the same magnitude left by Filippo Strozzi (not a descendant of Palla) in 1491 was worth at least 75 percent more in the local market owing to the increased purchasing power of the florin in the meantime. In 1528 the Venetian ambassador reported that no fewer than 80 Florentines had fortunes over 50,000 florins, which made them all about as wealthy as Palla Strozzi a century earlier; and 8 of these were worth at least twice as much. A few years later, in 1532, the estate of Jacopo Salviati in Rome amounted to 350,000 ducats. By the end of the century a dozen families in the small Tuscan town of Pescia—which had not been much more than a village in 1427—had patrimonies ranging from 20,000 to 50,000 scudi, which in purchasing power would have ranked them with the richest 25 men in the capital city as recorded in the Catasto of 1427.

At the middle of the seventeenth century (and allowing for inflation in the meantime) the Riccardi were eight times again as rich as Palla Strozzi (788,000 florins in 1655); and by the end of the century, with a fortune that went into seven figures (1,123,000 florins in 1691), this one family alone was worth almost one-tenth the total wealth of the city as capitalized in the 1427 Catasto. In the same period the annual income of the Riccardi rose from 22,000 to 36,000 ducats, whereas in the 1427 Catasto only 22 men reported estates of a total net worth as high as the former figure and only 8 as high as the latter. The Riccardi bought the former Medici palace and extensively enlarged it at a cost of three times (apart from the purchase price) of what it had cost to build originally. Their sumptuous transformation of the palace that in its day, two centuries earlier, was the most splendid in the city and that attracted the envious attention of princes throughout Italy is symptomatic of how

---

lira went from 1:4 to 1:7.5), while wages (in lire) remained stable; second, the erosion of the value of the florin (or now, ducat) by about half over the sixteenth century due to inflation of wages. The result is that the florin at the beginning of the seventeenth century was worth in the local economy slightly less than what it had been worth in the early fifteenth century. To index this change: a value of 100 in the early fifteenth century rose to 187.5 by the early sixteenth century and then fell to 93.8 by the seventeenth century. The same calculations are more or less valid for comparing values in gold currency across the same period in any Italian city. In other words, a seventeenth-century figure in gold currency was equivalent (in relation to the cost of labor) to approximately half its value at the beginning of the sixteenth century and to the same value at the beginning of the fifteenth century.

The data come from Arnaldo Segarizzi, *Relazioni degli ambasciatori veneti al Senato*, vol. 3 (Bari, 1916), pt. 1, p. 114; Pierre Hurtubise, *Une famille-témoin: Les Salviati* (Vatican City, 1985), p. 211; and Brown, *Pescia*, p. 124.

grand life became for a rich Florentine in the course of the sixteenth and early seventeenth centuries.

Evidence from elsewhere indicates how much richer the rich had become by the sixteenth century. In provincial Verona at midcentury a dozen or so men had fortunes in excess of 60,000 ducats, as rich as Palla Strozzi a century earlier in Florence.[59] In Genoa during the seven years at the end of the century his diary was open, Giulio Pallavicino noted the deaths of 10 men who left fortunes of over 125,000 scudi, the largest being worth half a million. The taxable wealth of 560 Genoese nobles averaged 31,335 scudi in 1575 and 50,179 scudi in 1624, while the patrimony of one of the wealthiest, the Spinola, reached 2 million scudi in 1636.[60] Delumeau estimated that in Rome around 1600 the richest barons earned as much as 30,000 scudi a year and the richest merchants earned even more—from 40,000 to 50,000 scudi.[61] In mid-seventeenth-century Venice (if we are to believe James Davis) there were some non-nobles so rich that the government could propose a fee of 60,000 ducats for the admission of five new families to the nobility, and subsequently new members actually paid as much as 100,000 ducats.[62]

The inflation of dowries (in real values) during these two centuries is one index of the rise in the level of private wealth. In fifteenth-century Florence a large dowry could amount to 2,000 florins, although there were some notable exceptions on occasion; at the end of the century Filippo Strozzi gave his daughter a dowry of 3,500 florins including the trousseau. Two centuries later dowries could easily reach 10,000 to 20,000 florins and more, the amount of a major fortune in the early fifteenth century; and the largest were much higher. In Genoa in the 1580s Pallavicino recorded twenty dowries (about one-sixth of those mentioned) over 20,000 ducats. In provincial Verona dowries reached as high as 10,000 ducats by the end of the century; and in the small Tuscan town of Pescia the highest dowries amounted to 3,000 to 4,000 scudi, the level they had been in the capital city a century earlier.[63]

59. Based on calculations made with data in Lanaro Sartori, *Un'oligarchia urbana*, pp. 153–55 and table on p. 168.

60. *Inventione di Giulio Pallavicino di scriver tutte le cose accadute alli tempi suoi (1583–1589)*, ed. Edoardo Grendi (Genoa, 1975); Kellenbenz, "Lo stato," p. 345 n.; Giorgio Doria e Rodolfo Savelli, "'Cittadini di governo' a Genova: Ricchezza e potere tra Cinque e Seicento," in *Gerarchie economiche e gerarchie sociali, secoli XII–XVIII*, ed. A. Guarducci (Prato, 1990), p. 487.

61. Jean Delumeau, *Rome au XVIe siècle* (Paris, 1975), pp. 457–58, 464.

62. Davis, *Decline of the Venetian Nobility*, pp. 106–14.

63. For the fifteenth century, see Samuel K. Cohn, Jr., *The Laboring Classes in Renaissance Florence* (New York, 1980), pp. 54–56. For later examples, see Malanima, *Riccardi*, p. 92; Litchfield, "Demographic Characteristics," p. 203; idem, *Emergence of a Bureaucracy*,

The level great fortunes reached in late Renaissance Italy was extraordinarily high even by the standards of private wealth in those countries in northern Europe undergoing the greatest economic expansion. Peter Burke came to the surprising conclusion that in the late seventeenth century, when Venice was in full decline, the average wealth of members of its elite was twice what it was in Amsterdam, the booming financial capital of the expanding world economy.[64] In mid-sixteenth-century England the wealthiest men in the kingdom are thought to have had incomes ranging (in equivalent Italian values) from 15,000 to 25,000 florins; a century later the average income of a peer of the realm reached the same level, equivalent to 20,000 to 25,000 florins.[65] In early seventeenth-century France the wealth of dukes and peers just outside the circle of royal princes and great court figures has been estimated to range from 1 million to 5 million livres; and the great Sully was worth just over this amount when he died in 1641. Such estates yielded revenues, at only about 3.5 percent, roughly equivalent 10,000 to 50,000 Italian scudi.[66]

Although all kinds of problems plague comparisons of this kind, especially where wealth consists largely in land that can often include unassessed labor service, these figures are suggestive, by way of contrast, of the extraordinary wealth of Italians even by standards of the great European monarchical states. They all pale to insignificance, however, when put beside the fortune of a great papal family in Rome such as the Borghese: their annual income over a twenty-nine-year

p. 43; Tim Carter, "Music and Patronage in Late Sixteenth-Century Florence: The Case of Jacopo Corsi (1561–1602)," *I Tatti Studies* 1 (1985), 62–63; Adam Manikowski, "The Tragic Consequences of a Florentine Nobleman's Marriage," in *Renaissance Studies in Honor of Craig Hugh Smyth*, ed. A. Morough et al. (Florence, 1985), 1:155–61; Alison Smith, "The Establishment of an Aristocratic Family in Renaissance Verona: The Verità from the Fifteenth to the Early Seventeenth Century" (Ph.D. diss., Johns Hopkins University, 1990), pp. 200–201; and Brown, *Pescia*, p. 42 n.

64. Peter Burke, *Venice and Amsterdam: A Study of Seventeenth-Century Elites* (London, 1974), pp. 60–61.

65. G. W. Bernard, *The Power of the Early Tudor Nobility: A Study of the Fourth and Fifth Earls of Shrewsbury* (Totowa, N.J., 1985), p. 173; Alan Simpson, *Wealth of the Gentry, 1540–1660* (Chicago, 1961), p. 60; Cooper, *Studies*, p. 23; Lawrence Stone, *Crisis of the Aristocracy, 1558–1641* (Oxford, 1965), p. 767. Equivalencies are roughly the same whether the conversion is made on the basis of exchange rates (in the mid-sixteenth century £1 = f.5; a century later £1 = f.4) or on the basis of man-years of labor (in England the daily wage of an unskilled worker went from about d.6 to d.8 during this period; in Florence it went from about s.15 to s.20).

66. Jean-Pierre Labatut, *Les ducs et pairs de France au XVII siècle* (Paris, 1972), pp. 262–64; Isabelle Aristide, *La fortune de Sully* (Paris, 1990), p. 94.

period at the beginning of the seventeenth century averaged 225,000 scudi—roughly equivalent to the income of no less a figure than Richelieu at the time of his death in 1642.[67] The Borghese earned in one year alone twice as much as the net worth of the richest man recorded in the Florentine tax records two centuries earlier.

Greater and more conspicuous consumption is, finally, another index of how much richer rich Italians became in the course of the Renaissance. Of the four outlets for consumption to satisfy basic human needs—food, clothing, housing, and religion—the latter two have left behind the greatest evidence in the form of the enormous artistic patrimony of Renaissance and Baroque Italy; and the rest of this book is directed to exploring some explanations for why the wealth of Italy found an outlet in this kind of consumption.

The rise of extravagance in expenditures for religious art can be recapitulated in the history of chapel decoration. In the fourteenth century a large fresco commission for a chapel—for example, in Santa Croce at Florence—cost as much as 500 florins; throughout the fifteenth century the price could go twice as high in real terms (about 1,000 florins) for something as grand as Ghirlandaio's frescoes in the main chapel at Santa Maria Novella; and by 1600 many painters of no great distinction, like Cesari and Roncalli, got chapel commissions for three times again as much (about 5,000 scudi). One of the culminating monuments of Italian religious art was the Cappella del Tesoro in the cathedral of Naples, begun in the early seventeenth century at a total projected cost of the extravagant sum of 90,000 ducats, considerably more (after inflation) than what it had cost to build the largest private palace—the Strozzi—in fifteenth-century Florence.

Architecture was by far the most important expenditure rich Italians made, and in the course of the Renaissance they became the most extravagant builders Europe had ever seen. The average home in fifteenth-century Florence cost as much as their builders probably had invested in business. Filippo Strozzi was prepared to invest more than one-third of the value of his entire estate in his home alone without counting its furnishings; and he (and his heirs) spent no less than one-third to one-half what Henry VII, king of England, paid out, in these very same years, for his great palace at Richmond, a building that "was destined to be the architectural symbol of the Tudor dynasty . . . a

67. Joseph Bergin, *Cardinal Richelieu: Power and the Pursuit of Wealth* (New Haven, 1985), pp. 254–55 (the figure is just over £1 million, exchanging into scudi at the rate of just over £5 per scudo); Volker Reinhardt, *Kardinal Scipione Borghese, 1605–1633* (Tübingen, 1984), pp. 96–98.

symbol [by which] all Europe would measure this upstart king."[68] A century and a half later a much richer Florentine banking family, the Riccardi, spent several times as much again for the acquisition and enlargement of the Medici palace (156,000 florins), which in its day had been one of the most magnificent in all of Italy; it cost them what the Earl of Salisbury, in exactly the same years, spent for Hatfield House (£39,000), which (as Lawrence Stone comments) could have been paid for only by "someone with access to the public funds, and as deeply corrupt as Salisbury."[69] With one of the greatest fortunes in Europe at the beginning of the seventeenth century, the Borghese spent one-eighth of their income over three decades for buildings of various kinds. The more rich Italians spent for buildings, the more they found themselves spending for the furnishing of these places, both domestic and ecclesiastical; hence, their investment in architecture had a multiplier effect in the expansion of their world of goods.

## DECLINE AND CONCLUSION

Notwithstanding the positive economic indicators that have been mentioned here, the eventual outcome of the secular trend of the Italian economy in the later Renaissance cannot be denied; and by the beginning of the seventeenth century, growth of the northern European economy had left Italy behind. Too little research has been conducted on the economic life of Italy in the later seventeenth century to permit anything more than the most general of impressions, but the sure sign that the economy ran down was demographic stagnation, which left Italy behind when the population of northwestern Europe began its rapid and irreversible growth in the seventeenth century. The Italian population instead reached a plateau in the early seventeenth century, with many of the great cities still not as large as they had been three centuries earlier, before the Black Death; nor were some destined to reach those levels again until the late eighteenth and early nineteenth centuries.[70]

The economic decline of Italy is often dramatized by reference to the

68. Gordon Kipling, *The Triumph of Honour: Burgundian Origins of the Elizabethan Renaissance* (Leiden, 1977), pp. 3–4.

69. Figures on the Riccardi come from Malanima, *Riccardi*, and the assumption is that the original Medici palace cost approximately what the Strozzi palace cost. Cf. Lawrence and Jeanne Stone, *An Open Elite? England 1540–1880* (Oxford, 1984), p. 354 (at this time £1 = f.4; the values work out to the same if translated into man-years of unskilled labor.

70. Amyard, "Fragilità di un'economia avanzata," surveys very sketchily the subsequent history of the Italian economy down to the nineteenth century.

population losses resulting from the disastrous plagues that hit the country in the early seventeenth century; but as tragic as these were, they were only momentary events, no more destined to mark economic decline than the plagues of the fourteenth century. Decline, rather, resulted from deep structural transformations, and these are not difficult to understand in their broad outlines. Above all was the relegation of the Mediterranean to a backwater of the expanding world economic system of Europe: with the circumvention of the Near East in the international traffic of spices from the Far East, Italians lost their role as intermediaries in international trade. Moreover, the entire Mediterranean was incorporated as a peripheral area into the world system now centering on Amsterdam and London. The Italians saw the collapse of their wool staple, with the consequent loss of Near Eastern markets and the invasion of their own domestic markets by northern cloths; and they were totally eclipsed in the world of international finance. For a time they continued to maintain their advantage in the silk market, partly owing to a geographical advantage, given the nature of the raw material; but eventually they lost out here, too, by the ability of other Europeans to catch up and also by the receding place of silk in the world of changing fashion.

The story of how Italy got left behind in the economic expansion of northwestern Europe lies outside the scope of this survey, but a brief review of reasons for this failure can serve as a concluding judgment of the Italian economic system. Above all, the Italians lacked the political basis for entering the competition for extra-European empire that permitted the development of capitalism into a world economic system. The Atlantic expansion in itself was not geographically beyond their reach. With a highly developed commercial network, centered in the Mediterranean and extending throughout western Europe, that had functioned well for centuries and was still operating well in the sixteenth century, however, no Italian state had the disposition to sponsor the kind of risky economic enterprises undertaken by the Portuguese monarchy and the Dutch oligarchy, both of which launched their operations from a base with no more geographical resources than several of the larger Italian states but with committed political support decisively thrown into the effort. Many Italian entrepreneurs instead tied their fortunes to Spain, only to find themselves eclipsed on the European stage as that power rapidly sank in the seventeenth century.

Moreover, Italian entrepreneurs never had sufficient political input into Spanish policy to inspire them to exploit their position through the reorganization of their highly individualistic firms into larger enterprises, such as the regulated companies of the English, the cartels of the south Germans, and the secret joint ventures undertaken by the Dutch to corner markets of particular commodities—not to mention the later stock companies of both the Dutch and English. Italians continued to operate on a small scale as they always had. For example, Florentines, including the Medici, had never made an effort to consolidate their position in international commerce and finance through monopoly organization, neither singly in an attempt to gain advantage over other Florentines nor collectively to strengthen the position of Florentines as a whole against outsiders. This disposition toward highly individualistic enterprise along with the inability to plug into political power precluded the kind of larger-scale operations that might have been able to tap larger shares of the rapidly growing supply of liquid capital in the sixteenth century and so meet the competition of the Germans, English, and Dutch.

If Italian capitalism thus failed to integrate itself into the expanding European state system and so take a place on the new stage of a world economic order, it also remained largely commercial and financial, not industrial in its orientation. Despite the availability of financing, the manufacturing sector revealed little imagination in meeting the foreign challenge. The silk industry underwent an expansion in the sixteenth century with the opening of workshops in the major northern Italian cities, but the cloth industries in general were structurally organized on a small scale; and since the industry utilized little capital equipment and underwent hardly any technological innovation (the notable exception was the hydraulic mill used for spinning silk), it offered little reinvestment possibilities for profits. For all the strength of the tradition in textiles, Italians failed to make any technological breakthrough in production, although in Lombardy and to a lesser extent in the Veneto further economic development extended into the stage of a proto-industrial revolution.

In explaining the loss of foreign markets and the failure to meet the competition of cheaper products made abroad, much has been made of conservative policies, still formulated within the corporate mode of the medieval mind, that resulted in obstructive taxes, rigid guild controls within the key urban industries, and higher labor costs as compared with northern Europe. Fundamental to the situation, however, was also a basic attitude about quality on the part of the elites who ran enterprises and directed government policy. These men were committed to luxury production; even as their markets were being flooded with cheaper Dutch and English cloths, they persisted in their conviction that quality was not to be compromised at any cost. Such an attitude about goods did not make much business sense in the economic context of the times.

That taste could becloud the business judgment of men with such vigorous entrepreneurial traditions is one mark of the mentality induced
by the material culture that they had created for themselves and that is
the object of this book to illuminate.

We have observed that the arts and crafts directed to satisfying the
demand for consumer goods, both domestic and religious, constituted
the most dynamic and imaginative sector of the economy. Fed by the
spending of ever-wealthier consumers, this sector showed considerable
development during the period when the forward sectors of the economy were losing their international position; but for all its vitality, it
constituted but a minuscule part of the total output of goods and services. Production was directed to the luxury market within Italy itself,
and the sector received hardly any investment, either by private persons
or by governments, to extend its markets abroad. The ever-higher
concentration of wealth at the top level of society and, conversely, the
limited downward redistribution of wealth precluded the eventual advance of this sector into the "revolutionary" stage when the dynamics
driving the market shifted from the demand to the supply side, with the
mass production of cheaper goods and new initiatives by producers
competing with one another to attract consumers into the market by
arousing and directing demand of large-scale production for a mass
market.

THIS SURVEY OF THE ECONOMIC DEVELOPMENT of Italy from the fourteenth through the sixteenth centuries has been directed to explaining
one phenomenon that is central to the thesis of this book: the continual
generation and accumulation of wealth that was the permissive cause
of consumption. An analysis with such a narrow focus, however, can
hardly reveal a comprehensive view of the economy. A long-run view
misses those ups and downs that mark the performance of any economy in the short run during which most people—entrepreneurs and
workers—live out their lives trying to make a living. What is most
notably lacking in this analysis has been any comment on the social
quality of the economy. Accumulation of wealth alone does not necessarily bring prosperity to the general population, and in this respect
the performance of the economy from the sixteenth century onward
left much to be desired. According to the widely accepted view, real
wages of the urban working classes rose sharply after the Black Death,
remained strong throughout most of the fifteenth century, but then
slowly declined in the course of the sixteenth century; while in the
countryside peasants—by far the largest mass of the population, for all
the growth of urban economies—remained pinned down to the land

by oppressive tenurial systems, especially sharecropping. The people who crowded into the two cities that underwent the most explosive growth in the sixteenth century—Naples and Rome—lived largely as parasites working in the service sector for survival wages rather than augmenting a productive labor force. As in any premodern capitalist economy, most people lived on the edge of disaster: they had little defense against natural catastrophes, famine, and disease (in Italy war was less a disruptive force), and the economy behaved capriciously in depriving them of a livelihood. Historians of late Renaissance Italy have had no difficulty in finding evidence of widespread poverty and misery, subjects that have contributed to the general picture of economic decline. The extent to which Italians were, in these respects, worse off than other Europeans, however, can hardly be assessed.

A balanced view of the economy of Italy would consider all these subjects and much more. Economic performance is not to be judged—as many economists and politicians in our own time seek to measure the performance of modern industrial economies—by the statistics of gross national product, aggregate private wealth, and consumer spending without considering the distribution of wealth, the extent of poverty, the level of unemployment, and other inequities in the social quality of economic life. The concern here, however, has been not with a global judgment of economic performance but solely with the accumulation of wealth as the background for understanding a new phase in the history of consumer spending.

IN MUCH OF THE HISTORIOGRAPHICAL TRADITION, increased disposable wealth has been a sufficient explanation for the emergence of the material culture of Renaissance Italy. According to the "Lopez thesis," disposable wealth increased because hard times after the mid-fourteenth century discouraged entrepreneurs from reinvesting capital in business enterprise. Here, however, a different argument has been made. First, wealth grew throughout the entire period from the fourteenth through the sixteenth centuries partly because the export of goods and services and political transfers from abroad resulted in a favorable balance of payments and partly because the economy continued to develop internally in the industrial and agricultural sectors. Second, this increasing wealth outpaced investment opportunities because commercial and financial outlets abroad slowly closed down and technological limitations precluded growth in capital-goods industries oriented around the staple at home; and once the political system was stabilized by the presence of a great foreign power, wealth was not burdened with the heavy cost of war. By the seventeenth century the center of the European economy had shifted from the Mediterranean to Holland and England; but if the expanding world system left Italy behind, the place was not exploited by the advanced economies, and its isolation meant only relative, not absolute, decline.

The level of disposable wealth is not the whole story, however. Effective demand depends also on the number of consumers and therefore on the distribution and redistribution of wealth. The structure of wealth in Italy was marked by heavy concentration in a large number of urban centers with well-developed markets and by relatively wide social distribution; in addition, the considerable mobility within the political, business, and ecclesiastical elites of Italy compared with those of the feudal kingdoms assured the frequent horizontal redistribution of wealth and consequently a constant renewal of demand. The eventual stabilization of elites in the later sixteenth century and the steady rise in the magnitude of private wealth probably indicate a greater concentration of wealth in the hands of fewer people and thus in the final analysis, as already observed, account for the eventual failure of the Italian economic system.

The timing of the Renaissance as a consumer phenomenon was very much a function of the political situation—the emergence of strong oligarchical and despotic governments in the towns, ending the secular instability of communal factionalism; the success of the popes in establishing an independent state in central Italy and transforming Rome into a European capital; the general, if precarious, stabilization of the political scene in the mid-fifteenth century; and the overwhelming presence of Spain in the sixteenth century, freezing the political system throughout the peninsula into permanent stability as well as transforming Naples into a significant new market and giving yet another infusion of wealth to Italian business interests. Given these political developments, the analysis of the economic system and the nature of wealth sketched out here goes a long way toward explaining the vigor of the luxury market, the geography of patronage (or the shifting of luxury markets), and the duration of luxury spending, with its ever-greater extravagance from the Renaissance to the Baroque. Likewise, the relative political stability in Italy after the mid-fifteenth century (excepting the interlude of the foreign invasions) in contrast to the mounting turbulence—and cost—of civil and religious wars and of the international power struggle in northern Europe helps explain why, for all the vigor of economic expansion in the north, luxury consumption was so much more brilliant a phenomenon in Italy.

# The Demand
# for Religious Art

THE CONSUMPTION MODEL

Liturgical Apparatus

Pictorial Forms

VARIABLES OF CONSUMER BEHAVIOR

Institutional Proliferation within
the Church

Lay Demand for Services

THE MATERIAL CULTURE OF
THE CHURCH AND
INCIPIENT CONSUMERISM

The Expansion and Filling Up of
Liturgical Space

The Internal Dynamics of Demand

The Generation of Pictorial Culture

A LL RELIGIONS HAVE INSPIRED some kind of artistic production, much of it serving directly the needs of worship and other practices of the cult itself. Of the world's great religions, Christianity has one of the richest artistic traditions, both in the variety and in the changing quality of its art; and much is known about the history of Christian art from the Middle Ages through the post–Counter Reformation epoch. Scholarship tends to regard this art as a reflection of religion and concentrates on the way religious ideas influence artistic production both stylistically and iconographically. Thus, within the chronological scope of this book, some of the problems that have attracted the greatest interest of art historians are how the Franciscan movement at the beginning of the period influenced the rise of naturalism and the representation of more human sentiments in painting, and how the Counter Reformation at the end of the period influenced style and content in its efforts to make art conform to standards of orthodoxy in religious practice and belief.

In the scholarly tradition, however, this art retains its primary identity as art rather than as religious object. Religion is therefore not a major organizational principle in dealing with the subject. Histories of medieval art approach a certain comprehensiveness in dealing with their materials if for no other reason than that subject matter is more exclusively religious; but they tend to focus on physical forms, iconographical traditions, workshops, and patrons rather than strive for a high level of generalization about the religious nature of art. In view of this arthistorical tradition, it is hardly surprising that historians of Christianity from the Middle Ages to the Counter Reformation generally ignore art and the material culture of religion altogether. If pressed, they, like the art historians, would recognize art's power to express religious sentiment and communicate ideas, but in the end they would probably consider much of it as a decorative accessory to the content and practice of religion that served in the "acculturation" of the masses.[1]

However much medieval art was inspired by religious feelings and ideas, its changing religious quality does not altogether explain the demand for it. Many people sense that the stylistic difference between a

1. See the perceptive comments of John Van Engen, "The Christian Middle Ages as an Historiographical Problem," *American Historical Review* 91 (1986), 548–52.

Romanesque and Gothic church reflects a different kind of religious sensibility, but it can hardly be assumed that a particular Gothic church was built just to satisfy a desire for a new kind of religious experience. What we might call independent or external forces impinge on the demand for a church—the need to replace a destroyed building, the need to accommodate a larger public or a larger clerical community, the desire to erect a monument to the pride or the power of a patron, or simply the desire to have a new building in the latest style. In short, the forces that converge in the demand for religious art are several, they vary from one place to another and from one time to another, and they have different degrees of relevance to the religious content and the aesthetic quality of the final product. Religious meaning as revealed in style, form, or content is not the only subject appropriate to the history of Christian art.

By sorting out all these variables that impinge on demand, we ought to be able to generalize about them and so build up a slightly different context for the history of religious art. Most Renaissance art was, after all, religious; and it is not immediately apparent why, in a place where, on the one hand, the religious public contracted as a result of the demographic disasters of the fourteenth century and, on the other, a vigorous secular culture arose in the fifteenth century, the demand for religious art soared to much greater heights than it had ever reached in the Age of Faith.

One approach to understanding why this happened is to consider art in the context of the overall material culture of religion. If we posit a consumption model consisting of all those things needed for religious practice, we can regard demand as having been generated by two kinds of variable forces: first, those dependent on the nature of the model itself; and the second, those external to the model. The first set of forces arose primarily out of changes in functions that generate demand for newer objects or the replacement of older ones; the second—the external forces—arose out of changing economic and social conditions that generated demand for more objects regardless of any changes in their specific intrinsic nature. The thirteenth century was decisive for the release of new forces of both kinds, and the momentum they gained in the following centuries accounts for much of the vitality of the art market in Renaissance Italy with respect at least to the level of production if not also to the quality of products.

## THE CONSUMPTION MODEL

### Liturgical Apparatus

Christianity was, almost from its inception, a religion oriented around things. In contrast to both Judaism and Islam, Christianity accepted the active role of powerful intermediaries between people and God: a self-perpetuating priestly elite presided over ritual in the exclusive exercise of the power to confer grace, and holy people were sanctified and revered as direct intercessors with the deity even after death. Both the mystery of ritual and the cult of the holy person readily lent themselves to the sanctification of things—things necessary to ritual and things associated with holy people; hence, a rich material culture grew up at the very center of the religion. Moreover, these durable goods were characterized by a high degree of luxury both in inherent materials and in craftsmanship.

The rituals of traditional Christianity centered on the sacraments, above all the celebration of the mass. The medieval world of religious goods, therefore, consisted of things the clergy needed to perform their essential liturgical function—reliquaries and monstrances; utensils, such as chalices, patens, caskets, pyxes, candlesticks, bells, ewers, cruets, ladles, cloths, and holy books; furnishings, such as altars, thrones, and lecterns; the accessories of the participants, such as scepters, croziers, censers, umbrellas, fans, and above all garments; and, finally, all the equipment, some of it of temporary duration, needed for public processions for the celebration of grander feast days. The requirements of the liturgy can be extended beyond these objects directly serving the performance of the ritual to include buildings—both churches, which provided priests with sanctified space for the essential rituals, and monasteries, which housed the regular clergy, whose prayers collectively performed the secular priests' services for the whole of society.

Reliquaries containing the remains of the holy people, who, at yet a higher level than priests and monks, further served society as divine intercessors, were at the center of this material culture. Since relics associated with holy people came themselves to share something of this holiness, the presence of such objects could alone sanctify space; hence, they were absolutely essential to religious practice. On the one hand, they attracted worshipers for ordinary rituals as well as pilgrims for special veneration; on the other hand, as mobile objects they circulated extensively through social space, being carried through the streets in processions, traded in the marketplace, stolen wherever they were to be found, and even taken home. Such special objects called for appropriately conspicuous containers from reliquaries to church buildings.

Collectively all these physical objects constitute the material culture of medieval religion, and they can be subsumed under the rubric of what will here be called the liturgical apparatus. Since virtually all the objects we have in mind when we talk about medieval art today are comprehended in this term, the liturgical apparatus can in fact be taken as the consumption model that defined the demand for the religious artwork of that epoch. Sacraments other than communion that were conferred outside the mass only modestly expanded this apparatus, the most significant objects being associated with baptism (baptisteries, baptismal fonts) and with death (tombs); beyond the sacraments, propaganda and private devotion also gave rise to other kinds of art forms. To the extent these things were to be found within churches, buildings, too, can be comprehended within the sphere of the liturgical apparatus as here defined, for buildings were essential to give focus and stability to all these holy things.

The basic forms of medieval church artwork go back to the beginnings of Christianity; and the liturgical apparatus in the narrow sense of the utensils, furnishings, accessories, and reliquaries directly incorporated into the ritual of the mass was largely in place by the ninth century. Vestments continued to undergo variation according to the specific liturgical occasion. The pulpit, altarpiece, and monstrance were among the few new items introduced in the high Middle Ages, and confessionals appear with the Counter Reformation. No other model, however, arose for a significantly different array of objects replacing the traditional liturgical apparatus, from utensils on the altar to buildings and their decoration. It was primarily in the architectural ambience that the model underwent its further growth—as opposed to the stylistic elaboration of its constituent parts. The elaboration and embellishment of ecclesiastical architecture from the eleventh century onward brought important art forms into existence, including murals, mosaics, stained glass windows, cast-bronze work, and monumental sculpture; but for the most part, the architectural component of the model, for all its stylistic evolution and embellishment with new kinds of artwork, remained fairly standard in its organization of liturgical space. The new forms of religious artwork that evolved in the later Middle Ages can for the most part be contained within the traditional model.

The great themes in the history of Christian art throughout the high Middle Ages and the Renaissance—new forms, stylistic developments, modes of production, religious meaning—were played out despite this inertia of liturgical tradition. Although conditions arose in the marketplace that were favorable for innovation in style, content, and techniques of production, the essential typology of the liturgical and devotional objects that constitute the artwork of the period did not change appreciably. The material substance of that art—what has here been called the liturgical apparatus—did not undergo changes that redefined basic functions and thereby introduced many new kinds of objects.

The Renaissance in the realm of religious art, therefore, is largely a matter of a change in taste and content, as art responded to new aesthetic and religious sensibilities. A priest from the earlier Middle Ages finding himself in a Renaissance church, after perhaps some initial disorientation due to the placement of the altar table, would have been familiar with most of the utensils and furnishings at the altar, and he would have easily found his way around in the liturgical space, however perplexed he might have been by the style in which all these things were made, if not also overwhelmed by the abundance of images that surrounded him. It was the conservative liturgical tradition, in fact, that limited the success of the centralized church so dear to Renaissance architects, who introduced this innovative form for aesthetic reasons without giving much thought to its inconvenience for the liturgy.

THE QUALIFICATION of so many of these objects as artwork derives from the luxury and skill that were lavished on their production. Although it is perhaps not surprising that objects of central importance to the practice of any religion come to be endowed with the beauty of rare materials and high-quality craftsmanship, the liturgical apparatus of Christianity underwent an extraordinarily rich artistic elaboration almost from the inception of the religion.

This penchant for luxury arose in part from the structuring of religious practice around a complex liturgy and a body of objects that required appropriate display. Since the mass was regarded as a drama performed exclusively by a priest and re-creating the most dramatic moments in the life of the deity, its performance was a veritable spectacle, involving the priest in much moving around and requiring that all those things needed for the execution of the ritual—from the priest isolated on the stage around the altar to the church itself—contribute to a mystical and dramatic impact on the lay public. All the material objects needed for such a performance, in other words, had a significant and conspicuous presence in what was in effect a theatrical performance, and they had to be endowed with the appropriate physical attributes of religious splendor. Moreover, the building in which this drama was played out received consecration for this specific purpose; and as sanctified space reflecting the heavenly city of God, it too demanded appropriate embellishment.

Another reason for the luxurious elaboration of the liturgical apparatus is cultural. Like most primitive peoples, the barbarians who overran the Roman world were fascinated by rare materials with luster effects—gold, silver, ivory, and gems—as representative of power; they were therefore to be displayed as precious objects, not hoarded away out of sight. Being symbols of power and authority, these things had become incorporated into the traditions of their gift culture as an appropriate offering to the gods in recognition of their majesty and power and in exchange for their favors. Such notions were easily appropriated by Christians and later, with the feudalization of the church, recast into the act of pious homage. Gifts were the supreme act of charity by which Christians could placate and appease God; they also brought grace and helped deceased relatives. Churchmen thus regarded conspicuous riches as the necessary attribute of their exclusive elitist position and of the majesty of the church itself. Moreover, through the doctrine of divine immanence in the physical world, Christians enhanced the spirituality of precious materials by charging their particular qualities of durability and luster with symbolic meaning. In the early twelfth century Abbot Suger wrote with passionate enthusiasm about the luxury he lavished on the decoration of liturgical space in the rebuilding of the church of Saint Denis, virtually endowing material splendor with theological content.

The criticism Suger received from Saint Bernard precisely on this score, and later challenges from groups like the Waldensians and the Franciscans directed against what they regarded as luxury-run-rampant among the clergy, are explicable only within a tradition of the religious appropriation and exaltation of luxury as a symbol of power designed to command reverence and obedience. In the thirteenth century Saint Thomas Aquinas, reworking classical concepts taken from Aristotle's *Ethics*, underpinned this tradition with philosophic arguments for the virtue of magnificence, justifying large expenditures for religious and public buildings. The repeated failure of persistent efforts to extol the ideal of poverty in the face of the growing material wealth of the church, so conspicuous in the luxury of its liturgical apparatus, attests the continuing power of this tradition right through the Counter Reformation.

The liturgical apparatus, in short, was endowed with the inherent qualities of luxury in its materials and craftsmanship in its production. Hence, a basic economic fact about its history is that demand for it required a high level of investment. To the extent that luxury means fine craftsmanship rather than just rarity or preciousness of materials, the numerous items included in this apparatus have gained recognition today as art objects. In the following discussion the term *church artwork* is to be understood as referring to the entirety of the liturgical apparatus as it has been described here. The proposition is not difficult to accept in the context of the historiography of medieval art, but it needs emphasis in a discussion of Renaissance art. It is an undeniable injustice, of course, to treat great art masterpieces of painting, sculpture, and architecture in this generic way as a category of durable goods within material culture, for they are thereby deprived of that essential quality that defines their status today as art; but by establishing the common denominator these objects shared with others that constituted the liturgical apparatus, we get closer to their original function and therefore to the occasion for their creation in the first place.

## Pictorial Forms

Another marked characteristic of church art is the prominence of imagery. The admission of the image into the church was undoubtedly the most momentous innovation in the history of Christian art, and it happened very early on in the history of the religion. In contrast to Judaism and to Islam, Christianity, with its early acceptance of holy people as intercessors after death and with the cult of relics, revealed a strong tendency to incorporate the image into its religious practices. As a religion founded on the theological tenet of incarnation of the deity and based on texts with considerable narrative content, including the drama commemorated in its most sacred rite, Christianity emphasized story in the discourse it used to win its way in the Roman Empire; and the religion had much material that lent itself to visual representation. The full impact of imagery on popular religious sensibilities was apparent in the development of mosaics and icons in the Byzantine world of the sixth and seventh centuries. The iconoclastic controversy, though evidence of a lingering fear of idolatry, could nevertheless have broken out only in a society in which the pictorial arts were regarded as an essential element of religious culture. Medievalists, who have been much concerned with the relation of literate culture to the illiterate masses and with what are called "textual communities," recognize the importance of images in the teaching of religious ideas and practices; but they have not altogether clarified how an increasingly pictorial communication—along with the sheer visual splendor of the liturgical apparatus in general—affected the Christianization of the masses and shaped the religious culture of the Middle Ages.

In the early centuries of Western Christianity, however, imagery was limited to small liturgical objects—above all, books—kept near the altar and not generally visible to the wider public, and one can wonder to what extent ordinary people were accustomed to images at all.[2] It was only from the eleventh century onward that imagery became more common, more public, and more monumental. Highly visible, public imagery appeared first in plastic objects such as reliquaries and sculpture; but soon other forms, such as stained glass, mosaics, mural painting, and decorated altar fronts, further expanded this public world of images. By this time tradition fully validated the pictorial arts for the didactic, devotional, and mnemonic functions that had been attributed to images by clerics as early as Gregory the Great and the victors in the iconoclastic controversy: images served as a medium for instruction about religious matters, they could have the inherent spiritual power to stimulate devotion, and they complemented reading as essential devices for the memorization, recollection, and hence comprehension of textual materials. Moreover, the medieval mind showed a characteristic penchant for the learned art of encapsulating theological and moral statements in visual signs and symbols. According to some, in fact, works of art deserved a special reverence since artists themselves, notwithstanding their lowly status as manual artisans, labored in the direct service of God and analogously to God as creators of images.[3]

Painted images began to proliferate inside Italian churches in the thirteenth century, and they took two basic forms that are central to the history of Italian art and largely distinguish it from art in the rest of medieval Europe—the wall fresco and panel painting. Mural decoration, both painting and mosaic, had been used in church interiors ever since Christians began building places of worship. Mosaics became a major art form for the decoration of churches in the Byzantine Empire from its very inception; and by the high Middle Ages in the West, the less expensive form of painted mural decoration could be found everywhere all across the map of Christian Europe, including many provincial churches. Beginning in the eleventh century in Italy, with the growth of the communes and closer contacts with Byzantium, mosaics were used extensively to decorate more prestigious churches both inside and out; and the new mendicant orders that appeared in the thirteenth century made major use of fresco for the embellishment of church interiors. Above all, the Franciscans and Dominicans adopted the medium as a major instrument for didactic purposes in conjunction with their preaching mission, often covering all available wall surface with illustrations as instructional aids to involve worshipers more emo-

2. Georges Duby, *The Age of the Cathedrals: Art and Society, 980–1420* (Chicago, 1981), p. 21.

3. Hans R. Hahnloser, "Du culte de l'image au moyen âge," in *Cristianesimo e ragion di stato: L'umanesimo e il demoniaco nell'arte*, ed. Enrico Castelli (Rome, 1953), pp. 225–33.

tionally in their teaching and enhance the architectural ambience for what was in a certain sense an extraliturgical service. The rapid proliferation of mendicant churches from the later thirteenth century onward generated that demand around which the early history of the art of fresco in Italy is written. Meanwhile in northern Europe, however, wall painting fell out of fashion and had little further development. Gothic architecture could hardly accommodate—aesthetically and physically—this kind of interior decoration; hence, there was not the demand for prestige work that might have stimulated the evolution of the form. The French Franciscans and Dominicans, for instance, failed to develop mural painting with anything like the originality in style and iconography of their Italian brothers.[4]

Panel painting, the other new pictorial form that came into its own in the thirteenth century, developed both as an accessory to the liturgy and as a devotional object outside the liturgical apparatus. Interest in painted images was probably aroused by the Byzantine icons that showed up among the vast numbers of reliquaries and relics flooding Italian markets in the thirteenth century as a consequence of commercial penetration by Italian merchants into the East in the wake of the crusades, especially following the Venetian conquest of Constantinople in 1204. Some icons of Christ and the holy figures associated with him were regarded as authoritative representations—if not as originals painted by Saint Luke, Nicodemus, and other holy men, at least as copies in a tradition going back to the originals; and these often became cult objects themselves, sharing with the sacraments and relics the power to mediate grace. As a portable object not placed on the altar or embedded in the fabric of the church, a panel painting could be taken outside the church; and outside it easily accommodated itself to the new kind of devotional piety that arose in the thirteenth century independent of traditional liturgical piety. With its diffusion in this freer market, it generated a new kind of demand for religious art and took on an inner life as a devotional object. The place panel painting eventually found in Italian religious practice was somewhat different from that of the Eastern icon in that it was not tied to the liturgy; it therefore had a larger potential market as well as freer range for iconographical development.[5]

4. Joan Evans, *Art in Medieval France* (Oxford, 1948), ch. 6.

5. Hans Belting, *Das Bild und sein Publikum im Mittelalter: Form und Funktion früher Bildtafeln der Passion* (Berlin, 1981); see also by Belting, "Die Reaktion der Kunst des 13. Jahrhunderts auf den Import von Reliquien und Ikonen," in *Il medio oriente e l'occidente nell'arte del XIII secolo*, ed. Belting (Bologna, 1982), pp. 35–53; and his "Icons and Roman Society in the Twelfth Century," in *Italian Church Decoration of the Middle Ages and Early*

Also in the thirteenth century a change in liturgical practice was introduced that is thought to have long-range implications for the history of religious art in Italy. As a result of the elaboration of theological notions about the host culminating in the promulgation of the doctrine of transubstantiation by the Fourth Lateran Council in 1215, a new emphasis was placed on seeing and adoring the consecrated host during the mass. The priestly act of transforming the bread into the body of Christ became a visible spectacle of high drama at the altar accompanied by the ringing of bells, special lighting effects, the burning of incense, and chanting so that for the laity, seeing the host took precedence even over receiving it. The exclusion of the laity from taking communion in both kinds and the infrequency with which it was taken at all only heightened its mystery.

If the new practice did not change the essential nature of the apparatus, it nevertheless meant an elaboration of liturgical performance, and obviously such a spectacle required an appropriate setting. The priest, who formerly said mass from behind the altar table facing the people, now performed his awesome act with his back to them. The utensils and furnishings associated with the host—pyxes and other receptacles for it, the monstrance to expose it between liturgical services and in processions, and the tabernacle as its visible storage place—were a major concern of the Lateran Council, and they subsequently became more elaborate. The tabernacle underwent a particularly interesting artistic evolution in fifteenth-century Tuscany as it moved from seclusion in the sacristy to a conspicuous monument on the side wall in the church and then to a central place on the altar table, where various solutions were worked out for its eventual accommodation.

The retable, or altarpiece, was another furnishing to undergo a rapid development beginning in the thirteenth century largely to complement the new liturgical arrangements, although such objects can be dated at least as far back as Carolingian times. Synodal legislation inspired by the Fourth Lateran Council's concern for the appropriate furnishings at the altar called for a conspicuous inscription or image at the altar to identify its titular saint. Since the priest now had his back to the congregation, the far side of the altar table lent itself to the invention of an appropriate backdrop to frame the ritual. One of the solutions was the painted altarpiece, and some of the earliest of these—for example, in the cathedral of Siena—were altar fronts appropriated for this purpose. The altarpiece evolved rapidly into a monumental work both to

*Renaissance: Functions, Forms, and Regional Traditions*, ed. William Tronzo (Bologna, 1989), p. 41.

identify the altar and to give focus and significance to what went on before it.[6]

FROM THE THIRTEENTH CENTURY ONWARD the religious world of Italians filled up with images in frescoes and altarpieces so rapidly and conspicuously as to mark a virtual watershed in the history of Christian art—if not also in the history of religious sensibilities; and by the sixteenth century people throughout most of northern and central Italy were playing out their religious lives, private and public, in the rich pictorial world we know as the Renaissance. The process by which Italian churches came to be filled up with murals and altarpieces started in Rome, in Tuscany, and to a lesser extent in Umbria, where they made their first appearance and had their early evolution; only slowly did they show up elsewhere. For instance, the altarpiece is not found in large quantities in other regions of northern Italy much before the fifteenth century. The eventual accommodation at the altar of both retable and tabernacle required a significant change in altar design, and solutions were a long time working themselves out. Still, at the end of the sixteenth century they were by no means standardized, and Carlo Borromeo was gravely concerned with the problem. Any generalization about the course of the history of the altarpiece in Italy as a whole must therefore be carefully qualified by geographical, chronological, and formal considerations. Moreover, as the altarpiece evolved as a formal object into a number of physical types, it took on a variety of functions arising out of its relation not only to its place in the larger decorative scheme of the altar and chapel but also to the liturgy and to the private intentions of its patron. Demand for the altarpiece, therefore, was a complex matter: it arose out of these various functions and evolved in distinct geographical and chronological patterns. In these terms it would be as difficult to generalize about the demand for altarpieces as it would be for us to see them not as individual works of art but as a specific kind of object with its own historical development.

Behind this complexity, however, is the basic fact that the altarpiece was indeed a distinct kind of object that in all its various forms nevertheless followed on the demand for the liturgical apparatus in general. For example, the influence of the Franciscans in particular on the subject matter in painting is well known, but so many pictures illustrating their ideas would not have been commissioned if there had not been new churches and altars to decorate. To say that Franciscan art arose from a

6. H. W. van Os, *Sienese Altarpieces 1215–1460: Form, Content, Function* (Groningen, 1984), 1:13–14.

new kind of religious spirituality or from new aesthetic notions is to explain why it looks the way it does, but this overlooks one of the permissive causes for the commissioning of it in the first place—the existence of new churches. The distinction is important to make in order to understand the rise of the pictorial arts within the manufacturing sector of the economy and the production of one of the most characteristic durable goods within the material culture of Renaissance Italy.

To recapitulate: in the thirteenth century new functions for the pictorial arts led to innovation within the liturgical apparatus, and the process of accommodation of these new products within the consumption model allowed considerable variation as production increased steadily across the fourteenth and fifteenth centuries. This diffusion, variation, and development of products had a complex historical development, and art-historical scholarship is directed to telling us all about this. The soaring demand that enlarged the market parameters for the production of all these things, however, cannot be altogether explained by the usual art-historical categories—the stylistic development of artists, the evolution of forms, the meaning of images, the specific needs and taste of patrons—since the demand for pictorial decoration depended on the prior existence of altars and churches to be decorated. In other words, while the demand for pictures did not necessarily derive from the demand for the liturgical apparatus, the liturgical apparatus was necessarily the prior condition for that demand. If, therefore, demand soared for pictures, it is likely it was also soaring for the entire liturgical apparatus of which they were just a part, from the altar to the church building itself; and to this extent forces independent of the liturgy account for the vigor of the Renaissance art market. The burden of the following discussion is to explain whence the demand arose that set off the extraordinary growth of what we can call the religious-art industry as a whole, including everything from luxury textiles for ecclesiastical garments to architecture for churches.

## VARIABLES OF CONSUMER BEHAVIOR

The market potential for pictorial artwork that opened up in the later thirteenth century went much beyond the furnishing of a fixed stock of churches and monasteries with altarpieces and frescoes. Demand was not just a matter of bringing the church's liturgical apparatus up to date according to a slightly enlarged consumption model for religious art. The new pictorial forms appeared in a market in which the demand for the entire liturgical apparatus was beginning to soar as a consequence of the erection of more altars in churches, the construction of more churches and religious houses, and the rebuilding of others. In fact, the remodeling, replacement, and enlargement of the entire physical plant of the church that got under way around 1300 reached boom proportions, and this general renewal sustained the demand for religious art of all kinds—painting, sculpture, and architecture as well as virtually the entire range of the minor arts—at an extraordinarily high level throughout the entire Renaissance, challenging producers to technical and stylistic innovations in their competition with one another in the market.

Since the religious realm underwent less of a change in its basic material culture as embodied in the liturgical apparatus than the secular realm, wealth alone might seem to have been the most important cause of the proliferation and elaboration of objects of religious art. Many of the developments in the history of religious art can in fact be explained on the demand side by greater wealth and on the supply side by producers' efforts to get a larger share of the market. As the wealth of Italy grew in the later Middle Ages and through the Renaissance, the rich could more easily afford the ever more elaborate and more luxurious decoration of chapels and churches, culminating in the extravagance of the Baroque; and the greater social diffusion of wealth can explain the success of painters, such as Neri di Bicci, in finding customers far down the social scale. New technology enabled artists to produce cheaper products, like the oil painters who could make larger pictures in less time and at lower prices and like the Della Robbia who could produce cheaper sculpture in glazed terra cotta. And what are the innovations in style associated with the Renaissance if not a kind of product innovation in fashion to win more of the market? Vasari says as much when he explains the preeminence of Florentine painters in the progress of art by referring to the more competitive—and therefore more challenging—market in which they had to work.

Nevertheless, religious art is not an ordinary consumer durable. Although most religious art was commissioned by private persons, the demand for it was not altogether a private matter: it had to accommodate itself to the church's needs and functions. The church created the structure through which private demand was channeled; and if demand in the Renaissance was strengthened by all those aspects of greater wealth surveyed in the previous discussion, it was because that structure facilitated the flow of wealth to the market. Since the liturgical apparatus serves the clergy for the performance of its professional activity, demand for religious artwork can be regarded as arising from pressure put on the church to expand its operations. This pressure, in turn, came from two quarters—the clergy, who, besides a vocation to serve the public, had its own reasons (as we shall see) for needing more churches and altars; and the laity, who sought an essential service for its spiritual benefit. Analyzed with reference to these two components, demand for religious artwork becomes a complex dynamic, shaped and augmented by a variety of different and often unrelated though converging forces that did not arise from, and were not conditioned by, the inherent nature of the liturgical apparatus itself. The task in the following discussion is to sort out some of the more important of these variables and to indicate the extent to which they were peculiar to the Italian scene—if not in kind, at least in degree.

## Institutional Proliferation within the Church

### Structural Transformations

The most obvious reason for rising demand from the clergy for the liturgical apparatus, apart from the desire to accommodate the laity's need for its services, might seem to be the growth in the number of priests and monks. The need to accommodate their liturgical obligations is in fact often cited to explain the addition of secondary altars around the apses of the great Gothic churches in the twelfth century. With the expansion of the mendicant orders in the next century, the number of clerics certainly grew, probably at a greater rate than the rapid rise of urban population at the same time. Although the demographic disasters of the fourteenth century struck the clergy as severely as any group—perhaps even more, because clergymen exposed themselves excessively to contagion from the sick and dead they attended—it continued to increase through the sixteenth century as a cohort within the total population. In Florence the number remained fairly stable from the time of Villani's estimate of about 1,500 to 1,600 in the early fourteenth century to 1427, but in the meanwhile the general population fell by more than half and perhaps as much as two-thirds (depending on whose estimate one accepts), so that the proportion of ecclesiastics doubled, if not tripled. The proportion more than doubled yet again by the mid-sixteenth century, by which time they numbered over 5,000 out of a population of less than 60,000. The population of nuns went up from 1,000 in 1427 to 2,500 in 1515, when fifteen of the largest convents averaged about 100 inmates, and to about 3,400 by the mid-sixteenth century, when about one-eighth of the female population lived in religious houses.[7]

---

7. David Herlihy and Christiane Klapisch, *Les Toscans et leurs familles* (Paris, 1978), p. 158 (the fourteenth-century figures, however, are based on Villani and therefore subject to debate).

The clergy's need for the liturgical apparatus, however, depended less on the size of its ranks than on its institutional organization. The institutional structure of the clergy was founded on a solid material basis, from the small parish church with a single altar equipped with the necessary liturgical utensils to the great monastery with its church and the full panoply of residential and service buildings around the cloister. Each foundation was a consumer and had substantial minimum needs for the liturgical apparatus, and this demand was not directly correlated to the number of clergy associated with it. Five monasteries each with only ten monks requires substantially more plant and equipment than one monastery with fifty monks. To the extent demand for the liturgical apparatus in fact depended on the number of foundation-consumers, it was more closely tied to an independent dynamic peculiar to the evolution of the institutional structure of the church than to either the number of clergy or the general demographic trend.

The architectural history of medieval Europe has been organized, consciously or unconsciously, around this aspect of the history of the church. The demographic growth and economic expansion of Europe from the eleventh century onward were accompanied by the strengthening of the episcopal structure of the church, with the emergence of powerful bishops, the expansion of the parish network, and the foundation of new monastic orders. By the twelfth century the growth of cities, with their concentrated populations and powerful resident bishops or communal governments, gave rise to the great age of cathedral building, while the consolidation of the feudal nobility brought increased patronage to monastic institutions serving its needs. In the thirteenth century a new division of the clergy—the mendicants—arose to cater to the specific needs of urban populations, and their buildings became major monuments on the urban scene. Students of medieval art generally regard the principal chapters in the history of medieval architecture as corresponding to all these phases in the institutional development of the church—first, the spread of monasticism; second, the concurrent building up of the parish structure of the secular church and the rise of the prestigious episcopal centers; and, third, the subsequent appearance of the preaching orders with their great urban churches and popular art forms.

Behind the vigorous demand for the extraordinary enlargement and renewal of the physical plant of the church that took place from the fourteenth through the sixteenth centuries was the continuing force of a dynamic seemingly endemic to the very structure of the late medieval church—the dynamic of institutional proliferation with its corollary of the propagation of new foundations. The production of much Renaissance art, in other words, supplied a market that was expanding as a result of organizational developments within the church. These developments, it is important to note, were largely independent of the course of demographic history, for the dynamic of institutional proliferation remained vigorous across the entire span of time we are interested in, while the population suffered immense losses in the fourteenth century and recovered slowly, only reaching its former level toward the end of the sixteenth century.

The discussion in the following pages is directed to describing this institutional proliferation within the church and to explaining why this dynamic of proliferation was especially powerful in Italy. The concern is not with the inherent spiritual quality of the religious movements behind the foundation of new institutions (nor therefore with the religious content of art) but with the pattern of organizational change. Structural change within the church explains the resulting kaleidoscopic configuration of new foundations and their demand for buildings and liturgical apparatus. For institutional proliferation was the essential dynamic behind much patronage of religious art.

THE HISTORY OF THE MEDIEVAL CHURCH is very much the story of the proliferation of institutions. Indeed, institutional proliferation was a notable structural feature in the growth and the development of the church as an organization. Organized almost from its inception around a self-perpetuating priestly caste based on the elitist, hierarchical, and monarchical principles inherent in the doctrines of the apostolic succession and papal supremacy, the church lacked the coercive power to command obedience according to a simple authoritarian model. Its genius as an institution, in fact, is to be found in its ability to absorb the innumerable religious movements that sprang up spontaneously as a developing European society underwent profound economic, social, and political transformations. Such movements always carried the threat of heresy and open clashes with the ecclesiastical establishment, and the history of medieval Christianity is not without its moments of violent internal conflict; but most movements eventually gained official recognition—or, rather, were successfully coopted by the official church. This flexibility required compromise to prevent the centrifugal forces from getting out of hand, and the instrument of compromise was institutional identity. As a result, institutions proliferated within the body of the church, and hence the medieval church grew as a loose and increasingly complex organization.

The proliferation of institutions was of two kinds. First was the process by which spontaneous movements arising from outside the ecclesiastical structure eventually gained official status and were integrated into the structure. Proliferation increased as the rapid pace of economic, social, and political change that overtook Europe from the eleventh century onward aroused new forms of religious piety and as new cultural interests changed intellectuals' understanding of their religion. This dynamic was particularly vigorous in Italy because of the extraordinary urban development there and also because of the inextricable involvement of the papacy in political affairs.

A second dynamic of proliferation was internal reform, the process by which dissident splinter groups within established institutions broke away from the parent organization to form yet new institutions. Often the kind of accommodation with the establishment that led to the formation of a new institution involved a modification of the movement's original aspirations, and with the passing of time such an institution was likely to be plagued by reformers seeking to recover what they considered hopelessly compromised causes— hence yet another round of proliferation, as such splinter groups, fired by religious zeal and seeking their own autonomy, broke off from established organizations and set up their own. Such reform movements, furthermore, released a dynamic for the propagation of foundations. The reform dynamic is perhaps inherent in any religious organization, but it was all the more vigorous in a loose institutional structure like that of the medieval church.

The church's perennial problem in dealing with these expansive tendencies was to maintain the delicate and dangerous balance between orthodoxy and heresy, sectarianism and compromise. If it demonstrated considerable flexibility in meeting the particular religious needs of an increasingly diverse and complex society, this was often less a matter of choice than necessity. Although the papacy was a centralizing agency, the authoritarian ideals of the great thirteenth-century popes Innocent III and Boniface VIII were far from universally accepted; and in any case the papacy did not have the power to overcome the precarious political situation in Italy and to make its limited authority felt over the great distances in Europe. Not until the Counter Reformation did the popes get a firmer grip on ecclesiastical affairs and finally realize somewhat more of the potential for authoritarian power inherent in the basic organizational principles of the church from its very beginning. By that time, however, the reform forces in northern Europe were already out of control and had rent forever the fabric of Christendom.

A pattern of four successive phases of institutional proliferation can be identified in the evolution of the ecclesiastical structure from the high Middle Ages to the Counter Reformation, each following somewhat different lines of development and diversification yet all propagating new foundations: the first in the eleventh and twelfth centuries, with the growth of the secular clergy through the episcopal and parish network and with the organization of new monastic orders for Benedictine monks and canons regular; the second in the thirteenth century, with the emergence of the mendicants as an entirely new division of the clergy alongside the secular and regular clergy; the third from the fourteenth to the sixteenth centuries, with reform movements within both the monastic and mendicant orders; the fourth in the sixteenth century, with the reform of the secular clergy. This last reform constitutes a kind of finale to the entire process of the church's institutional evolution: it effectively counteracted once and for all the vigorous centrifugal forces of the medieval and Renaissance church by putting into place the centralized, hierarchical, and authoritarian organization of the modern Catholic church.

THE FIRST PHASE OF INSTITUTIONAL GROWTH was set off by the political stabilization and economic recovery of Europe around 1000 A.D. With the enormous surge in population and the appearance of towns at this time, bishops consolidated their administrative centers and laid out the basic parish network that remained in place for the rest of the Middle Ages. This strengthening of the infrastructure of the secular clergy entailed massive investment in physical plant from great cathedrals to small rural churches. It was, perhaps, the greatest period for building in the history of Christianity. Given the undeveloped state of the European economy at the time, this building nourished the roots of artisan traditions in the production of the liturgical apparatus, even though much of the building and furnishing of rural churches remained modest.

Contemporaneously the reinvigoration of the regular clergy, inspired by the reform of Cluny, led to the construction of many new monastic houses. An eremitical movement of ascetic reforms, the Cluniacs sought to combat popular heresies and simoniacal clerics, but they eventually returned to their original monastic impulse. Nevertheless, the movement changed the structure of the monastic division of the church by introducing higher-level associations of houses, or congregations, for the purpose of consolidating reform and founding new houses. The vigor of some of these congregations in the propagation of new foundations was such that they took on an identity as new orders: the Camaldolesi, Vallombrosans, and Cistercians in the eleventh century and subsequently, around 1100, the Carthusians, Grandmontines, Fontevrists, Savignaics, and, in Italy, the Pulsanesi and Albi. Most of these orders, with links to the rural nobility, ignored the growing towns and established their houses in remote places in the countryside.

The same spirit of reform and corporatism within the regular clergy took hold of that sector of the secular clergy—the canons—attached to cathedrals at a time when they were beginning to emerge as centers of wealth and power as a result of the growth of towns and the emergence of feudal government. These clerics sought their own identity by organizing themselves according to rules going back to Saint Augustine. Their houses associated with one another in congregations, such as the Premonstratensians; and these canons regular, as they were called, were brought together in the loosely organized order of the Augustinian (or Austin) Canons. The military orders represented a third movement of institutional innovation and proliferation that arose at this time. Although inspired by a different kind of religious zeal in the spirit of the crusades, these orders were also organized on the monastic model and had ties to the rural nobility; and they came to constitute a distinct if small subdivision within the clergy.

This monastic phase in the development of the structure of the medieval church was marked by the foundation of new orders and congregations and by the propagation within these institutions of numerous houses based more or less on the monastic model; and the demand of these new houses accounted for much of the art and architecture of the high Middle Ages. Because the material support for new houses as well as for cathedrals came from the dominant class in an agrarian economy, this demand was more substantial in northern, feudal Europe than in Italy, where the rural nobility was less well entrenched but not yet displaced by the nascent urban elite. This is why so much of the history of art and architecture of the high Middle Ages, from the tenth into the thirteenth century, is written around evidence from northern Europe.

THE SUBSEQUENT PHASES OF INSTITUTIONAL DEVELOPMENT, however, are much more marked in Italy. The second phase came in the thirteenth century as a response to the new spirituality arising out of the urbanization of increasingly larger numbers of Europeans. The proliferation of institutions in this urban phase proceeded with greater intensity in the propagation of new foundations, followed a different pattern, and left a much more complex organizational structure in its wake; and it swept over Italy with more force than elsewhere. With it the demand for liturgical apparatus began to soar, stimulating the productive forces that created the religious art of the Renaissance.

In what we might call a process of epigenesis, spontaneous movements arising outside the traditional structure of the regular and secular clergy dedicated themselves to the spiritual needs of urban populations that were not being attended to by the established church. Already in the twelfth century the Humiliati, a semi-lay order dedicated to penitential work in towns, and other mass movements (such as the Cathars and the Waldensians) growing up around popular evangelical preachers and catering to townsmen raised such serious threats of heresy that by the thirteenth century the church recognized the need to incorporate such movements into its organization. To this end it created a new division within the clergy known as the mendicants; and the new orders—Franciscans, Dominicans, Carmelites, Servites, and Augustinian (or Austin) Friars, all established by the mid-thirteenth century—were remarkably prolific in founding new houses. Moreover, catering to the needs of the urban population, the mendicant orders involved the laity in the life of the order; and the consequence of this infrastructural accommodation of both men and women was yet another set of institutions—the so-called second order for women and the third orders for the laity (Tertiaries)—that propagated myriads of satellite communities. In the fifteenth century the Franciscans further refined this structure by dividing the Tertiaries into two groups, one of members who continued to live at home, the other of both men and women who lived in communities (the Third Order Regular).

The incorporation of women into the institutional structure of the church was one of the most notable features of urban life in late medieval Italy, and the phenomenon conditioned the demand for the liturgical apparatus in a particular way. Urban elites encouraged the foundation of convents, since they regarded cloistered women as serving a civic function in their role as spiritual intermediaries for the city. Many were minuscule communities, some having evolved from small informal gatherings. Hence they were more mutable and proliferated more vigorously. Female houses were on the whole much smaller than male houses; and in many towns they outnumbered male houses, it not being uncommon to find two and even more convents under the same rule in one city. In the later Renaissance the move of women to nunneries was largely an upper-class phenomenon resulting partly from a desire to provide for unmarried daughters in a period when patrimonies faced the threat of sharply rising dowries. In Florence, for instance, the ratio of daughters who were nuns to those who were married went from 39:100 to 102:100 across the sixteenth and seventeenth centuries; and in seventeenth-century Milan one-half to three-fourths of the daughters of noble families were in convents. Moreover, given their social background, women tended to bring more luxury into the convent than men, since nuns often brought with them not only dowries, which passed to the community as a whole, but also their own private resources. Wealth, therefore, emerged as a pronounced feature of cloistered female life, especially in the later sixteenth century. Much of it was released on the market to be spent for religious artwork.[8]

Urbanization thus induced considerable expansion of the institutional structure of the church. Cities also pulled the orders of the regular clergy irresistibly into their orbit and conditioned the further institutional development of the older monastic division of the clergy. Benedictine houses, especially those near towns, were drawn out of their cloistered isolation: they increasingly opened themselves up to laymen through a variety of services, including preaching, spiritual guidance, and charity in the name of lay penitents; they accepted lay men and women into their houses; and monks themselves began to move freely in the outside world. The new orders among them, in fact, resembled the mendicants. Thus the Celestines (1254), although organized as monks, modified their Benedictine rule to include both preaching and confessing, while both the new Benedictine orders of Sylvestrines (1231) and Olivetans (1319) tended to locate their monasteries in towns rather than in the isolation of the countryside. Likewise, the older eremitical orders like the Camaldolesi, as well as the Cistercians, dedicated to agricultural work, felt the need to set up new houses in towns. In fact, the only Camaldolesi house still true to its eremitical origins at the end of the fifteenth century was the mother house itself at Camaldoli. Most of the new Carthusian houses that proliferated in Italy at the end of the Middle Ages as never before were to be found just outside city walls as monumental burial grounds for their urban patrons.[9]

This second or urban phase of institutional proliferation, in short, was much more vigorous than the first. There were more new orders, and most of them constituted an entirely new division within the church; they sprang up at a rapid pace within just a few years of one

8. See in general Gabriella Zarri, "Aspetti dello sviluppo degli ordini religiosi in Italia tra Quattro e Cinquecento. Studi e problemi," in Strutture ecclesiastiche in Italia e in Germania prima della Riforma, ed. P. Prodi and P. Johanek (Bologna, 1984), pp. 207–57 (with further bibliography); and also, for the situation in seventeenth-century Rome, Marilyn R. Dunn, "Nuns as Patrons: The Decoration of S. Marta al Collegio Romano," Art Bulletin 70 (1988), 450–51 (with further bibliography). The Florentine ratios come from Enrico Stumpo, "Il consolidamento della grande proprietà ecclesiastica nell'età della Controriforma," in the Einaudi Storia d'Italia: Annali, vol. 9 (Turin, 1986), p. 273.

9. Gregorio Penco, Medioevo monastico (Rome, 1988), pp. 427–30. For a case study of the urban pull on monastic life, see Duane J. Osheim, A Tuscan Monastery and Its Social World: San Michele of Guamo (1156–1348) (Rome, 1989), ch. 5.

another; many of these orders reached out to incorporate women and laymen on an unprecedented scale; and, with the growing concentrations of urban population as the theater of action in which they competed with one another for support, they had a built-in dynamic for the propagation of new foundations unlike anything experienced by the monastic movement of the previous centuries. The regular clergy, however, was not left altogether behind: it too responded with new orders more oriented to urban conditions and with many new foundations within cities.

REFORM GAVE RISE TO THE THIRD PHASE of institutional proliferation, which therefore followed on the second both structurally and chronologically. In contrast to the previous monastic and urban phases, this growth was less a matter of new orders than internal division within the traditional structure of the orders, both mendicant and monastic. The new dynamic arose from movements within the orders that resulted in the creation of an intermediate level of associations to promote reform, thereby generating an infrastructural proliferation of congregations and the propagation of new houses. The process began in the fourteenth century and remained vigorous into the early sixteenth century, restlessly stirring up all the orders in an effort to return to what were conceived as original principles. The reformers were in effect splinter groups breaking away from parent institutions to reorganize older houses or to organize separate ones; and like-minded reformers from various houses united with one another in autonomous congregations within their orders to spearhead vigorous opposition movements from within and to gain the support of yet other houses. The establishment of a reform house did not necessarily mean a new foundation, but in Italy it often did. Moreover, the renewal explicit in the reform of an existing house, since it was usually achieved at the high emotional cost of a reform effort within a closed community, often signaled the occasion for refurbishing older quarters, if not the building of a new house. Arising from within the complex structure built up during the urban phase of the institutional evolution of the church, the reform movement was all the more effective in propagating new foundations.

Restlessness for reform particularly unsettled the mendicants, who held strong, idealistic notions about their role in urban life in contrast to the traditional roles of the secular and regular clergy. In the course of gaining acceptance by the church authorities, they had to adjust to the realities of life within the institutional organization the church imposed on them. This compromise bred discontent that eventually erupted in reform programs. Thus was born what is called the Observant movement, dedicated to the original intentions of the orders' founders as understood by the reformers. Observants made their appearance within most of the orders. They typically organized like-minded reformers within the same order into formal associations of houses called congregations, complete with their own vicars-general; and these formal reform institutions found additional strength in the aggressive stance they often had to take in the face of both the resistance of traditional elements within their own orders (called the Conventuals) and the opposition of constituted ecclesiastical authorities. Forces other than religious reform, of course, came into play within these movements, such as the vigorous personalities of the men involved on both sides, the intense zeal of some communities, and the special interest of political and church authorities (about which more will be said in due course).

The Observant movement within the Franciscan order is the best known. Originally dedicated to organizing a brotherhood around the model of poverty and renunciation laid down by Christ, the order found itself increasingly involved in problems of the material conditions of life arising from the institutional ownership of property. Compromise continually aroused the indignation of men who wanted to return to the ideals of the founder. The Spiritual Franciscans were an early movement of reform; their most extreme members, known as the Fraticelli, were a constant heretical challenge to the order until their numbers dwindled in the fifteenth century. At the end of the fourteenth century an Observant movement within the Franciscans got under way and soon enjoyed much organizational success. The Observants were vigorous and often outright hostile in their opposition to the Conventuals. By the early sixteenth century they had 600 houses in Italy alone, as many houses as the Conventuals—a growth that represented a doubling of Franciscan houses over the preceding century and a half. In 1517 the order was officially divided between the two rules. Moreover, other movements within the Franciscans eventually gained recognition as new orders—the Minims of San Francesco di Paolo, founded in the mid-fifteenth century, and the Capuchins, founded in the 1530s, both of which had many houses by the end of the sixteenth century.

Other orders experienced the rise of reform movements and congregations within their ranks in the later fourteenth and fifteenth centuries. The Dominicans, after the Franciscans the largest of the mendicant orders, were also torn apart by splinter groups and reformers, although eventually the Observants effected the reform of the entire order, thereby precluding the formal division that overtook the Franciscans. In the sixteenth century the Dominicans numbered over 300 houses plus more than 200 smaller establishments. Among the Augustinian Friars, who began organizing themselves into congregations in the late thirteenth century, the first congregation dedicated to a formal Observant movement dates from the early fifteenth century; and although the movement died down by the end of the century, the Augustinians ended up with 179 new houses divided in five congregations as compared with 333 unreformed houses. The first Observant group of the Servites was founded in 1411, that of the Carmelites the next year; the Humiliati had three congregations in Italy by the end of the fifteenth century.[10]

Reform movements also sprang up among regular monks and canons, who heretofore had shown little proclivity for corporate organization beyond their own communities. Monte Oliveto, founded as a new Benedictine house near Siena in the early fourteenth century, expanded into a congregation with 30 houses by the end of the century and more than 200 by 1500. The Congregation of Santa Giustina, founded at Padua in the early fifteenth century, directed its energies to reforming already established Benedictine houses, such as the Vallombrosans. Its organization of the Cassinese Congregation in 1504 became the largest and strongest of the associations of Benedictine monasteries in Italy. Italian Camaldolesi organized a congregation at the end of the fifteenth century and two more early in the next century. A reform movement within the Italian Cistercians resulted in the formation of a congregation that broke away from Cîteaux in 1497; and by the seventeenth century it had three congregations in Italy. Reform movements among the Austin canons led to the organization of a number of congregations; one of these, springing from a monastery reformed in 1401, had 11 houses by 1421, when it was officially recognized as the Lateran Canons, and 39 houses by 1485. Other congregations of canons were of more strictly regional importance—like the Alghensi Canons, founded in 1404 by young Venetian aristocrats, which eventually had houses throughout the Veneto.

The Observant movement was a general phenomenon throughout the orders of regular and mendicant clergy in the later fourteenth and fifteenth centuries; it was just one expression of the restlessness and increasing agitation for reform that disturbed the late medieval church. The same energy was channeled into the foundation of new orders. The Jesuates, an organization approved in 1367 and confined to Italy, started off as laymen dedicated to works of mercy and only much later admitted priests. The Swedish order of Bridgettines opened its first house in Italy a few years after its approval in 1370. Probably the most successful

---

10. Some of the statistics come from Zarri, "Aspetti dello sviluppo degli ordini religiosi," p. 223.

of the new orders were the Hieronymites. Founded in Spain in 1373, they soon had three congregations in Italy and by the end of the sixteenth century counted about 100 houses among them. The most severe of the older monastic orders, the Carthusians, underwent its greatest expansion in Italy in the late fourteenth and early fifteenth centuries.

All this proliferation within the religious orders was a general European phenomenon at the end of the Middle Ages and was not confined only to Italy. Most of the reform movements within the orders and new orders mentioned above showed up also in northern Europe. Erasmus, for one, lamented the internal divisions among the orders and the variety of their dress, inspired by the fashion among these different groups to set themselves off from one another. New orders and reorganizations within orders, however, did not necessarily mean an increase in the total number of religious houses. In northern Europe the Observant movement tended to absorb local Conventual houses rather than set up separate monasteries; and in England the number of houses of all kinds actually declined from the mid-fourteenth century to the eve of the Reformation. Given the general decline of the population everywhere in Europe in the fourteenth century, which then did not regain its former levels until the seventeenth century, it is hardly surprising that most religious communities also lost members and many eventually disappeared.

The scene was very different in Italy, however, where—notwithstanding the same demographic pattern—the institutional developments within the ecclesiastical structure spawned a more vigorous proliferation of new houses. The contrast is perhaps most marked in the history of female houses: whereas both their numbers and population fall off sharply in northern Europe at the end of the Middle Ages, they flourished in Italy, as noted above. Statistical data relevant to institutional proliferation in general, however, are hard to come by, and there is no clear map of new foundations available. Most of the new orders that have been mentioned were in fact Italian in origin and had their greatest success in Italy. Some were popular in Italy but had hardly any success abroad. The Sylvestrines, Lateran Canons, and Jesuates were essentially Italian orders. The Celestines at their height had two-thirds of their houses in Italy. The Servites did not appear in France until the late fifteenth century—two centuries after their foundation—and had only 6 houses by 1550. The Minims had only 13 houses in France by 1550.

Evidence from the history of the Franciscan movement, by far the most popular of these orders, can be taken as indicative of the general situation. Already by 1316 Italy had 567 friaries, as compared with

France with only 247 and Germany with 203, and more than twice as many nunneries as in both these other places combined. By the early sixteenth century new Observant houses numbered 600 in Italy as compared with 6 in England, 9 in Scotland, 16 in Holland, and just over 100 in France. Taken all together there were almost 50 percent more Franciscan houses alone in Italy (about 1,200) than there were monasteries, friaries, and nunneries of all kinds in the whole of England (just over 800). After the twofold increase in the number of Franciscan houses over the previous century and a half, fourteen Italian towns had 3 or more houses, most of which had been founded in the previous century, whereas in the rest of Europe only five towns had more than 2 houses and only fifteen had more than 1. In Lombardy alone (for which there is a statistical survey), 61 new Observant foundations were established in the fifteenth century and 21 more in the sixteenth century, when 52 Capuchin houses were also opened—all together, more than half the number of new foundations by all the mendicant orders in France from 1350 to 1550. The small town of Prato, with a population of just over five thousand in the sixteenth century, had no fewer than 9 houses of the various mendicant orders. Moreover, at the beginning of the fifteenth century, 250 of the 400 houses of the Franciscan Second Order of Saint Clare (the Poor Clares) were in Italy. As for the Third Order of Tertiaries, there is little evidence for them outside of Italy.[11]

THE FINAL PHASE IN THE STRUCTURAL EVOLUTION of the church came in the sixteenth century with the Counter Reformation, and it was also—at least initially—primarily an Italian phenomenon. It consisted of yet another wave of new institutions as well as renewal, both spiritual and physical, of the entire complex structure of the church as it had evolved up to that moment. Although a few older orders continued to spawn reform movements from within—for instance, the Carmelite Scalzi and the Capuchins within the Franciscans—it was now the secular clergy who seized the initiative. Up to this point the secular clergy, rendered inert largely as a result of having fallen victim to the rapacious

11. Statistics on houses can be found in John R. H. Moorman, *Medieval Franciscan Houses* (New York, 1983); Wolfgang Braunfels, *Monasteries of Western Europe: The Architecture of the Orders* (Princeton, 1972), p. 129; David Knowles and R. Neville Hadcock, *Medieval Religious Houses: England and Wales* (London, 1953), p. 364; *Il Francescanesimo in Lombardia: Storia e arte* (Milan, 1983), pp. 36–37; and Richard W. Emery, *The Friars in Medieval France: A Catalogue of French Mendicant Convents, 1200–1550* (New York, 1962), pp. 21–22. The towns selected for comparison are those that had a population of over twenty thousand around 1500 as listed in Jan de Vries, *European Urbanization, 1500–1800* (London, 1984).

use of benefices by the upper classes, had been eclipsed by the proliferation of orders and houses within the other divisions of the clergy. Indeed, both the emergence of the mendicant orders as a distinctly new category of clergy dedicated to the concerns of the urban masses and the spontaneous organization by laymen themselves into confraternities (discussed below) can be seen as a consequence of the weakness of the parish structure of the secular church. Clearly, the secular clergy was not meeting the religious needs of the laity. The deplorable decay of the physical plant of parish churches, lamented in the numerous visitations that got under way after the Council of Trent, marked the extent to which the functions of the secular clergy had been usurped by other institutions within the church.[12]

The reform movement among the secular clergy sought to get control over the dissipating forces of proliferation that had left the church with such an amorphous structure; but if they eventually achieved this by strengthening the central papal and episcopal framework of the ecclesiastical structure, their program unfolded through yet another new set of institutions. In the early sixteenth century, with reform movements running rife throughout the other divisions of the church and the Protestant Reformation gaining ground north of the Alps, some Italian secular priests began seriously to face the need for their own reformation. They joined together to subject their lives to disciplinary rules by organizing themselves into congregations, and out of these came the so-called New Orders—Theatines, Barnabites, Jesuits, Oratorians of Saint Philip Neri, Somaschi—all vigorous in promoting reform and prolific in setting up new houses throughout Italy. Moreover, since education was an important part of their program, their physical facilities, including schools and colleges for training both priests and laymen, could be as imposing as traditional religious houses. Hence, these New Orders released another new wave of spending, which extended well into the seventeenth century, to set themselves up for operation with the full complement of the liturgical apparatus.

The same spirit of reform among the secular clergy began also to move bishops to renounce absenteeism and to take up residence in their own cathedrals and tend to local affairs. They sought more administrative control by tightening their grip on the institutions within their diocese—chapters, parishes, and confraternities. The popes directed much effort to exerting authority over the loose structure of the church in order to bring some order to the welter of institutions that had grown

12. Adriano Prosperi, "Le istituzioni ecclesiastiche e le idee religiose," in *Il Rinascimento nelle corti padane: Società e cultura* (Bari, 1977), p. 143.

up within its various divisions. These reforms did the job of stabilizing the structure of the church and directing its further development along completely different lines defined now by the more centralized, bureaucratic, and authoritarian model of the modern Catholic church.

THE VIGOROUS DYNAMIC OF PROLIFERATION and propagation within the institutional structure of the late medieval church was a major force for generating demand for buildings and the liturgical apparatus that in effect resulted in an enormous expansion of the physical plant of the church. At each phase, new or reformed ecclesiastical institutions had to have the appropriate buildings to house their communities and the necessary liturgical accouterments to perform their religious functions. Buildings assured stability and durability to those communities, especially those of friars, who had a natural tendency to move around. They also made a public statement about the presence of the religious community, and in an urban world this was important in winning the support of the laity through the services offered by the community. A new building, or major rebuilding of existing buildings in instances when a reform movement took over an older establishment, was a kind of advertisement essential to the success of a new foundation.

The statistical data for the physical building of new foundations are not yet complete enough to permit us to draw a graph representing the demand curves corresponding to the phases of institutional proliferation described here. With this kind of information we could document specific moments and places of patronage and measure their relative impact on the market: in other words, we could identify specific art markets, as defined in quantitative terms, in time and space and so correlate their patterns with the chronology and geography of Italian Renaissance art as we now understand it in qualitative terms.

The general pattern over the long run, however, is clear enough: it marks a continual rise of demand through the last three of the four phases of the history recounted here, from the end of the thirteenth through the sixteenth centuries, and much of this demand was concentrated in Italy. In the urban phase the mendicant movement not only propagated new houses at a rate much higher than the regular clergy had in the earlier phase, but it created an infrastructure of institutions for large numbers of women and laymen organized into their own communities. In the next phase reform movements among both regulars and mendicants occasioned the foundation of even more houses as well as the rebuilding of older ones. In the final phase the secular clergy created numerous institutions of its own that gave rise to another wave of new foundations. The ultimate objective of this last movement, however, was to reestablish papal control over the church's entire structure throughout all its divisions, hence extinguishing once and for all the restless proliferation that had characterized the history of the medieval church. Yet, by promoting a thoroughgoing liturgical reform throughout the church, it generated one final spurt of demand for the renewal of the entire physical plant of the church as well, with the result that enormous resources were poured into the market for the liturgical apparatus in all divisions of the clergy.

One of the chief reforms inspired by the spirit of the Council of Trent was to make the liturgy at once more accessible and more impressive in order to involve the worshiper more actively. This renewal of the efficacy of the cult itself required nothing less than a program for the physical rehabilitation of churches. It entailed clearing away the clutter and disorder of accumulated religious paraphernalia and restoring altars to a pristine purity. The great model bishop—so considered at the time and ever since—was Carlo Borromeo, of Milan. His treatise (1577) of instructions for cleaning up churches became the standard manual on the subject, although it largely codified a body of practice growing up at the time among other reform-minded bishops. Borromeo was called the "cardinal sacristan" because of the zeal with which he attended to the most minute details of church arrangements. Altars were to be appropriately located and set off architecturally, no longer just put up casually against columns and here and there along the walls, and they were to have railings to keep out the public; the high altar was to be elevated on three sides by steps up to it; the tabernacle on it was to be given conspicuous prominence and appropriately decorated; the space in front of the high altar was to be enlarged and a balustrade erected around it to separate this zone from the congregation as a kind of stage; all utensils, furnishings, and decoration were to be of the most splendid kind; pictorial decoration was to be severely appropriate in iconography and in visual effects—one could go on and on with Borromeo's instructions for the restoration of churches, in effect describing what began to happen to churches all over Italy.

Monastic and mendicant communities, too, were caught up in this reform effort to bring the mass closer to the participants, and the remodeling problems in their churches were no less serious. Heretofore many of these churches had enormous interior structures of rood screens and enclosures extending from the altar well into the nave that separated monks and friars from the public, but now these were ripped out to expose the altar fully, leaving the clergy to build a choir area for themselves behind the altar. These renovations posed monumental redecoration problems in the main body of the church.

This physical renewal within all the divisions of the church was not specifically legislated by Trent but grew out of the spirit of reform that possessed the men who gathered at Trent and who felt the urgency of elevating the cult to a new level of dignity and efficacy. If the restless proliferation of institutions in the late medieval church had spawned the seemingly endless propagation of new foundations, now all of these came in for a general overhaul. There was hardly a church anywhere in Italy that did not get redecorated in one way or another. In strictly quantitative terms, the productive forces that sustained this renewal and enlargement of Italy's artistic patrimony in the religious sphere well into the seventeenth century had never reached, nor were ever again to reach, such a high level. The Counter Reformation thus came as the climax in the long rise of demand for religious artwork that stretched over the entire Renaissance. The fact that so much of the physical plant of the church that was refurbished at that time remains intact over three hundred years later (and more would have survived had it not been for recent historicist efforts at "restoration") marks the success of the Counter Reformation in suppressing much of the internal dynamic of institutional evolution that had made the late medieval church such a powerful consumer in the art market.[13]

## Why Italy?

In his study contrasting the church in Italy with the church in England in the thirteenth century, Robert Brentano remarked the "different humors . . . different personalities . . . [and] clear difference in their styles."[14] Behind this difference was the most basic condition of Italian civilization: its urban setting. The city, with its monetized marketplace, was inherently a place of constant social change and uprootedness, much more than the countryside. In the urban setting traditional religious values had to confront new attitudes and notions; and what was often an ensuing clash generated new kinds of concerns and practices—forcing the merchant, for instance, to deal with his insecurity and guilt through penance and charity, and the poor to seek solace in religious devotions. Religious expression of these changes was much more likely to take an institutional form in the city, where there was a far greater

13. The story of Borromeo's influence in his own diocese is recounted by Maria Luisa Gatti Perer, "Cultura e socialità dell'altare barocco nell'antica Diocesi di Milano," *Arte Lombarda* 42–43 (1975), 11–66; for the problems of redecorating monastic churches, see Marcia Hall, *Renovation and Counter-Reformation: Vasari and Duke Cosimo in Sta Maria Novella and Sta Croce, 1565–1577* (Oxford, 1979).

14. Robert Brentano, *Two Churches: England and Italy in the Thirteenth Century* (Princeton, 1968), p. 352.

proclivity for different forms of association, than among the scattered populations in the countryside. Given the rapid development of the Italian economy, the intricacies of Italian politics both within and without the city-state, and the complex texture of urban society in general, the pace of change in Italian cities was arguably greater than in most cities elsewhere, and therefore they were more religiously volatile. In any case, the fact that Italy was simply more urbanized in the first place meant a more restless religious energy and therefore a greater challenge to the church's ability to meet the spiritual needs of the people.

Statistics—such as they are—reveal the basic difference about the urban scene in Italy. Before the Black Death, Italy was by far the most urbanized area in Europe: it had the three regions with the most concentration of urban population—those of Milan, Venice, and Florence—and each exceeded the fourth—that of Ghent—by more than 50 percent. Eleven cities had a population of over 40,000, as compared with only eight or nine in the rest of Europe; over seventy had a population of 10,000 to 40,000, as compared with only about fifty for the rest of Europe; and well over one hundred were in the next category going down to around 5,000. Moreover, most of these cities were concentrated in the Po Valley and central Italy, an area that counted as many cities with a population of over 20,000 as France, the Low Countries, England, and the Empire combined.

Italian cities suffered great losses with the plagues of the fourteenth century, many never again regaining their earlier levels of population; meanwhile, in the later Middle Ages northern Europe became more urban. Still, at the end of the fifteenth century, however, Italy counted between a fourth and a third of all European cities with a population of over 10,000 and more than half (ten out of eighteen) of those with a population of over 40,000. Italy had a larger concentration of urban population than any other place in Europe, with north Italy alone accounting for about 20 percent of the total urban population of western Europe. One-eighth of the population of the entire peninsula lived in cities, three times the proportion in France and four times that in Germany and England. Although the Low Countries had a substantially higher percentage of the total population living in towns, Italy had twice as large an urban population in absolute numbers; collectively, Venice, Milan, Genoa, and Florence alone had as many people as lived in all the twenty-one cities in Flanders and the Low Countries with a population of over 10,000. In short, urban growth had been much more rapid in Italy, and the rest of Europe had not caught up by the end of the Middle Ages. In the Po Valley, moreover, most cities had recovered from earlier losses by the latter half of the sixteenth century, some becoming larger than they ever had been before; and some cities elsewhere—Genoa and Venice, but above all Rome and Naples—underwent vigorous growth.[15]

If Italian religious life was more urban oriented than in the north, it was also subject to a church with a different structure. In northern Europe the church was fully integrated into the feudal system: the great monasteries were themselves powerful landowners, and cathedral chapters were thoroughly penetrated by the feudal nobility. By the end of the Middle Ages, northern European monarchs, taking advantage of the weakness of the papacy resulting from the schism and subsequently the failure of the conciliar movement, had gone a long way toward the establishment of a "national" church under their control. This veritable constitutional revolution, as it has been called, hardly extended into Italy. The development of a territorial church within the various city-states was limited in Italy, so that church and state never consolidated their relation into anything like a state church. This was largely a result of the greater political role the church was forced to play in Italy, both by the pope as a head of state himself and by bishops as contenders in the local arena of urban politics during the Investiture Controversy. More-over, the church itself lacked a highly centralized authority. The popes failed to stabilize the internal structure of the church. Subject to a variety of external pressures, they created and suppressed dioceses, changed their boundaries, shifted monastic houses from one order to another, readily approved new movements such as the Observants—all of which gave rise to a certain instability and discord within the church and contributed greatly to the continual failure of reform movements within the orders. At the local level bishops had little control over parishes, many of which were under the patronage of private persons or monasteries; and when the mendicant orders appeared, they brought many parishes under their purview. Likewise, cathedral chapters en-joyed a certain autonomy, and in many towns the cathedral itself was under civic rather than episcopal management. In his comparison of the churches of England and Italy, Brentano so stressed the "insubstan-tiality" and the "administrative unimportance" of the Italian diocese already in the thirteenth century that in the end he felt compelled to

15. Maria Ginatempo and Lucia Sandri, *L'Italia delle città: Il popolamento urbano tra Medioevo e Rinascimento (secoli XIII–XVI)* (Florence, 1990), pp. 195–222; Josiah Cox Russell, *Medieval Regions and Their Cities* (Newton Abbot, 1972), p. 235; de Vries, *European Urbanization*, app. 1; P. M. M. Klep, "Urban Decline in Brabant: The Traditional-ization of Investments and Labour (1374–1896)," in *The Rise and Decline of Urban Industries in Italy and in the Low Countries (Late Middle Ages—Early Modern Times)*, ed. H. Van der Wee (Leuven, 1988), pp. 266–67.

caution that "Italy was not, of course, completely without any bishops who took their jobs seriously."[16]

Recent studies have emphasized the close relation between civil society and religious organization and how the city moved into the gap left by weak episcopal authority to support and even sponsor new institutions, a situation that obviously contributed to their proliferation. The remarkable success of the Observant movement, for example, has been partly attributed to the vigorous support it had from newer urban elites and despots who took the opportunity to establish their credentials in the religious life of the city in opposition to traditional ecclesiastical authority tied to the interests of an older political class that was being replaced. Rulers also saw in these movements the possibility of creating something like a state church. Thus Venice supported new congregations of Austin Friars, Franciscans, Camaldolesi, and Carmelites to promote a strong territorial Venetian church; Siena's political interests strongly influenced the Observant movement among the Augustinians, which had originated there; the Gonzaga at Mantua encouraged the effort to introduce the Observant movement in Carmelite houses throughout their territories; and the d'Este at Ferrara patronized Observant movements in monastic houses to enhance the sanctity of their state.[17]

Sometimes states regarded support of these religious movements in the wider context of foreign policy, as a way of extending their influence abroad. For this same reason many states supported local congregations to reduce influence from abroad by other congregations and resisted penetration of new congregations from abroad associated with other states. The Venetians encouraged the diffusion of the reforms sponsored by the Congregation of Santa Giustina at Padua as a way to promote their influence in monasteries abroad; and Florence zealously supported Franciscan Observants, both defending new houses from the Conventuals and encouraging expansion. Relations between reform congregations could therefore be exacerbated by the political relations of their patrons. When the Lombard Congregation of Dominican Ob-

16. Brentano, *Two Churches*, p. 189; Giorgio Chittolini, "Stati regionali e istituzioni ecclesiastiche nell'Italia centrosettentrionale del Quattrocento," in *Storia d'Italia: Annali*, vol. 9 (1986), pp. 190–91.

17. Chittolini, "Stati regionali e istituzioni ecclesiastiche," pp. 174–77; Prosperi, "Istituzioni ecclesiastiche," p. 135; Zarri, "Aspetti dello sviluppo degli ordini religiosi," p. 209 (with bibliography). For instances of private support of new foundations, see Nicolai Rubinstein, "Lay Patronage and Observant Reform in Fifteenth-Century Florence," in *Christianity and the Renaissance: Images and Religious Imagination in the Quattrocento*, ed. T. Verdon and J. Henderson (Syracuse, N.Y., 1990), pp. 64–82.

servants sought to enlist houses throughout Italy, the opposition to it by Savonarola's congregation in Florence was undoubtedly related to political considerations. The attitude of the Florentine ruling class toward reform within the Servite order encapsulated the general Italian situation. Although a Florentine order, the Observant movement grew up outside Florence, in north Italy; and the Florentine government supported efforts of the community at the Santissima Annunziata to resist being absorbed into it. The city won papal approval for separation of this church as well as the mother house at Monte Senario (in 1447 and 1473, respectively) from the Observant movement on the grounds that Florentine friars would therefore be free to return to Florence and so liberate themselves from the Lombard Observants.[18]

The political aspect of the reform movements was more pronounced in Italy because the peninsula was so politically fragmented and the rivalry between states so intense. One cannot deny the genuine religious feelings with which some princes and elites promoted reform movements as well as other welfare and confraternal institutions, but their support almost always had political implications. Patronage of this kind further stimulated institutional proliferation and also introduced a prestige factor that raised the level of competition among institutions and hence amplified demand for an appropriate physical expression of the status they sought.

This ecclesiastical situation in a period generally marked by doctrinal confusion favored the birth of new religious institutions and assured their autonomy and freedom from traditional ecclesiastical authorities; and this proliferation in turn meant increasing disparity and variety. The considerable fluidity that resulted among Italian religious institutions is another variable in the quantitative assessment of the consumer presence in the market for religious artwork. In contrast, for example, to English monasteries, which enjoyed the economic stability of extensive and well-managed rural estates, the fortunes of Italian religious houses were tied to the fluid economy of the city and dependent on volatile public support: they might suddenly enjoy a windfall of good fortune with a large bequest from a rich merchant or with a flood of requests for private chapels, or they might be devastated by the loss of public support as a result of negative attitudes about wealth that periodically surfaced in popular movements.[19] Many of the smaller institutions such as nunneries and hospices were subject to rapidly changing

18. Roberto Bizzocchi, *Chiesa e potere nella Toscana del Quattrocento* (Bologna, 1987), pp. 78–81.
19. A point made by Brentano, *Two Churches*, p. 351.

fortune, and the fortunes of others fluctuated with rises and falls in their membership rosters. Finally, the winds of reform could breathe new life into an institution so it could attract funds for refurbishing its quarters, something that happened frequently, if sporadically, in the fourteenth and fifteenth centuries and more generally with the Counter Reformation in the sixteenth century.

These Italian institutions, in short, were forever moving up and down in the ranking order of wealth; in the process, some were absorbed by others, and some disappeared—for example, a convent in Florence, according to a 1478 tax document, absorbed the nuns from no fewer than six others that had been closed down.[20] Whenever institutional quarters passed from one hand to another, however, the passage likely marked the occasion for refurbishing to a greater or lesser degree as a signal of a new regime. Hence, to the extent that in all this fluidity there was upward mobility in economic status, it had the effect of renewing demand and hence sustaining the force of demand beyond the initial impetus arising from the proliferation of new institutions. Demand was thus amplified by a high incidence of renewal as consumers came and went in the fluid urban markets of late medieval Italy. It is enough to read through a book like the Paatzes' catalogue-history of Florentine churches to get a sense of how often many of these foundations were rebuilt and rebuilt anew across the entire Renaissance according to their changing fortunes, with the major surges coming first at the end of the thirteenth century, then in the later fourteenth and fifteenth centuries, and then again in the later sixteenth century.

The most powerful component force within this dynamic of proliferation and fluidity within the structure of the church at the end of the Middle Ages was a process not of the secularization of the church but of the laicization of religion, a process initiated largely from outside the sacramental church of the secular clergy to satisfy the increasing religious restlessness of the urban laity. In a very real sense, the institutional proliferation and fragmentation that arose from this restlessness marked the extent to which the secular church got left behind in tending to the needs of the laity. This process of laicization was a powerful force in arousing the demand that enlarged the material culture of the church.

When, with the Counter Reformation, the secular clergy finally got around to putting its house in order, redecoration and rebuilding of churches were central to the reform program; and given the immense size and diffusion of the secular clergy, this reform gave rise to the

---

20. Gene Brucker, "Monasteries, Friaries, and Nunneries in Quattrocento Florence," in Verdon and Henderson, *Christianity and the Renaissance*, pp. 42–62.

veritable boom in the production of the liturgical apparatus we associate with the late Renaissance and Baroque in art and architecture. By this time the physical plant of the church in Italy was more extensive than it was in northern Europe, so that there was much more renovation to be done to bring churches in line with Counter Reformation standards; and the great wealth that was continuing to accumulate in Italy could be tapped to finance the effort. Moreover, the internal stability of the political order in Italy, now isolated from the European theater of power politics, favored what can be called "the great rebuilding" within the ecclesiastical patrimony, whereas northern Europe at this time, by way of contrast, was racked by religious wars and overrun by iconoclasts. This last great period in the history of religious art in the West was almost exclusively an Italian phenomenon.

## Lay Demand for Services

At the same time the church was expanding its physical facilities to accommodate the institutional proliferation arising from within its formal structure, it was also under increasing pressure from the laity for services that entailed further outlay for liturgical apparatus. In fact, much of the dynamic of proliferation and propagation examined in the previous section arose out of clerics' perception of the needs of the lay public and their desire to offer new and more services. The two phenomena are closely interrelated: the real costs incurred by the propagation of new foundations were met not by dipping into institutional coffers but, in effect, by selling services to the laity at the local level of each new foundation. New or remodeled buildings complete with their panoply of liturgical objects paid for themselves by attracting more business. In economic terms, the church offered an essential service in the tertiary sector that entailed considerable investment in durable goods and plant; and it so successfully aroused the demand for its services that the public began to take its own initiatives to satisfy its demand.

The most obvious correlation between propagation of new foundations and the market for the clergy's services might seem to be demographic. The great rise of population in Europe accompanying its economic takeoff from the eleventh century onward generated demand for more religious services. By the end of the thirteenth century almost four thousand churches of one kind or another had sprung up in that small part of Tuscany corresponding today to no more than the dioceses of Florence and Fiesole.[21] Florence itself had about fifty parish

21. Italo Moretti, "Espansione demografica, sviluppo economico, e pievi romaniche: Il caso del contado fiorentino," *Ricerche storiche* 13 (1983), 34.

churches, and Venice had closer to seventy. The growth of urban concentrations in Italy helps account for the rapid expansion of the mendicant orders in the thirteenth century. Many of their communities—like
the Franciscans at Santa Croce and the Dominicans at Santa Maria
Novella in Florence—had to rebuild their original churches into larger
structures already before the century was out; in addition, the friars
invaded the territory of the secular church by opening their own parish
churches.

This simple correlation of demography and demand, however, cannot be made for the later period of the Renaissance. The population
reached the apex of its growth in the early fourteenth century, when it
was drastically reduced by the cycle of plagues associated with the
Black Death. The recovery was slow, stretching over the entire period
we are interested in; and the population did not again reach its former
height until the seventeenth century, with many Italian cities still remaining at a level appreciably lower than in 1300. The two cities that
experienced the most significant population rise in the sixteenth
century—Rome and Naples—did in fact become major markets for
liturgical apparatus, partly in response to the needs of a larger population; and both cities figure prominently in the history of later Renaissance art. Yet despite the general demographic trend, with its sharp fall
and slow recovery from the fourteenth to the seventeenth century, the
demand for religious art continued its upward curve across the entire
period.

Demand for the church's services clearly depended not only on the
number of consumers but also on the variety and extent of their spiritual needs. In the thirteenth century, as already remarked, the pressure on
the church from the mounting population concentrations in Italian
cities was compounded by new kinds of spiritual problems that heightened religious sensibilities of urban dwellers, so that at the same time
the church found itself ministering to more souls, these people had an
even greater need for the church's services. In part this religious restlessness can be attributed to the problems of uprootedness, fluidity, precar-
iousness, and violence attendant on the uncontrolled and rapid urban
growth that outpaced the development of the appropriate political institutions to deal with the harsh realities of urban living. Heretical and
confraternal movements, new devotional cults, and more extreme
kinds of religious experiences were the characteristic and spontaneous
expressions in the spiritual world of this developing urban society, a
world inextricably bound up with the mendicant movement.

Spiritual restlessness mounted in intensity with the economic and
social problems created by the growth of population that in the four-

teenth century began to reach the upper limits of what the economy could support. The subsequent fall in population, however, did not bring any relief to the religious situation. On the contrary, according to a commonplace in the historical literature about popular religion throughout Europe at the end of the Middle Ages, both the demographic disasters of the fourteenth century and the devastation of frequent wars—in Italy arising from the political anarchy before the establishment of the precarious balance of power in the mid-fifteenth century—further heightened the intensity of spiritual concerns. In other words, with the mounting spiritual restlessness from the fourteenth century onward, the level of individual demand for religious services may have risen in inverse relation to the fall in the number of consumers, in effect more than counterbalancing the decline of population.

What has been called here spiritual restlessness must not be understood as simply a response to harsh conditions of life. The lay piety of the later Middle Ages that scholars of the last generation have so much emphasized has somewhat obscured a fundamental shift in Christian culture. From the eleventh century onward the laity increasingly sought to participate more directly in the sacred life that heretofore had been the preserve of the priestly caste. This evoked a response from the church, which most notably took the form of the mendicant movement, to cater to this new spirituality; but these new expectations also prompted the laity to search for its own outlets, releasing a dynamic that here will be referred to as the laicization of religion.[22]

The objective of the ensuing discussion is to enquire not into the underlying influences that shaped the spirituality of the later Middle Ages and Renaissance but into how this spirituality generated the material culture of the church. Religious restlessness was not an intangible, purely spiritual state of mind. In ministering to it the clergy institutionalized its services by inspiring and directing new forms of piety that in effect stimulated demand for its services and thereby impinged also on the demand for liturgical apparatus. The clergy came up with devices to meet the spiritual problems of a changing society, to focus the growing restlessness on legitimate practices, and to keep the laicization of religion within acceptable bounds. The mendicant movement as a whole represented an institutional device to meet the needs of urban masses; other devices included confraternities, the cult of the saints, indulgences, and the practice of commemorative and votive masses. To the extent these institutions, instruments, and practices became a part of habitual behavior, demand for them outlived the immediate spiritual

22. Van Engen, "Christian Middle Ages," pp. 547–48.

needs they originally addressed, to be sustained eventually by custom. Thus the rising demand for the church's services throughout the later Middle Ages takes its own upward course independent of the number of consumers linked to demographic movements. In a sense, what we have here is a veritable religious consumerism centering on demand for services but not without implications also for the demand for material goods, a consumerism stimulated and renewed by the providers of these services and sustained at an ever-higher level by custom. The deepest roots of the consumerism of the West may well lie in this aspect of medieval religion.

Two forces, therefore, converge in the demand for increased services from the clergy—the clergy's initiatives to stimulate and channel demand by providing new services and the laity's initiatives to seek more services; the following discussion is directed to explaining how this demand for the clergy's services impinged directly on the demand for the liturgical apparatus and enlarged the material culture of the church.

## Church Initiatives

Commemorative masses. Perhaps the single most important new practice introduced into the religious lives of Europeans that called for expanded service from the clergy arose from the doctrine of indulgences. This doctrine was based on the notion of purgatory, which developed with the theology of life after death and gained widespread popularity in the thirteenth century. Purgatory created what has been called a distinct "age group" of the population, people beyond life but not yet at their final destination and still in relation with the living through the practice of the cult;[23] and indulgences were the instruments of communication conceived to benefit both one's self and others after death. In a sense, indulgences reified the gift exchange that determined the structure of relations between believer and divinity.

The indulgence was a financial instrument that opened up to the general population the kind of investment the aristocracy had long been making. In building churches and monasteries the landed feudal nobility in effect bought commemoration, and they could count on family networks both inside and outside the clergy to tend to their memory. From the thirteenth century onward this new instrument enabled others to take up the practice—first, the wealthy laity, and then an ever-wider segment of the urban population who could invest more modest funds and found their social support groups instead in ecclesiastical institutions and confraternities. It is not surprising, therefore, that in-

23. John Bossy, *Christianity in the West, 1400–1700* (Oxford, 1985), p. 30.

dulgences have been seen as a monetary device, developed in the context of a growing market economy, by which the church was able to increase its liquid income and urban workers could offer their support without loss of time. The practice served to bind the church and the new urban population in a monetary nexus to the convenience of both. Money, moreover, served as a lubricant that accelerated the flow of demand and services.

If death became a more highly individualized personal concern as compared with the more generalized approach of an earlier period, it also became highly socialized through the material culture that grew up around the practices associated with it. The practice required concrete investment in the next life—for endowments to pay for commemorative masses, for altars for the celebration of these masses, for tombs to remind heirs of their duty—and the construction of a social apparatus to maintain these practices. It is often argued that the fourteenth-century plagues heightened these demands the dead made on the living. To meet the crushing demand for masses, the church needed more and more priests, some of whom found this their sole activity; and the continuing rise in the number of priests in the face of general demographic decline is probably related to the increased demand for their services. More priests needed more altars where they could execute their responsibilities. The mendicants in particular greatly enhanced the importance of secondary altars by moving relics from relatively secluded crypts to prominent places in the main body of the church and by promoting the saying of masses for the dead. With more altars, more endowments for masses, and more priests, what have been called "veritable mass factories" grew up to meet the demand.[24] In fifteenth-century Florence, the clergy at some churches had to see to the serving of as many as a hundred masses every day.[25]

The cult of the saints.    The theology of purgatory and the practice of indulgences promoted saints as divine intercessors, and a revitalized cult of the saints was another service provided by the church for which there was growing demand and which required the appropriate apparatus—altars and chapels with all their accouterments, including decorations. The cult dated from late antiquity but picked up notably in the thirteenth century and flourished throughout the end of the Middle Ages and the Renaissance, nowhere more than in Italy.

24. Francis Oakley, *The Western Church in the Later Middle Ages* (Ithaca, N.Y., 1979), p. 118.

25. Robert Gaston, "Liturgy and Patronage in San Lorenzo, Florence," in *Patronage, Art, and Society in Renaissance Italy*, ed. F. W. Kent and P. Simons (Oxford, 1987), p. 130.

Several scholars have recently tried to quantify and interpret the phenomenon of the increase in the number of saints in Italy during this period. Although their figures are somewhat different, their conclusions agree on the prominence of Italy in the history of European saints from the thirteenth to the fifteenth century.[26] Whereas in the eleventh and twelfth centuries one-fifth of the new saints were Italian, the proportion grew to closer to three-fourths in the fourteenth century and to two-thirds in the fifteenth century before falling back to the earlier level in the sixteenth century. As many as two hundred new saints have been counted in Italy from the thirteenth to the mid-sixteenth century, three and a half times more than in France. Of the processes for papal canonization that were formally drawn up in the thirteenth and the first half of the fourteenth century, about one-third were Italian (slightly more English saints actually made it to canonization); but the vast majority of the new saints that captured the popular imagination did not receive official recognition at the time. In the fourteenth century many towns in northern and central Italy had a local holy figure, and a great center like Florence could claim as many as a dozen. The catalogue of "questi Santi novellini" numbered half as many as the original saints, lamented the Florentine storyteller Franco Sacchetti in the third quarter of the fourteenth century; and, while he was on the subject of the fickleness of fashions in religious practices, he went on to deride the numerous cults of the Virgin that kept springing up everywhere in Florence and had people running from one shrine to another to keep up with the latest version.[27]

One of the chief reasons saints proliferated in Italy more than elsewhere is the politicization of their cults. Many Italian saints were local figures associated with particular towns; and in a city-state system such as Italy's, governments had political motives for promoting a cult around a local saint, who could excite patriotism within the city and help in the conquest of the loyalties of the rural population within the orbit of the town's influence.[28] Moreover, cults were invigorated by the proliferation of orders, each with its founders and protagonists,

---

26. Quantitative data can be found in Rudolph M. Bell and Donald Weinstein, *Saints and Society: The Two Worlds of Western Christendom, 1000–1700* (Chicago, 1982); Denys Hay, *The Church in Italy in the Fifteenth Century* (Cambridge, 1977); and André Vauchez, *La sainteté en occident aux derniers siècles du moyen âge* (Paris, 1981).

27. Franco Sacchetti, *La battaglia delle belle donne, le lettere, le esposizioni di vangeli*, ed. Alberto Chiari (Bari, 1938), pp. 99–104.

28. André Vauchez, "Patronage des saints et religion civique dans l'Italie communale à la fin du Moyen Age," in *Patronage and Public in the Trecento*, ed. Vincent Moleta (Florence, 1986), pp. 59–80.

and by rivalries among them, each promoting its own favorites. As a result of the reform movements that arose among the regular and mendicant clergy in the fourteenth and fifteenth centuries, many splinter groups that broke away from the orders to establish their own houses and congregations often championed local saints, or saints who had emerged from their midst, to gain credibility, legitimacy, and support. To a certain extent, too, some saints were instruments of social promotion by new families, by older ones threatened with decline, and by families seeking local authority in the countryside at places associated with the origins of saintly ancestors where the family owned property.[29] All this agitation for canonization brought about by political interests—ecclesiastical and secular, communal and familial—was more intense in Italy because of some of the conditions already discussed: on the one hand, towns were more numerous and autonomous and institutional proliferation within the orders more vigorous, and, on the other, the church was a much more amorphous structure.

However politicized the cult of the saints was in Italy, it nevertheless dug deep roots into the religious sensibilities of ordinary folk, and it took on particular qualities as compared with the rest of Europe.[30] The cults arose above all in the towns of north and central Italy, and they captured the new popular religious feelings that were erupting in the urban environment. Indeed, the movement represented in a very real way the popularization of a religion that had earlier been highly elitist in its general tenor. André Vauchez calls this the "modernization" of Italian sainthood. Italian saints were predominantly merchants, friars, and women, in contrast to the north European model comprising martyrs, bishops, and princes. Moreover, they were usually local figures, of much more immediate familiarity to their public than earlier saints, who had long been dead and hence shrouded in the idealization of historical myth. Finally, late medieval saints became much more humanized than their predecessors: their cults caught something of the new devotional mood as well as some of the fanaticism so peculiar to popular religion at the end of the Middle Ages, and so they were able to establish a direct emotional relation with the worshiper.

The enthusiasm with which Italians accepted the intercession of saints accounts for the abandonment of traditional non-Christian names in all their variety and originality—one thinks of all the Floren-

29. Anna Benvenuti Papi, "S. Zanobi: Memoria episcopale, tradizioni civiche, e dignità familiari," in *I ceti dirigenti nella Toscana del Quattrocento* (Atti del V Convegno, 1982; Florence, 1987), pp. 111–15.

30. Vauchez, *Sainteté en occident*, pp. 165–287.

tine names of the thirteenth century that, like Machiavello, Guicciar-
dino, and Strozzo, eventually became surnames—for the standardized
list of modern names representing protecting saints. With this kind of
cult growing up around them, saints saw their powers slowly expanded
from that of divine intercessor to that of protector against the dangers
and evils that people had to confront every day. This aspect of the cult
reached its extreme in the fifteenth century with the popular assignment
of protection against very specific evils, some of the most insignificant
kind, to individual saints, a practice that eventually aroused scathing
criticism and satire. In these ways the cult reshaped itself according to
changing religious concerns, a process that helps account for its extraordinary vitality through the fifteenth century.[31]

The cult of the saints affected the demand for art not only by requiring more liturgical apparatus to accommodate the increased occasions
for votive masses but also by calling for its own apparatus. As the cult
grew, it lost its exclusive focus on the tomb as an object of pilgrimage,
to become diffused among altars elsewhere; and two particular objects
the cult required at the altar were a reliquary and an image of the saint.

The veneration of relics goes back at least as far as Saint Augustine
and was well established by the Carolingian period; but in the thirteenth
century its popularity became so much more widespread as to be a new
phenomenon. Relics as well as Byzantine reliquaries poured into Italy
from the East as a result of the conquest of Constantinople in 1204 and
the growing contact between the East and West thereafter. A lively
trade in these objects ensued, with Italy as the center of a distribution
network extending over all of western Europe. These new relics inspired their own cults, which were vigorously promoted partly in fund-
raising efforts by the churches where they ended up. Older Western
cults also became much more visible, as relics were brought out of the
crypt, where they had heretofore been hidden away with the tomb of
the saint, and moved to altars. At the same time, the proliferation of
contemporary saints increased the supply of holy objects associated
with saints, especially, of course, in Italy. As a result of the new craze,
relics came to have such mystical properties that the popular imagination was prepared to grasp anything as a cult object. The most trivial
object associated with a holy person qualified for recognition, and the
invention of things associated with Christ himself—a piece of the
swaddling clothes, a strand of his beard, a straw from the manger—
scandalized many religious reformers by the time of the Reformation.

31. Richard Kieckhefer, *Unquiet Souls: Fourteenth-Century Saints and Their Religious
Milieu* (Chicago, 1984), pp. 114–15; and Vauchez, *Sainteté en occident.*

Enormous collections of relics were built up and put on view on special occasions; and their popularity was frequently exploited to raise income from worshipers, to the extent that by the sixteenth century catalogues were published to advertise them.

Since relics had to be displayed with an appropriate sumptuousness, the growth of the cult was a boon to the production of reliquaries. The Fourth Lateran Council, held amidst the first wave of the new imports, gave impetus to the demand for more luxurious reliquaries by decreeing that relics were to be housed in appropriate shrines; subsequently the popes set an example by donating costly utensils to Roman churches.[32] Rich Byzantine reliquaries were themselves often treated as relics and inserted in their own mountings, and they provided models for Western imitation, Italy being a particularly important center of production. As the cult grew, however, new forms were designed to give maximum exposure to the relic itself inside, and these receptacles became subject to further stylistic and formal elaboration as the artisans who worked in the precious materials required to produce them took advantage of the expanding market opportunities. The goldsmith's craft, in fact, was a growth industry in the Renaissance, and its importance for the training of painters, sculptors, and architects has been abundantly documented.

Once synodal decrees required an altar to have an inscription or an image indicating to whom it was dedicated, images of saints became an important part of the altar equipment. Images of Mary proliferated with particular rapidity as a focus for the Marian devotion because so few relics of her survived, and many of these images became cult objects themselves. Likewise, saints' cults greatly increased the range of images in the pictorial world of religious practice. Images were used to propagandize the cult and to induce devotion; and to the extent an image could acquire the same powers associated with the tomb or relics of the saint, it could become as essential to the altar as these other, more concrete marks of the saint's presence. The ascendancy of the image in Italy as a cult object is perhaps also due to the fact that, with so many saints being near-contemporaries, their remains were not subject to dismemberment for relics. In Italy, in any case, the image usually took the form of a picture, whereas wood or stone sculpture was more common in the north.

Also of increasing importance to the apparatus of a cult along with

32. Michele Maccarrone, "'Cura animarum' e 'parochialis sacerdos' nelle costituzioni del IV concilio lateranense (1215): Applicazioni in Italia nel sec. XIII," in *Pievi e parrocchie in Italia nel basso medioevo (sec. XIII–XV)* (Rome, 1984), 1:156–57.

reliquaries and altar pictures, especially in the fourteenth century, was mural painting depicting the stories of saints as propaganda to arouse popular support for local cults by inspiring pilgrims to the proper devotion and establishing the basic iconography for the edification of the public. The great basilica dedicated to Saint Francis at Assisi is only the most notable example of such a propaganda campaign. Many cults were carefully directed by interested parties—a religious house, the local authorities—in what have been called genuine grass-roots movements that made it difficult for the papacy to reject eventual appeals for canonization. In fact, most of these late medieval saints achieved their status in the minds and practices of the people long before they were officially canonized. Painting could play an important role in such a campaign, and indeed, the diffusion of cults in Italy was probably directly related to the rise of this popular communication medium.[33]

### Lay Initiatives

The laity, too, took its own initiatives to assure itself of the church's services. Organizing themselves into confraternities, people transformed individual needs into corporate demand. They also bought liens on the services of the clergy through endowments. Some literally privatized liturgical space for themselves by buying chapels in churches and by building them in their own homes. The laity in general, finally, went one step further to develop its own forms of entirely private devotion; and if this kind of lay piety largely dispensed with the direct need for the clergy's services and therefore for the liturgical apparatus, its own needs for material objects generated demand for what might be called paraliturgical apparatus. In short, the laity came to represent a powerful force in the market for religious artwork, and this demand was much less structured than that which arose within the church. The church had encouraged consumption in connection with its services; and, not surprisingly, once the public entered the growing market for such things, it began to generate demand for itself.

Confraternities.  As the church evolved into a more complex and amorphous structure with the proliferation of institutions dominated by a religious elite, other kinds of institutions organized by the laity came to be included, to a greater or lesser extent, within the collectivity of the church in the sense that they were organized for religious pur-

33. See, for example, Julian Gardner, "The Cappellone di San Nicola at Tolentino: Some Functions of a Fourteenth-Century Fresco Cycle," in Tronzo, *Italian Church Decoration*, esp. pp. 108–10 and 117.

poses and accepted clerical leadership. This process of the organization of lay groups and then their incorporation into the church—or at least their recognition under the auspices of the church—might be considered another distinct phase of the proliferation of institutions within the structure of the church at the end of the Middle Ages discussed in the previous section. The development occurred concurrently with the evolution of the ecclesiastical structure from the thirteenth century onward, and it too is notable for an extraordinary propagation of foundations. The confraternal movement was an aspect of the laicization of the church, representing one stage beyond the mendicant movement within the clergy in its generation of highly independent and localized institutions that remained outside the orbit of the official ecclesiastical structure until the later Renaissance. For purposes of description here, these institutions can be categorized into confraternities and welfare foundations, although the two were not necessarily mutually exclusive.

In some essential respect, guilds were a kind of protoconfraternal movement. A guild was defined primarily by the economic activity of its members, who joined together for mutual benefits in a nascent urban society not yet firmly in place under a clearly defined public authority. At the time no such group could organize itself without a strong social and religious program, and in fact some guilds may have had their origins as confraternities. In any event, guilds organized religious celebrations of all kinds, from private worship to participation in public ceremonies. Religion was central to their existence, and all probably had a private oratory in their halls if not also a public chapel in a church. With guilds numbering in the dozens in larger towns (outside Tuscany, where guild government reduced their numbers), they augmented the demand for liturgical apparatus. In Venice, which had about a hundred guilds, as many as fifty altarpieces have been identified that were executed for guilds in the Renaissance down to 1610.[34]

Spontaneous religious movements among the laity independent of guild interests began to spring up in the thirteenth century as expressions of the spiritual restlessness among the growing urban populations already noted, the same restlessness that inspired the mendicant movement. These were movements in the sense that people organized themselves into groups for common religious activities; and they were served by the clergy, above all the mendicants, who appropriated the spirit of the movement in their Third Orders. Confraternities thus appeared as another tier of institutions alongside the mendicant

---

34. Peter Humfrey and Richard Mackenney, "The Venetian Trade Guilds as Patrons of Art in the Renaissance," *Burlington Magazine* 128 (1986), 317–30.

orders—if not indeed a further extension of the mendicants beyond the Tertiaries—to involve the laity actively in devotional and penitential exercises, charity and other good works, and spiritual self-discipline in general. Above all, however, they represented a group effort, often for people too poor to do anything on their own, to celebrate the rites of death, including burial, and to memorialize the dead through commemorative masses and acts of charity.

The popularity of confraternities among all classes exposed the weak parochial foundation of urban religion: the laity regarded confraternities as a more effective link to the sacramental church, and in fact, most early confraternities were not parish oriented. They have often been seen as inspired by the same forces that gave rise to the mendicant orders; but unlike the Third Order they sought to create a sacred community on their own, outside the constituted ecclesiastical institutions. Although many had statutes, they were largely free from the discipline of any ecclesiastical authority, and they did not join together into higher-level associations. As small autonomous groups, they were directly responsive to fashions and fluctuations of lay piety as well as to changing social pressures in the volatile environment of towns; and they proliferated boundlessly in the late thirteenth and fourteenth centuries, coming and going on the urban scene with great frequency as they rode the crest of emotions arising out of plagues, political disorders, economic crises, millennial expectations, and a host of other problems embedded in the social reality of people's existence. The popularity of confraternities was due in general to new attitudes toward death and to a strong need for corporate sociability in dealing with the problem. By 1300, confraternities generally fell into two categories— those dedicated to praising the divinity (*laudesi*) and those dedicated to rigorous penitential self-discipline (flagellants); but subsequently these distinctions tended to erode as confraternities took on a more generalized devotional character.[35]

The confraternal movement went through distinct phases according to the changing religious temper of the times, and as new organizations and functions thereby came into existence, demand was renewed for all those things needed for their religious activities. In contrast to the amorphous and spontaneous character of the earlier movement, a new wave of confraternities came in the wake of schism and conciliar movements in the fifteenth century that were more oriented to church reform

---

35. For a good overview of the subject based on a thorough evaluation of the historiographical tradition, see the general remarks of James R. Banker, *Death in the Community: Memorialization and Confraternities in an Italian Commune in the Late Middle Ages* (Athens, Ga., 1988).

and therefore more closely linked to the secular church; and yet another wave of new foundations came as reform picked up momentum in the sixteenth century in response to the general malaise of the church following the sack of Rome and the Protestant successes in northern Europe. These new confraternities focused their practices on such things as Marian devotions, the sacraments, the rosary, and Christian doctrine; and with the desire of single groups to establish common ground with like-minded groups in other places, and with efforts of the secular church finally to bring them under its control, these later devotional confraternities were prone to establish more organizational solidarity among themselves than did the earlier *laudesi* and flagellant groups. The Tridentine reforms reinforced these structures, and the process was also facilitated by the printing press, which permitted the circulation of common rules. Indeed, confraternities enjoyed a considerable revival in the sixteenth century as a major instrument by which the secular clergy, now for the first time, systematically mobilized the laity for its program of reform.

One approach toward consolidation was to organize new confraternities under episcopal auspices, such as those dedicated to the Holy Sacrament that Paul III encouraged in each parish as a vital aspect of his reform program. In the Milanese diocese this program, pursued with zeal by Carlo Borromeo, resulted in the organization of such confraternities in over five hundred parishes (more than two-thirds the total number) by the end of the sixteenth century. In Brescia the percentage was even higher, and in Venice most parish churches had an altar for this confraternity.[36] At a higher level was the archiconfraternity, endowed by the papacy with privileges and indulgence-granting powers and authorized to associate local groups with it. The archiconfraternity was an aggregate corporate organization under papal control with a network of confraternities that extended through all of Italy. The regular clergy also took a more active role in organizing confraternities around specific cults, such as those dedicated to the Madonna of the Rosary sponsored by the Dominicans. The Counter Reformation thus gave yet another boost to the proliferation of confraternities, bringing into existence a completely new generation of these institutions with which their modern history really begins. By the seventeenth century myriads of confraternities were scattered across the religious map of Italy; but by

---

36. P. Hills, "Piety and Patronage in Cinquecento Venice: Tintoretto and the Scuole del Sacramento," *Art History* 6 (1983), 30–43; Richard Mackenney, *Tradesmen and Traders: The World of the Guilds in Venice and Europe, c.1250–c.1650* (London, 1987), p. 48 (on Milan); Daniele Montanari, *Disciplinamento in terra veneta: La diocesi di Brescia nella seconda metà del XVI secolo* (Bologna, 1987), p. 211.

this time, in sharp contrast to the confraternal world of three hundred years earlier, they were largely under clerical control and often tied to one another in larger associations under the official auspices of the church.

The confraternal movement, in short, spawned an extraordinary propagation of foundations across the fourteenth, fifteenth, and six-teenth centuries, with considerable fluidity in their ranks. In Florence, 51 confraternities were founded in the fourteenth century and 87 more in the fifteenth century. In Genoa, 56 existed in 1480, 74 more were founded in the next hundred years, and at least 124 more appeared after 1582 down to the end of the eighteenth century, when there were more than 200 in existence. In Venice, statutes were approved for 45 new confraternities between 1360 and 1476, 210 different confraternity stan-dards were counted at a public funeral by Marin Sanudo in 1501, 119 confraternities participated in the procession of the doge's funeral in 1519, and 357 existed in the eighteenth century. The small town of Borgo San Sepolcro, with a population of about five thousand, saw 14 new confraternities spring up in the early fourteenth century, and other small towns like Norcia and Spello had about a dozen in the later sixteenth century. With the structural changes that brought greater parochial control over confraternities in the later period, they spread rapidly into parishes in the countryside. In the absence of further statis-tical materials it is impossible to chart the precise patterns in the secular trend of the proliferation of these institutions. Their ranks seemed to have been subject to considerable and erratic fluidity from their first appearance in the thirteenth century until the sixteenth century, when a massive number of new foundations appeared within the more stable structure provided by a reinvigorated secular church.[37]

37. Banker, *Death in the Community*, p. 110 (Borgo San Sepolcro); John Henderson, "Religious Confraternities and Death in Early Renaissance Florence," in *Florence and Italy: Renaissance Studies in Honour of Nicolai Rubinstein*, ed. P. Denley and C. Elam (London, 1988), p. 384; Edoardo Grendi, "Morfologia e dinamica della vita associativa urbana. Le confraternite a Genova fra i secoli XVI e XVII," *Atti della società ligure di storia patria*, n.s., 5, no. 79 (1965), 241–311; idem, "Le confraternite come fenomeno associativo e reli-gioso," in *Società, chiesa, e vita religiosa nell'Ancien Régime*, ed. Carlo Russo (Naples, 1976), pp. 115–86. On Venice, see Mackenney, *Tradesmen and Traders*, p. 48; Sanudo's observa-tion is cited by Peter Humfrey, "Competitive Devotions: The Venetian *Scuole Piccole* as Donors of Altarpieces in the Years around 1500," *Art Bulletin* 70 (1988), 405. On the vitality of confraternities in this period in general, see G. Alberigo, "Contributi alla storia delle Confraternite dei Disciplinati e della spiritualità laicale nei secc. XV e XVI," in *Il movimento dei disciplinati nel settimo centenario dal suo inizio*, ed. L. Scaramucci (Perugia, 1986), pp. 156–252; Danilo Zardin, "Le confraternite in Italia settentrionale fra XV e XVIII secolo," *Società e storia* 10 (1987), 81–137; and Christopher Black, *Italian Confrater-nities in the Sixteenth Century* (Cambridge, 1989), esp. pp. 50–57.

Confraternities were important new consumers in the market for religious artwork. Despite the distinct emotional tone of the early confraternities, all were similar, among other things, in their strong emphasis on liturgical practices. Some, especially those in the earlier period, assembled only occasionally, perhaps no more than several times a year, and so perhaps had little or no need to spend money for an altar; but the later ones became important consumers of goods. They often had to provide themselves with liturgical apparatus, some eventually going so far as to set up their own altars or chapels within churches. Once they were brought under the control of the secular church, they lived according to a more disciplined regimen and had more need of an altar in a church as a focus for funerals, masses for the dead, and devotions in general. Many went on to obtain an entire chapel, if not indeed an oratory or a more elaborate building complex like the famous Scuole Grandi of Venice. In fact, there was a general tendency in the later fifteenth and sixteenth centuries for confraternities to acquire their own quarters outside an established church.

Confraternities also took an increasingly prominent place in civic life, both in the greater participation in processions on public holidays and in the redirection of their activities to the performance of a social function, such as ministering to the spiritual needs of prisoners and those condemned to die and providing dowries for poor girls. This involvement in ceremonies and the heightened consciousness of a civic role aroused a greater desire for the conspicuous expression of their status. Their expenditures included, if not altars, chapels, or oratories, most certainly large and costly banners used in public processions, which were often painted by prominent artists. In Genoa the growing sumptuousness of confraternities, especially in ceremonial display, came under such criticism that in 1530 the authorities tried to limit them.

The increased pace of proliferation of confraternities from the fourteenth to the seventeenth century, in short, was accompanied by their transformation into more institutionalized organizations complete with the ownership of property. This meant an exponentially greater increase in the demand for the liturgical services of the church with all the material goods, including artwork, necessary for those services; and the fluidity within their ranks assured a continual renewal of that demand.[38] As they came under the control of more powerful institutions,

---

38. See, for instance, the observations of Gabriele De Rosa, "Problemi della storiografia confraternale," in *Le confraternite romane: Esperienza religiosa, società, committenza artistica*, ed. Luigi Fiorani (Rome, 1984), p. 26; and for Genoa, Grendi, "Morfologia e dinamica," pp. 292–98.

their material foundations were strengthened—whether that was under the auspices of a government or of the secular church. The *scuole* in Venice probably represent the highest expression of conspicuous prestige a confraternity could reach under civic auspices. The parochially controlled confraternities of the Counter Reformation era were major new consumers in the growing art market of later Renaissance and Baroque Italy. For instance, in Cremona at the end of the sixteenth century, confraternities along with schools and charitable institutions were much more important for the commissioning of new altar paintings than families and private individuals.[39]

Social welfare was another activity that generated a proliferation of institutions at the end of the Middle Ages, most of which, like confraternities, were organized around groups with a corporate religious commitment.[40] Hospices multiplied in the thirteenth and fourteenth centuries as a response to an increased urban consciousness of the problems of pilgrims, the poor, the sick, the aged, and orphans. Their history roughly falls into three phases. Initially they proliferated spontaneously, growing up in connection with confraternities and monasteries or founded by single benefactors. Then, in the fourteenth century, they tended to specialize in just one function, such as caring for orphans or the sick; and within this latter function some specialized further in dealing only with plague victims, with victims of venereal disease, or with convalescents. Finally, from the fifteenth century onward, governments began to intervene to effect a more efficient administration of public welfare, particularly with hospitals, by consolidating them in single establishments. Ravenna, for instance, which earlier had twenty-seven hospices, had only six at the beginning of the sixteenth century, and later in the century this number was reduced to two. Brescia in 1562 had six hospices, each with its own specialty: a general hospital for the poor, one for incurables, an orphanage, a home for the elderly, a home for the poor, and a hostel for the wandering poor. Although many of these earlier institutions were, of course, minuscule operations, even the smallest required quarters to house their wards and their resident staff, who for the most part were religious or quasi-religious groups. Their physical arrangements followed the monastic model in being organized around a cloister and including a chapel or church, and the quarters of the larger institutions had to be built in a

39. To judge from the exhibition catalogue *I Campi e la cultura artistica cremonese del Cinquecento* (Milan, 1985), passim.

40. Alessandro Pastore, "Strutture assistenziali fra chiesa e stati nell'Italia della Controriforma," *Storia d'Italia: Annali*, vol. 9 (1986), p. 435; Montanari, *Disciplinamento in terra veneta*, pp. 245–46.

manner commensurate with the importance of their public role.

An altogether different kind of welfare institution was the Monte di Pietà. Originating under Franciscan auspices at the end of the fifteenth century, the Monte was a kind of lending and pawn bank set up in an increasingly monetized economy to protect the poor from exploitation through distress loans from Jewish moneylenders. These institutions spread rapidly throughout Italy: in 1515 there were 185 Monti, many in places that were hardly large enough to qualify as towns. In the diocese of Brescia at the end of the century, there were 44, although a number of these in small rural communities trafficked more in grain than in money for the benefit of local peasants. As already noted, in some larger centers Monti gained such financial strength resulting from the influx of excess capital that they eventually fell victim to exploitation by local governments pressed for new sources of income. Monti established themselves as prominent public institutions even in small towns, and they housed their operations in a distinctive public palace that was often the most conspicuous secular building after the town hall. In Brescia the local Monte enlarged its premises in the course of the sixteenth century to stretch along the entire side of the central public square, and in many smaller places they were the only public buildings of any prominence at all.

Privatization of the church.   For the urban resident driven by the preoccupation with death that focused on the cult of purgatory, purchase of commemorative masses and association with confraternities sharpened what John Bossy has called "the sense of family property in the dead," resulting in "a sort of enclosure movement in the territory of the dead, destined to accommodate the claims of family ownership."[41] This same movement, beyond obtaining a lien on clerical activities for private purposes through the endowment of commemorative masses, included also the appropriation of liturgical space as personal property. Once the mendicants, ever anxious to build bridges of all kinds to a wide public, won papal approval for granting the privilege of burial in their churches, lay people could erect a tomb as a memory image that reminded heirs and descendants of their duty to offer commemorative masses. They could also make an outright purchase of the altar itself where the masses were to be said; and it was just another step again to finance the building of an entire chapel to accommodate the altar and perhaps also family tombs. A new kind of piety thus arose in the celebration of death that shifted its focus from earlier ascetic ideals of

41. Bossy, *Christianity in the West*, p. 33.

worldly denunciation to a cult of remembrance organized around things as concrete signs.[42]

In generating this material culture, the dead served the living on this side of life as well as beyond the grave, for their continuing presence in physical objects not only reminded survivors of their spiritual duty but also enhanced the worldly prestige of their families. Following along this path, the demand for the physical accommodations of churches took a new direction, where the objective was what we might call the privatization, if not also the secularization, of the liturgical apparatus. The building of tombs, altars, and chapels and the endowment of commemorative masses to maintain this property became a major expenditure for those who could afford them. The private altar had to be fitted out with all the necessary ecclesiastical furniture, utensils, and decoration; and the chapel opened up, in addition, the possibility of a large range of architectural, sculptural, and painted embellishment. These things were a major occasion for the commissioning of much ecclesiastical art throughout the period under examination. Moreover, the necessity of making physical accommodations to this end largely accounts for the success in the building of new churches by the mendicant and reformed orders; and many of these communities opened their entire quarters—and not just the church—to the new demand.

Private oratories and churches go back almost to the beginning of Christianity; but until these new developments in the thirteenth century, they were not numerous outside the great feudal and ecclesiastical aristocracy. Then, a prodigious proliferation of private altars and chapels began that continued across the entire period we are examining. The rich were the first to move in, but by the fifteenth century ordinary people were also looking for space. The Florentine chapter in this history is well documented. The earliest chapels there appear around the transepts (and therefore near the high altar) of the great mendicant churches, such as those built by the Bardi, Peruzzi, and other families at Santa Croce. The richest men, or the ones who could drive the hardest bargain (like the Alberti, again at Santa Croce), took over the patronage of the high altar itself, whence the space could extend into the nave to incorporate the entire choir area. Others moved into equally prestigious areas such as the sacristy (the Medici at San Lorenzo) or the chapter room (the Pazzi at Santa Croce). Once these zones had been appropriated, large chapel spaces could be built on as additions to the nave, as at Santa Trinita and the Santi Apostoli; and when an artist like Bru-

---

42. Samuel K. Cohn, *The Cult of Remembrance and the Black Death: Six Renaissance Cities in Central Italy* (Baltimore, 1992), dates this shift to the later fourteenth century.

nelleschi got such a commission—from the Barbadori for a chapel at Santa Felicita and from the Ridolfi for one at San Jacopo sopr'Arno—the chapel became a prominent architectural monument in itself.

The ultimate step was to build a completely new church planned from the beginning to maximize the space for private chapels—and to pay for it by selling off chapels pro rata. Thus the demand for chapels became a catalyst for rebuilding in the fifteenth century. Brunelleschi took this demand so much for granted that he made all of his churches chapel-lined—eight around the rotunda of Santa Maria degli Angeli, sixteen down the two sides of the nave at San Lorenzo, thirty-eight around the entire circumference of Santo Spirito except for the façade. Thereafter, most new church building in Florence and elsewhere followed this scheme, whether it was the great tribune at the Santissima Annunziata or a traditional nave structure, such as San Giuseppe, San Salvatore al Monte, and Santa Maria Maddalena dei Pazzi. It has been estimated that there were six hundred chapels scattered throughout Florentine churches in the fifteenth century,[43] and this is not to count the innumerable side altars that went up in those churches where extensive rebuilding of enlarged chapel-space was not possible, often because the church—like Santa Croce of the Franciscans, Santa Maria Novella of the Dominicans, and the cathedral itself (where, in fact, Brunelleschi had plans for adding side chapels)—was simply too large to make it economically feasible to undertake such extensive remodeling. The size of many of these new or rebuilt monastic churches depended more on the demand for private chapel space than on the number of friars or monks in the community or on the wealth of the foundation. Chapels, like any piece of private property, were bought and sold, such events being the occasion for physical redecoration.

A collective portrait of the Florentine patron will help illustrate this enthusiasm for chapel building. Chapel builders about whom something is known included people far down into the middling ranks of the hierarchy of wealth—a modest wool manufacturer, a bank broker, a goldsmith, a teacher of commercial arithmetic, a sculptor. A man of more substantial wealth might have chapels in more than one church—one in his parish church, another in the neighborhood mendicant church, perhaps another in a monastic church of an order he particularly favored; and he might have yet another chapel in a country place where he and his family owned property. A chapel might be a place tradi-

43. Creighton Gilbert, "The Patron of Starnina's Frescoes," in *Studies in Late Medieval and Renaissance Painting in Honor of Millard Meiss*, ed. Irving Lavin and John Plummer (New York, 1977), 1:189 n.

tionally associated with his family and built in cooperation with a large family group, or it might be an entirely private place; it might contain the patron's tomb, or it might serve only for commemorative masses in his memory. Filippo Strozzi bequeathed his chapel at Santa Maria Novella to his descendants as a burial vault; but Francesco Sassetti showed no concern in his testament for his heirs' use of his chapel at Santa Trinita, and Leonardo Bartolini explicitly stated in his will that his chapel at Cestello belonged to him alone and not to anyone else in his family. A survey of thirteen of the sixteen chapels built at the new Cistercian church of Cestello from 1480 to 1526 sharpens this collective portrait of the chapel builder: hardly any lived in the neighborhood and most lived far away, six are known to have had family chapels in other churches, three had associations with a third chapel in yet another church, only four are buried in their chapels at Cestello. At least three of these chapels changed hands within a generation of their building and yet again in the sixteenth century.[44]

The process of privatization of liturgical space did not stop with the building of churches; it included also the carving out of liturgical space in the private realm. Again, from the very beginnings of Christianity, prominent persons had chapels in their homes, and the feudal aristocracy continued this practice throughout the Middle Ages. In the cities of Italy chapels were to be found in princely residences, but they were less common in private homes. In fifteenth-century Florence, for instance, private palaces in the city did not have chapels as self-contained functional liturgical spaces, although a few families had portable altars, for which it was not easy to get the appropriate authorization. The Medici palace is about the only exception on record, with its famous chapel decorated by Benozzo Gozzoli; but in fact the palace served a quasi-public function, given the role of the family in civic affairs. Chapel building in Florence went through yet another phase in the sixteenth century, however, when the rich also began to install chapels in their residences; and by the seventeenth century the palaces of the rich generally had chapels, some more than one, probably in part to accommodate their large staffs of servants. Two were inserted into the Strozzi palace, one for each branch of the family living there; and when the Riccardi rebuilt the former Medici palace for their residence, they added

44. Alison Luchs, *Cestello, a Cistercian Church of the Florentine Renaissance* (New York, 1977), ch. 3; other comments on chapel building are made by Richard Goldthwaite, *The Building of Renaissance Florence: An Economic and Social History* (Baltimore, 1980), pp. 99–102. The vicissitudes of chapels can be traced in W. and E. Paatz, *Die Kirchen von Florenz*, 6 vols. (Frankfurt am Main, 1940–54).

no fewer than four chapels, having closed the older one dating from the fifteenth century.

Rich townsmen throughout Italy also built chapels within the complex of buildings associated with their property in the countryside, and these too proliferated with the building of villas and the formation of larger, more compact estates from the fifteenth century onward. These chapels were normally not inside the villa itself but built as a separate structure, a kind of oratory serving as the family chapel. Palladio's villas, for instance, do not have chapels inside the house itself, but some, like Maser, have chapels nearby on their property opening on a public road. Being also accessible to peasants who lived in the vicinity, such a chapel was not just a monument to the presence of the family on the local scene; in offering a basic service to peasants, it could serve to consolidate the social position of the landlord in the rural world. Thus outside the city as inside, the rich, indulging in their passion for building chapels, enlarged the physical plant of the church. The myriads of chapels that sprang up on private estates all over the Italian countryside accompanying the "return to the land" of the upper classes constituted in effect a new and densely populated tier of highly localized and private facilities supplementing the parish structure of the rural church.

The appropriation of liturgical space by private interests contributed to its expansion in three ways. First, laymen carved out personal property within existing churches, both by invading them piecemeal to build tombs, altars, and chapels and by seizing direct possession of these in the form of patronage rights. Having so appropriated liturgical space as their own, they renovated it and inflated it with their own liturgical apparatus. Every church in Italy was fair game for private possessiveness. Second, in setting up semipublic chapels on their country estates, the rich created an entirely new, private, and densely populated tier of buildings within the rural structure of the church below the parish level. Finally, with the construction of chapels in their own homes, they created yet another tier of private sacred space below the parish level within the structure of the urban church. By the early seventeenth century a moderately prosperous family was likely to have a chapel in its town palace, another in its parish or other neighborhood church, and a third attached to its country villa. The wealthy had several more, perhaps in each place, not to mention patronage rights they might have had over entire churches.

Burial, commemorative masses, remembrance, and family pride were not the only reasons for the incursion into church space and for the privatization of altars and chapels. More worldly explanations for the appropriation of the church for private interests include a profound change in the relations between ecclesiastical institutions and the upper classes at the end of the Middle Ages. From the thirteenth century onward rich and powerful laymen expanded their patronage over ecclesiastical appointments, gradually replacing the traditional electoral system by one of private nominations to benefices both large and small. The legal right of private patronage received doctrinal justification in the twelfth century, and the growing importance of papal reservations thereafter opened opportunities for men with connections to exploit the situation to their own advantage. Patronage rights gave them access to revenues, enhanced their prestige, and enlarged their clientage network; and with the sharpening of dynastic concern for keeping patrimonies intact and free from generational partitions, the rich regarded the church as a place where they could establish younger sons so they could reduce liens on their estates.

Italian urban elites, moreover, were in a better position than any other in Europe to assert direct influence on the papacy; they had to deal with the pope as a political power once he was back in Rome after the Avignon period and forced to fend for himself in the Italian state system, and many had influence through the Italian bankers and merchants at Rome who dominated papal finances. They also enjoyed exceptional opportunities to launch relatives on ambitious ecclesiastical careers leading to positions of immense power and wealth in the growing bureaucracy that had its birth during the Avignon period. Moreover, central governments in Lombardy, Florence, Venice, and the other leading Italian states had no effective check on the papal system of benefices, so that even the most local of elites could take possession of small benefices of chapters and endowed chapels in their vicinity through direct channels to Rome that sidestepped the state. In short, in Italy the church became fair—and fairly easy—game for exploitation for everything from local benefices to curial posts and even the papacy itself. The possession of these offices became so common among the upper classes that in the early seventeenth century, when urban elites were thrashing around to define their status, the presence of highly placed clerics on a family tree could well be considered a qualifying attribute of nobility.[45]

Again, the best evidence comes from Florence, where this situation

---

45. Paolo Prodi, "Istituzioni ecclesiastiche e mondo nobiliare," in *Patriziati e aristocrazie nobiliari*, ed. C. Mozzarelli and Pierangelo Schiera (Trent, 1978), pp. 64–77; Chittolini, "Stati regionali e istituzioni ecclesiastiche," pp. 168–70; and the same scholar's comment in *Gli Sforza, la chiesa lombarda, la corte di Roma*, ed. Chittolini (Naples, 1989), pp. xv–xvi.

has been studied by Roberto Bizzocchi.[46] The process of aristocratization of the Florentine church accelerated in the fifteenth century. By the beginning of the next century, patronage of 11 of the city's 52 parishes, 23 of the 50 rural baptismal churches (*pievi*), and 164 of the 333 remaining rural parishes was in private hands; and many of these places had come under private patronage for the first time in the course of the fifteenth century. Bizzocchi has shown how the Buondelmonte family, which had long had patronage rights over the church at Impruneta, expanded the chapter into a network of subordinate client churches and then went on to finance a canonry in the cathedral of Florence. Canonries in the cathedral were a special target for the patronage ambitions of Florentine families. The number of prebends increased under these family pressures, going from twelve in 1300 to thirty-eight in 1500, by which time sixteen belonged to families who had entered in the fifteenth century and only three belonged to older families represented before 1300. In nearby Prato, a town with a population of only five thousand in 1500 (representing a fall of perhaps more than 50 percent over the preceding two centuries), the number of canonries doubled (to become fourteen) in the fifteenth century, mostly to accommodate leading families; and with the enlarged chapter a new hierarchical structure was created within the institution to further satisfy family ambitions for signs of distinction.[47] In addition to canonries, chaplaincies also proliferated under the aegis of family interest; in Florence they more than doubled in the fifteenth century, and in Prato their numbers swelled four- to fivefold in the same period. These statistics reflect the extraordinary mobility within the urban elites of Italy, in contrast to France and Germany, where, for instance, chapters, being securely in the hands of the landed aristocracy, were much more stable institutions. Canonries and chaplaincies carried with them patronage rights over chapels and churches; and these took their places alongside the other altars and chapels a great family might possess.

The incursion into the ecclesiastical realm by private interests followed many routes. It has been described as the aristocratization of the

---

46. Bizzocchi, *Chiesa e potere*, and also his article "Chiesa e aristocrazia della Firenze del Quattrocento," *Archivio storico italiano* 142 (1984), 191–282. Bizzocchi thinks that the process of aristocratization was more developed in Florence than in other Italian towns; but for Venice, see Paolo Prodi, "The Structure and Organization of the Church in Renaissance Venice: Suggestions for Research," in *Renaissance Venice*, ed. J. R. Hale (Totowa, N.J., 1973), p. 417. In any case, the Florentine phenomenon is worth putting in relief given the city's importance in the history of art.

47. Mario Rosa, "La chiesa e la città," in *Prato, storia di una città*, vol. 2, ed. E. Fasano Guarini (Prato, 1986), pp. 503–78.

church at the end of the Middle Ages, and it resulted in the appropriation of church space for private display. The physical assertion of ownership in a church obviously served as a reminder to descendants of their obligation to recall the dead in their prayers, and it is not quite correct to say (as many scholars have) that the building of chapels and tombs in the Renaissance represents secular selfishness. Yet, however pious the motivations for carving out one's own religious space in a church, hardly any rich Italian could be oblivious to his public presence in such a place and therefore to the opportunity it provided for the demonstration of wealth and status for himself and for his family in the future. Hence magnificence—that distinctive rationalization for conspicuous consumption in the Renaissance that will be discussed in the third part of this book—came into play also in the market for religious artwork. In fifteenth-century Florence Bishop Antonino tried to persuade men to pay for repairs to existing structures rather than spend so much seeking publicity for themselves by building new ones, and Savonarola ranted against those who gave nothing to the poor but spent lavishly for a chapel just to display their family arms; but not even such powerful voices were heeded. The endowment of private chapels and entire churches, in the city and in the countryside, became in itself, as Borghini declared later in the sixteenth century, a sign of nobility, "an act of magnificence by great and generous souls."[48]

By the end of our period a considerable percentage of liturgical space must have been in private hands, and the growth and development of this property constitutes much of the enlargement and renewal of the physical plant of the church that took place from the fourteenth through the sixteenth century. The demand and resources the rich brought to the market largely financed the proliferation of religious institutions and the propagation of new foundations already described. Through this process of the privatization of the church, the secular consumption model to be examined later on in this study was extended to incorporate also liturgical apparatus, thereby opening a channel for directing vigorous consumer demand; and the enormous private resources poured into the market account for the boom in the production of religious artwork in the Renaissance and Baroque periods.

The practice of intercession in favor of departed beloved ones or for the sake of one's own future also opened the floodgates to a soaring demand for what might be called extraliturgical devices. Tombs in churches were projected not only as memorials to the fame of the dead but also as reminders to descendants for liturgical commemoration.

48. Bizzocchi, *Chiesa e potere*, p. 46.

Many panel paintings purchased for private space in the home probably had the same function. The commemorative function of portraits, although entirely secular in their appearance, may explain the extraordinary popularity of them, especially in the early Renaissance.[49] Devotional pictures, too, could be transformed into commemorative objects. Several owners of devotional pictures by Giovanni Bellini, for instance, made testamentary provisions for them to be set up as altar pictures in churches with the explicit intention that they become commemorative objects to assure prayers for the dead testators and their families.[50] Although all these things had no official liturgical function, it is likely that they were utilized as private devices for commemoration and intercession in ways that, consciously or unconsciously, substituted for the services of the clergy. Taken all together, these objects made up a realm of material culture organized around religious practices that expanded rapidly outside the confines of liturgical space. This kind of panel painting, therefore, cannot be contained in our construct of the liturgical apparatus; and with its appearance in the private domestic world, our hypothetical consumption model has to be expanded to take in the production of religious art for a growing market outside ecclesiastical circles. This new demand obviously accounts for much of the increased production of art in the Renaissance.

## THE MATERIAL CULTURE OF THE CHURCH AND INCIPIENT CONSUMERISM

Beginning in the thirteenth century, Italy experienced an increase in the production of liturgical apparatus, from altars with the entire panoply of utensils, furnishings, and accessories, to the full complement of the necessary buildings; and the pace of this production continued to rise through the fourteenth to seventeenth centuries. This increased production was due not so much to liturgical innovation as to all the exogenous forces reviewed here arising out of the structural evolution of the church and the greater demand for its services.

These forces were all part of a phenomenon that has been called here a spiritual restlessness among the laity and that resulted in a process of the laicization of religion. This process began in the thirteenth century and continued until the Counter Reformation, when the secular clergy

49. Rab Hatfield, "Five Early Renaissance Portraits," *Art Bulletin* 47 (1965), 315–34.

50. Rona Goffen, *Piety and Patronage in Renaissance Venice: Bellini, Titian, and the Franciscans* (New Haven and London, 1986), pp. 90–95, 101–2; this happened in the Netherlands as well: Peter Humfrey, in *The Altarpiece in the Renaissance*, ed. Humfrey and Martin Kemp (Cambridge, 1990), p. 54.

once and for all reasserted its secure control over lay religious practices and sensibilities. Laicization consisted, on the one hand, of greater efforts by the clergy to incorporate the laity into its own institutions and, on the other, of initiatives by the laity to appropriate sacred space for itself. The mendicant movement taken in its entirety—its emergence in the thirteenth century as a new kind of clergy distinct from the regular and secular varieties; the organization of Second Orders for women and of Third Orders for the laity in general; the proliferation of these orders, the rapid and widespread propagation of houses, and their internal divisions—all this represented a gigantic effort by the church to reach out more energetically to the laity, particularly the masses crowding into the growing towns and cities. Likewise, the doctrine of purgatory, with its practice of commemorative masses for the dead, and the cult of the saints, with its further possibilities for divine intercession, aroused the demand of the laity for church services. What is more, these doctrines gave laypersons the wherewithal to take more initiative themselves to satisfy their religious needs. For example, the cults of many of the new saints who won their way into the hearts of Italians arose as local lay movements independent of official canonization. With the confraternal movement, groups of laypersons went so far as to create sacred space for themselves, and private persons went further, both by buying into churches and by carving out consecrated liturgical space for themselves in their private domestic worlds. An extreme lay initiative was the practice of devotions that grew up around religious objects, especially pictures, that people bought in ever-greater quantities for the privacy of their homes—a practice that threatened to take religious sensibilities altogether outside the orbit of the church's control and into the hands of the individual.

This spiritual restlessness among the laity at the end of the Middle Ages impinged mightily on the demand for all those things that constitute the material culture of religion in late medieval, Renaissance, and Baroque Italy. Demand in the market for religious artwork soared to new heights as more and more individual and institutional consumers crowded into it. If institutional proliferation within the church theoretically meant the fragmentation of the church's wealth in the hands of more clerical consumers for the liturgical apparatus, in fact the propagation of new foundations occurred at a time when the church was able to tap more and more of Italy's immense wealth by generating demand for its services. The dynamic growth and transformation of the institutional infrastructure of the church in fact occurred largely because new foundations had the possibility of scrambling to get their share of these outside sources of wealth. The result was direct investment from the private sector in the enlargement or renewal of the church's physical plant. In fact, the soaring demand from the laity, both individually and collectively in confraternities, for commemorative and votive masses and for its own private liturgical space in churches provided much of the wherewithal to sustain the real costs of building, remodeling, and enlarging the physical facilities of the church and of filling churches up with the necessary liturgical equipment, not to mention private forms of devotional art—to pay, in short, for all the religious artwork produced in the Renaissance. Another result of the church's success in marketing its services through goods, however, was the extension of possessiveness of lay persons into the material world of religion; and their direct participation in the market for religious goods exposed religious sensibilities to an incipient consumerism.

### The Expansion and Filling Up of Liturgical Space

Statistics to document the filling up of liturgical space and to measure the rise in the production of artwork are hard to come by. For some places we have figures for the increase in the number of churches. Florence, one of the largest cities in Italy, had 126 institutions with something that might be called a church at one time or another before the Black Death, including about 50 parish churches. Notwithstanding the demographic disasters of the fourteenth century, the physical plant of the Florentine church continued to expand. Over the next three hundred years, during which time the city regained barely three-fourths of the population it had had at the time of Dante, about 75 older churches were extensively rebuilt and about 65 new ones built. In 1427 there were 17 monasteries within the city walls and 12 more in the suburbs just outside. At the same time, convents numbered 27 in the city plus 21 in the suburbs; by the end of the century they numbered 37 in the city and 17 outside the walls; and in 1552 they totaled 56. Between 30 and 35 hospices of one kind or another can be counted at any one time in the fifteenth century. Confraternities numbered 43 in the mid-fourteenth century and 96 a century later; 156 have been identified as having existed at one time or another before 1500. Monastic houses numbered 19 in the fifteenth century, with most of the orders and Observant movements represented.[51]

Odds and ends of figures from other places confirm the pattern. In

51. Estimates of the number of institutions and their population have been attempted by Henderson, "Religious Confraternities and Death," p. 384; and Charles de La Roncière, "Les confréries en Toscane aux XIV et XV siècles d'après les travaux récents," in Fiorani, *Confraternite romane*, p. 51; for religious houses, see Brucker, "Monasteries, Friaries, and Nunneries"; and Bizzocchi, *Chiesa e potere*, p. 31.

the provincial town of Borgo San Sepolcro, the population growth to about 5,000 in the thirteenth century was accompanied by an increase of ecclesiastical institutions from 3, all monasteries, to 16 with the addition of 2 secular churches, 4 male mendicant houses, and 7 convents, to which must be added 1 major confraternity and 8 hospices; and then 14 more confraternities sprang up in the first half of the fourteenth century. In the fifteenth century, towns that had been much larger before the Black Death still had an extraordinary number of churches: Treviso, with about 9,000 inhabitants, counted 19 churches besides its cathedral, 12 religious houses, and 15 hospices; Pistoia, reduced to half the size of Treviso, had 29 parish churches and 11 hospices; and Prato, about the same size as Pistoia at the time, had 9 parish churches plus 5 monastic foundations (and 5 more arose in the sixteenth century).

Moreover, in many places the number of churches tended to grow from the fifteenth through the sixteenth centuries even though the population did not return to earlier preplague levels. Genoa in 1535 had 76 churches, 23 oratories, and 35 religious houses; a century later there were 90 churches, 19 oratories, and 53 houses, most of which were new or completely rebuilt structures. Bologna in the thirteenth century, a much smaller place than Florence and Genoa at the time, had 94 churches; in the early seventeenth century, according to a guide to the churches of the city (which was approximately the same size as Florence at that time but now an administrative center in the papal states), the number had grown to 188, of which 62 were associated with religious houses and 32 either were new or had been largely rebuilt since the mid-sixteenth century. During the next century the total number grew to 270—a 50 percent increase—and the list gives us a more precise designation of their use: 24 belonged to colleges, schools, and *monti*, 42 to convents, 32 to monasteries, 68 to confraternal organizations, and 24 to guilds. In Verona, a city of about 25,000 to 30,000 inhabitants, the number of churches went from about 70 in the fifteenth century to 90 at the middle of the seventeenth century. In the mid-seventeenth century Naples had almost 100 male houses alone; and in the next century remote towns in Sicily with no more than 10,000 inhabitants could have from 15 to 20 religious houses and as many as a dozen parish churches.[52]

52. Giorgio Doria, "Investimenti della nobiltà genovese nell'edilizia di prestigio (1530–1630)," *Studi storici* 27 (1986), 18 n.; Matteo Mainardi, *Origine e fondatione di tutte le chiese . . . di Bologna* (Bologna, 1633); Luigi Montieri, *Catalogo di tutte le Chiese . . . di Bologna* (Bologna, n.d. [but during pontificate of Benedetto XIV]); Giorgio Borelli, *Città e campagna in età preindustriale, XVI–XVIII secolo* (Verona, 1986), p. 360; Luigi Pesce, *La chiesa di Treviso nel primo Quattrocento* (Rome, 1987), 1:142–59 and vol. 2, apps.; Rosa, "Chiesa e la città"; Banker, *Death in the Community*, pp. 21–32; David Herlihy, *Medieval and Renais-*

Comparative figures for cities outside Italy are hard to come by. Lyon in the mid-sixteenth century, the third largest city in France with a population of 60,000 to 70,000, had, besides its cathedral, only 7 parish and 4 collegiate churches and 9 male houses. In the thirteenth century, before the rise of the mendicants, Cologne, the largest city in Germany with a population of about 40,000, had a cathedral, 16 parish and 11 collegiate churches, and 10 monastic houses (including nunneries); but many important German towns—Frankfurt, Bamberg, Wurzburg, Ulm—had only 1 parish church. On the eve of the Reformation the great imperial city of Nuremberg, whose population of about 20,000 ranked it among the top half-dozen cities in Germany, had only 2 parish churches (along with 2 other churches, 2 hospitals, 2 convents, and 8 monasteries); and Strasbourg (about the same size) had 7 parish and 5 collegiate churches and 19 religious houses. A better count has been taken for a much smaller place at the same time: Biberach in southern Germany, which, with a population of about 5,000 inhabitants, was about the size of Prato and Pistoia. It had only 10 churches, of which 1 was a convent (there were no monasteries) and several little more than chapels; and there were no more than 38 altars all together. The principal church was the single parish church with its 18 altars.[53]

While Italian churches increased in number, they were also filling up with altars. Additional altars had begun to appear in major churches from the eleventh century onward largely as a response to the need to accommodate more priests, but in the course of the thirteenth century altars began to proliferate at a much higher pace to satisfy the new popular demand for more commemorative and votive masses and to provide local cults and confraternities with their own liturgical identity. According to a panegyric of Milan written in 1288, there were 200 churches with 480 altars in the city and 2,050 churches with 2,600 altars in the countryside—a low ratio of altars to churches compared with the situation a century and a half later, when Alberti threw up his hands in dismay at the contemporary practice of crowding the churches with

_sance Pistoia: The Social History of an Italian Town, 1200–1430_ (New Haven, 1967), pp. 244, 248; Enrico Bacco, _Naples: An Early Guide_, ed. and trans. E. Gardiner (New York, 1991), pp. 50–54.

53. Philip T. Hoffman, _Church and Community in the Diocese of Lyon, 1500–1789_ (New Haven, 1984), pp. 11–16; John B. Freed, _The Friars in German Society in the Thirteenth Century_ (Cambridge, Mass., 1977), p. 80; Gerald Strauss, _Nuremberg in the Sixteenth Century_ (New York, 1966), p. 157; Thomas Brady, _Ruling Class, Regime, and Reformation at Strasbourg_ (Leiden, 1978), p. 217; Christopher S. Wood, "In Defense of Images: Two Local Rejoinders to the Zwinglian Iconoclasm," _Sixteenth Century Journal_ 19 (1988), 25–44.

altars, interrupting his text at this point to say that it was useless to continue on with the subject.[54] Yet another century later, when bishops were fired by Counter Reformation zeal to bring some order to the centuries' accumulation of liturgical apparatus in many churches, they must have shared the experience of the bishop of Brescia, who, on journeying into the countryside to assess the state of the cult in his diocese, found churches cluttered with myriads of altars, some attached to columns and some also in the vestibules. No wonder Carlo Borromeo issued instructions for cleaning out these unsightly accretions of time and restoring dignity to the place of the cult, insisting that each altar be placed, if not in its own chapel, at least in a framed niche to define it architecturally in its own space.[55]

In the towns of north and central Italy the density of churches, and of altars within them, must have been far higher than in any other part of Europe, not counting also chapels in private palaces and the dense stratum of semipublic chapels on private estates throughout the countryside. Notwithstanding the increase in demand for secular painting, the major part of the output of almost all Italian painters, including the very greatest, was directed to meeting the demand for religious pictures. To the enlightened reformers of the late eighteenth century, intent on weeding out inefficiencies, the excessive number of churches and religious houses in relation to the population more than justified the vigor with which they closed down so many of them, cleaning them out of their centuries' accumulation of artwork—an act that ruthlessly uprooted and dispersed throughout the world art market a large part of Italy's huge artistic patrimony.

## The Internal Dynamics of Demand

Demand has its own internal dynamics. The very energy of an expanding consumer society such as the one described here can generate other forces that are released within the confines of the market itself and amplify demand. If one consumer does something that catches the attention of others so that they are inspired to follow his or her lead, that consumer's behavior is said to have a demonstration effect in the market that arouses further demand. If in the attempt to outdo one another consumers go beyond imitation, competition becomes an even more powerful force in generating demand for new things, more expensive

54. Leon Battista Alberti, *L'architettura*, ed. Giovanni Orlandi (Milan, 1966), 2:628; the Milanese text is cited in Giorgio Cracco, "La 'cura animarum' nella cultura laica del tardo Medioevo (lo specchio delle 'laudes civitatum')," in *Pievi e parrocchie*, 1:561.

55. Montanari, *Disciplinamento in terra veneta*, p. 93; Gatti Perer, "Cultura e socialità dell'altare barocco," pp. 17–18.

things, or simply more things. If, finally, the terms of competition are enlarged to include taste, which then begins to change with ever-greater frequency as consumers seek to keep ahead of one another, another powerful dynamic—fashion—is introduced into the market, assuring a continuing renewal of demand so that it is able to maintain and even increase its momentum. In other words, the demonstration effect can set off a kind of chain reaction, releasing new forces such as competition and fashion that converge into, and amplify, demand.

Throughout the Middle Ages the demonstration effect was operative in the market for religious artwork. The development of Gothic architecture in the cathedrals of the Ile de France is generally seen in these terms, and it has been shown how innovation in mosaic decoration of thirteenth-century Roman churches led to attempts to update older work.[56] Many contracts surviving from the later fourteenth century in Italy document explicit instructions for the imitation of an existing work. In a traditional preindustrial economy in which the role of the artist was not yet highly developed, the client could point to something close at hand that represented more or less the model to be followed. Contracts of this kind do not necessarily mean that exact imitation was required; the intention was probably to give only general indications of what was desired in the easiest way possible. For example, when in 1546 Count Giovanni Antonio Caracciolo made provisions in his will for the decoration of his family chapel in Naples, he cited a sculpted image and two tombs, each in separate chapels in other churches, to give an idea of what he wanted.[57]

In this kind of market the appearance of something new or arresting in its difference caught the attention of other potential consumers. For example, an altarpiece painted by Foppa in Genoa about 1483 was designated the model in two subsequent contracts for altarpieces in other churches in the city; likewise, the *Coronation of the Virgin* Ghirlandaio painted for a Franciscan church in provincial Narni around 1485 immediately aroused other houses of the order in the vicinity to commission copies, including a convent near Perugia that twenty years later commissioned the young Raphael to do a picture like it.[58] When docu-

---

56. William Tronzo, "Apse Decoration, the Liturgy, and the Perception of Art in Medieval Rome: S. Maria in Trastevere and S. Maria Maggiore," in *Italian Church Decoration*, pp. 167–93.

57. Maria Antonietta Visceglia, "Corpo e sepoltura nei testamenti della nobiltà napoletana XVI–XVIII secolo," *Quaderni storici* 17 (1982), 605.

58. Jocelyn Ffoulkes and Rodolfo Maiocchi, *Vicenzo Foppa of Brescia, Founder of the Lombard School: His Life and Works* (London and New York, 1909), pp. 133–34; Roger Jones and Nicholas Penny, *Raphael* (New Haven, 1983), pp. 16–17.

mentation is otherwise lacking, this pattern of the diffusion of imitative or similar works through the network of a religious order can often be accounted for in this way. The fresco cycles in the great church of Saint Francis at Assisi were obvious models for other churches in the order; and in Siena the polyptychs that appeared in Franciscan and Dominican churches in the early fourteenth century seem to have set a fashion for a new art form that subsequently not only spread through provincial houses of these orders but also was taken up by other orders that previously had shown no interest in multipanel paintings. Similarly, the wall-type rood screens frescoed by Foppa in two Observant Franciscan churches in Lombardy were widely imitated within the order throughout the region at the end of the fifteenth century.[59]

It is just one step from imitation to open competition, but it can be a big step for the further growth of an already expanding and crowded market. As far back as the fifth century, inscriptions attest that competition was a strong motive for church building.[60] Raul Glaber thought competition explained why there were so many beautiful churches in the eleventh century, and not long afterward the great abbot-builder Suger admitted as much about his own motivations. This competitive impulse has also been inferred from the sequence of Gothic cathedrals whose vaults rose higher and higher—at Paris, Chartres, Rheims, Amiens—until finally (in 1284) at Beauvais they came tumbling down. In the context of Italian urban civilization, public buildings that were particularly expressive of status figured in the rivalries among communes; and the formulation of the concept of magnificence in the Renaissance fully rationalized open competition among private builders.

As a result of internal factions within religious orders as well as rivalry among individual institutions for popular support, the spirit of competition also permeated the market for religious artwork. As laymen appropriated church space for their own altars and chapels, or acquired benefices with control over an entire church, demand got an additional boost from all the obsessions and rivalries of the social and political worlds. It has been inferred from some of the contracts of the kind cited above, in which consumers clearly had an eye on other works, that competition was indeed lurking behind these envious glances, although few are as explicit as Raphael's 1505 commission to paint a picture like the one Ghirlandaio had done twenty years earlier

59. Alessandro Nova, "I tramezzi in Lombardia fra XV e XVI secolo: scene della Passione e devozione francescana," in *Il francescanesimo in Lombardia* (Milan, 1983), pp. 197–215.

60. Bryan Ward-Perkins, *From Classical Antiquity to the Middle Ages: Urban Public Building in Northern and Central Italy, AD 300–850* (Oxford, 1984), pp. 75–77.

but "of higher perfection, if it is possible."[61] As this instance of patronage by a Franciscan house indicates, not even the mendicants, with their disdain for wealth, were immune to the competitive spirit. In 1422 the Dominicans of Santa Maria Novella in Florence, becoming only too conscious of the building going on all around them, appointed a committee to consider extensive rebuilding "in order to imitate the other churches and to work for the embellishment of the monastery";[62] in 1521 the Dominicans of San Niccolò in Venice successfully blocked the plans of Observant Franciscans to erect a church they felt would have been too near their own.[63]

Confraternities, too, felt the pressures to outdo one another, especially on the occasions of the public processions in which they participated on great holidays, when they could conspicuously demonstrate their status—occasions that gave social and political overtones to the performance of a basic religious function. This competition with others could consume so much of the patrimony of confraternities that a marked concern with the problem came to be written into later statutes.[64] In Venice the government injected a strong civic spirit into the rivalry among those confraternities it recognized as having the special status of *grande*, thereby committing them to ambitious building programs to outdo one another; but also among the dozens of small confraternities in Venice, competition has been cited as the most important motive for the commissioning of ambitious altarpieces.[65] Rivalry among such patrons is one reason that they sometimes sponsored formal competitions among artists to get the best products possible.

Once released in the marketplace, competition amplifies demand by setting new standards for consumption that usually involve greater magnitude of expenditure. The cathedrals of Siena, Florence, Bologna, and Milan in the fourteenth and fifteenth centuries are notable examples of competition among communes to have a bigger building or one built with more expensive materials or with more elaborate and monumental sculptural decoration. The Florentines, besides trying to outdo them all

---

61. Vincenzo Golzio, *Raffaello nei documenti, nelle testimonianze dei contemporanei e nella letteratura del suo secolo* (Vatican City, 1936), pp. 11–13.

62. Gene Brucker, *Renaissance Florence* (Berkeley, 1969), p. 34.

63. Goffen, *Piety and Patronage*, p. 5.

64. Roberto Rusconi, "Confraternite, compagnie e devozioni," in *Storia d'Italia: Annali*, vol. 9 (1986), p. 497.

65. Patricia Fortini Brown, "Honor and Necessity: The Dynamics of Patronage in the Confraternities of Renaissance Venice," *Studi veneziani* 14 (1987), 207; Humfrey, "Competitive Devotions," p. 405.

in their grandiose program for free-standing, greater-than-life-sized sculptures on the façade and campanile and for colossal figures high up on the drum of the cupola, declared yet other grounds for competition—daring technology—when they decided to accept Brunelleschi's plan for covering the crossing of their cathedral. Once they got their new cathedral, they continued their extravagance inside with luxurious and innovative internal appointments. Competition can thus account for a powerful disposition to spend more and more for religious artwork, and these expenditures can take several forms depending on what the stakes of competition are—size, quantity, inherent luxury, craftsmanship.

Introduce, finally, taste into this complex of notions about what the stakes are, and a dynamic for change dependent on fashion is released that can further amplify demand. When the desire arose, in the thirteenth century, to have a picture on the high altar of their cathedral, the Sienese were content to transfer an altar front to the altar table; but once such an object enjoyed so much public prominence, the desire arose to increase its grandeur—and so by the end of the century they commissioned the great *Maestà* by Duccio. In fifteenth-century Venice, where pictorial style changed rapidly, guilds who had chapels in major churches and saw their colleagues put up altar tables in more up-to-date styles felt the pressure to follow suit even when they had had a picture painted not too many years earlier. In sixteenth-century Florence the grand duke took advantage of Tridentine reforms calling for the cleaning out of the centuries' accumulation of clutter in church interiors to justify the refurbishing of both Santa Croce and Santa Maria Novella according to the latest aesthetic criteria, which dictated side altars evenly spaced and of equal size.

Fashion arouses demand not necessarily for more things or something of greater magnitude but for something different; and if the new object is in fact cheaper, its replacement frequency following rapid change of fashion may stimulate growth of productive forces that more than make up for its decline in value. Taste is therefore a dynamic above all for renewal, and it possesses its own momentum. This momentum counted for much in the history of secular art in the Italian Renaissance, eventually constituting a good part of the demand factor—to the point that, perhaps for the first time in the history of art, artists themselves were in a position to move in aggressively and win a commanding position over the market. Domenico Veneziano's famous letter to Piero de' Medici in 1438 is perhaps the earliest extant expression of how for both producer and client competition was beginning to impinge on the market: he promises to produce a picture as marvelous as any that could be done by other prominent painters, and he is sure his work will bring Piero much honor.

Painters of religious pictures, moreover, realized the considerable potential of their products for variation as pictorial forms responsive to changing fashions and taste and to changing ideas, attitudes, and sentiments arising from religious sensibilities. Painting had the potential for rendering images with infinite variety; and once this capability was exploited to enhance the efficacy of images in inviting the observer to respond, powerful new rhetorical possibilities opened up. Panel paintings in particular, by freeing the painted image both from the strictly liturgical context of the altar and from the narrative context of mural painting, had a potential for psychological meaning heretofore unknown; and the change toward naturalism, realism, and secular subject matter gave painting of all kinds a new social role outside the performance of the liturgy. Thus charged with all kinds of cultural and psychological meaning, painting became responsive to an enormous variety of influences—doctrine, popular spiritual movements, political propaganda, social values, psychological needs. Painting, therefore, became the ready instrument of a new kind of mass religion. Its history in the later Middle Ages is very much the story of how it realized its market potential as a popular art form responsive to devotional movements and freed from the control of the church.

This enlargement of the content of painting gave the artist greater possibilities for developing new techniques of representing images and refining his own style. All these elements increasingly went into the taste for a picture. The content of art thus broadened considerably; and as a result of this extraordinary sensitivity to changes in the larger world, the pace of change within the pictorial arts accelerated from the fourteenth century onward. Moreover, to the extent that these influences vary over time, they increased the susceptibility of art to change and variety; hence taste, including fashion, came increasingly to the fore in the art market. In short, the industry was successful in meeting the growing demand through product and process innovation—by introducing new and accessible, useful, malleable, and changeable products.

The market potential for the pictorial arts was enormous: for mural decoration it was nothing less than the walls of every church, for altar pictures nothing less than all the altars in those churches, and for panel painting nothing less than every home and even every room in the home. Murals and painting on wood were relatively inexpensive compared with the earlier pictorial forms of mosaics and sculpted images made from materials with high intrinsic value or requiring intensive labor input, and costs of the materials of painting fell lower as time wore on—that is, as the market expanded. The industry was highly flexible in its organization; and by introducing new and cheaper products, it was successful in arousing demand to levels never before achieved. By the sixteenth century, artisans were enjoying an expanding market in which, to a greater degree than ever before in the history of the West, a premium was put on innovation and invention. Vasari observed this situation with great insight: his concept of progress in the arts was rooted in his understanding of what was happening in a marketplace in which artisans struggling for a living kept raising the ante in their competition to capture more of the market. Once the producer takes the initiative and is able to shift control of the market from the demand to the supply side, the consumer economy is born.

## The Generation of Pictorial Culture

From the end of the thirteenth century onward, as Italians found their religious experiences focused increasingly on new pictorial forms, their lives came to be filled with images. Theirs was a pictorial world much more dense with images than that known by most other Europeans. Johan Huizinga, commenting on northern attitudes toward art at the end of the Middle Ages, remarked that the craving for symbolism and allegory became an obsession to convert every mental concept into a pictorial image, so that at all levels of society "art in these times was still wrapped up in life." For the Italians more than for other Europeans, however, the converse was also true: life was completely wrapped up in art.

In the Byzantine world icons were a source of spiritual powers associated with the holy people and emperors they represented. When they were imported into Italy in the thirteenth century, they brought something of their mystery with them; but images in the West did not have the sanctity they had in the East, where they were closely tied to the liturgy. As pictorial forms evolved in the looser religious society of the West, therefore, new rhetorical possibilities opened up. The didactic function of pictures was developed by the friars in association with their preaching mission, and devotional images such as the Pietà appeared that had nothing to do with the narrative tradition of the Bible or with any liturgical function. Along with these iconographical innovations, figures of Christ, the Madonna, and the saints became humanized in their depiction, so that the observer could establish a personal and emotional relation with them. All this enriched the pictorial culture of Europeans—and nowhere more so than in Italy.

By the end of the fifteenth century, production of pictorial decoration of churches in Italy had reached a much higher level than in most other parts of Europe. The painted altarpiece, in contrast to the sculpted form so much more common in northern Europe (except for Flanders), probably became a standard fixture; and today it is hard to imagine an Italian church without pictures at its various altar tables. The growth in the size of these pictures is itself impressive: the evolution of the typical altarpiece from the end of the thirteenth century onward, until it reached the enormous proportions of the pictures sixteenth-century artists painted in the normal course of their work, can be replayed by a walk through the chronologically organized galleries of any major museum.

As no other Europeans, including the Flemish, Italians became accustomed to seeing the walls of their churches covered with images. Within a century of the first great fresco cycles, mendicant churches in many Italian towns were entirely frescoed from floor to ceiling; and the painting of walls extended deep into the inner recesses of monasteries—to refectories, chapter rooms, cloisters—converting interior architecture into pictorial decoration.[66] If frescoed walls are not so much in evidence today as altarpieces, it is chiefly because so many were painted over as the result of the new architectural aesthetic that came to dominate taste in the fifteenth century. Yet, however successful Renaissance architects were in recovering the blank wall for their own aesthetic, the pictorial impulse broke through again in the sixteenth century—apparently first in a major way at the Cathedral, San Sigismondo, and other churches of Cremona. Moreover, vaulted ceilings and cupolas along with wall surfaces were appropriated for pictorial decoration that dissolved architecture and enveloped worshipers with images now in an illusionistic way they had never experienced in the earlier mendicant churches. Some major sixteenth-century artists spent most of their time painting extensive chapel cycles. Domenichino worked almost exclusively on just one project, the Cappella del Tesoro in Naples, for the last decade of his life.

The communal ethos also found outlets in the representative arts of painting and sculpture. Sacred images proliferated in the street and squares not just to incite private devotion but to enlist the holy in the effort to maintain public order.[67] Beginning in the thirteenth century, painted rooms in public places depicted the values underlying good government and commemorated historical events in the life of

66. A process never systematically studied, according to Braunfels, *Monasteries of Western Europe*, p. 142.

67. Edward Muir, "The Virgin on the Street Corner: The Place of the Sacred in Italian Cities," in *Religion and Culture in the Renaissance and Reformation*, ed. S. Ozment (Kirksville, Mo., 1989), p. 25.

the commune. In the fourteenth and fifteenth centuries residents of some towns—above all, Florentines—expressed their public indignation against convicted enemies of the public interest—bankrupts, debtors, forgers, traitors—by having them painted, so that they were fully recognizable, on the exterior walls of government buildings at street level for all to see, making the place into what has been termed a "negative church" where sinners of all kinds were displayed.[68] By the later fifteenth century people in the streets also encountered images on a grand scale in the frescoes and sgraffiti that decorated entire palace façades in many cities. These major art forms, along with the *pittura infamante* on communal buildings, have long since been lost (and therefore hardly studied) through the wear of time, so that it is impossible for us to re-create the extensive pictorial world that engulfed many Italians as they went through the streets on their daily tasks.

Finally, with the rise of devotional piety and the diffusion of inexpensive panel paintings throughout the marketplace, Italians could take pictures home with them and into their private lives. At the beginning of the fifteenth century the cardinal Giovanni Dominici emphasized the importance of having paintings in the home, especially pictures of child saints and young virgins, for the religious edification of children; he would "make the home like a temple with paintings." Contemporary inventories from Florence reveal how common—and how numerous—pictures came to be in the workshops and homes of people of modest wealth, often showing up in every room, including the kitchen; and servants owned them as well. The surviving record book of Neri di Bicci documents the profitability of this popular market for one of the painters who supplied it, and the careers of Lorenzo Lotto in the Marches and of the Bassano in the Veneto are evidence that the popular taste for painting had spread also into the provinces.

By the fifteenth century, images in the private world of the upper classes, as in the public world, began to become secularized. The tradition of decorating palaces with chivalric scenes and gardens populated with great personages and ancestors goes back at least as far as the papal palace at Avignon and continued in Verona, Ferrara, Pavia, Mantua, and other princely centers at the end of the fourteenth century. A 1414 contract for fresco decoration in the home of Nicolò Grimaldi in Genoa refers to similar scenes in three other houses in this merchant city,[69] and

68. The characterization comes from Samuel Y. Edgerton, "Icons of Justice," *Past and Present* 89 (1980), 28–38.

69. Antonia Borlandi, "Pittura politica e committenza nel primo Quattrocento genovese," *Renaissance Studies in Honor of Craig Hugh Smyth*, ed. A. Morough et al. (Florence, 1985), 2:71.

interior frescoes survive from the fifteenth century in Florence (all in villas), Ferrara, Mantua, and elsewhere, not to mention the increasing literary references to them by such writers as Sabadino degli Arienti. By the sixteenth century the rich and powerful were much possessed by the fashion for decorating the interior walls and ceilings of their palaces with vast scenes filled with historical and literary materials of some significance to their own lives. Advisors helped them work out learned programs of all kinds, and in his manual of 1587 Armenini included a section on the appropriate subjects for decoration of private palaces. The Campi worked extensively in private palaces of Cremona; Nosadella was known above all as a fresco painter of private houses, although most of his work is lost; and Prospero Fontana spent most of his time as an interior decorator traveling around northern Italy to Genoa, Bologna, Florence, Parma, and Rome. These and other sixteenth-century painters, like Pordenone, made the major part of their living frescoing private homes both inside and out. Meanwhile, in the fifteenth century, pictures with secular subject matter began to appear on chests (a principal item of furniture at the time) and then increasingly in panel paintings on walls—a subject we shall return to below. Finally, many of the other art forms developed in Renaissance Italy—painted and transparent smalto, niello, maiolica, wood intarsia, ecclesiastical garments, stained glass—were perfected largely as pictorial forms laden with illustrative material in a naturalistic style that was a virtuoso defiance of the inherent physical limitations of these media, so strong was the pictorial impulse of the age.

This expansion of the pictorial arts beginning in the later thirteenth century and the extent to which Italians eventually found themselves encountering images in churches, on the streets, in their homes, and even on dishes at the dinner table have never been adequately assessed. Pictures had a profound effect on the religious mentality by sharpening the sensibility to images and even conditioning modes of expression. Italians found their religious lives increasingly caught up in a pictorial world that came to exist on its own terms as a new kind of reality located somewhere between this world and God's realm. Images, once they were isolated on panels and detached from both a liturgical context and larger decorative schemes, could invite contemplative penetration into the holy realm, involving the viewer in an intimate and private psychological experience: they acquired miraculous powers and commonly came to speak to observers, to act on them, and to react to them. Saint Giovanni Gualberto and Saint Francis underwent conversions while contemplating the crucifix, and many visionaries from Saint Catherine of Siena in the fourteenth century to the Counter Reformation saints of the later sixteenth century were influenced if not in fact stimulated by pictures.[70] Images could, of course, also work miracles, especially images of the Virgin; and the large number of new churches constructed in the fifteenth century and variously dedicated to Santa Maria—delle Carceri, della Consolazione, delle Grazie, della Quercia—attests the frequency of such events. By the fifteenth century Italians commonly expressed their private gratitude for the miraculous intercession of saints in the solution of their personal problems by leaving a picture as an ex-voto recording the event at the appropriate shrine, usually a highly frequented pilgrimage site. Not surprisingly with this kind of pictorial sensibility, people on their deathbeds wanted to fix their attention on images of holy figures, and confraternities sprang up to minister to criminals condemned to death by brandishing holy images before their eyes even as they ascended the scaffold.[71]

The importance of the image for the ritual of prayer within one's own household, where in the private exercise of their religious devotions Italians found their attention increasingly fixed on pictures, has been illustrated by Richard Trexler's analysis of evidence from fifteenth-century Florence. Giovanni Morelli describes in his record book how he concentrates on images, weeps before them, kisses and embraces them, and then prays to them. Contemporary anecdotes (which, if not reporting reality, reflect a certain verisimilitude) illustrate how, as in any human relation, tension could arise between the image and its interlocutor: a shoemaker, angered by a picture of Saint John because it had given an unsatisfactory answer to a question about his wife's faithfulness, defiantly expresses his deep sense of betrayal after years of devotion to the image, curses it, and announces his abandonment of it; another man whose son died despite appeals to an image of Christ hurls his rage at the image, telling it he would have done better to have appealed to another image of Christ nearby.[72] With the secularization of the pictorial world in the Renaissance, images could also threaten the moral health of the soul, if we can accept the suggestion of Carlo Ginzburg that by the sixteenth century priest-confessors had come to regard sight as the sense most susceptible to sin and images as the

70. Millard Meiss, *Painting in Florence and Siena after the Black Death* (Princeton, 1951), ch. 5; Mario Fanti, "Voglia di Paradiso: Mistici, pittori, e committenti a Bologna fra Cinquecento e Seicento," in *Dall'avanguardia dei Carracci al secolo barocco: Bologna, 1580–1600*, ed. Andrea Emiliani (Bologna, 1988), p. 90.

71. Samuel Y. Edgerton, "A Little-Known 'Purpose of Art' in the Italian Renaissance," *Art History* 2 (1979), 45–61.

72. Richard Trexler, *Public Life in Renaissance Florence* (New York, 1980), pp. 119–21, 176–80; Hahnloser, "Culte de l'image au moyen âge," pp. 225–33.

occasion for the most serious sin they had to deal with—lust.

The expanding pictorial world of the Italians was also one in which they themselves entered. Frescoes—from the *pittura infamante* on the external walls of the town hall to major scenes decorating the interiors of both princely palaces and churches—were crowded with contemporary portraits, including often the artist himself peering out at the public. Ghirlandaio's numerous fresco cycles in the Sassetti chapel at Santa Trinita, the Tornabuoni chapel at Santa Maria Novella, and elsewhere are the most notable examples of religious scenes transformed into group portraits. In his discussion of how to compose a painted scene, Alberti advised the insertion of portraits of well-known persons so that the viewer could have greater empathy with the picture. No scene—historical or contemporary, secular or religious—was out of bounds. Court personalities and citizens at Milan under the Sforza got themselves depicted in Leonardo's *Last Supper* (as Antonio de Beatis remarks in his travel journal of 1517–18), and Michelangelo put himself and others into his *Last Judgment* in the Sistine Chapel. Nor has any society ever gone in so enthusiastically for portraiture as a separate form. After religious works, portraits constituted the most important output of many artists and the most numerous kind of picture found in many homes. Scholars have never been able to explain satisfactorily just what Italians saw in these kinds of visual representations of themselves—propitiation, family piety, propaganda, pride, remembrance, introspection—but obviously their sense of themselves was conditioned by the experience of occupying a world of representational art and by the knowledge of being ever on view even apart from their personal presence.[73]

Before the elaboration of secular art in the Renaissance, painting in the religious tradition aroused an awareness of the pleasure in beauty. Communal documents from the early fourteenth century explicitly state this criterion for public projects, and the history of Giotto's fame in fourteenth-century Florence testifies to the extent such sensibilities were diffused throughout society. The impact painting began to make also on intellectuals as a special kind of activity is manifest in the reputation Giotto enjoyed already within the generation following his death. Boccaccio recognized a distinction in the ways the artist appealed to the ignorant and to the wise; and in his testament Petrarch observed that the ignorant were incapable of appreciating the beauty of the picture of the Virgin by Giotto he owned.

73. Enrico Castelnuovo, "Il significato del ritratto pittorico nella società," in the Einaudi *Storia d'Italia*, vol. 5 (Turin, 1972), pp. 1033–94, offers little discussion of function and does not resolve the problem of the popularity of this form.

Beginning with Alberti in the fifteenth century, the art of painting—
still primarily a religious medium—came in for serious intellectual
discussion. In the medieval tradition pictures and symbols had long
been regarded as a necessary adjunct to reading in the way they acted on
the memory and hence helped in the recollection and even comprehension of a text,[74] but now the humanists enlarged the power of the image
by incorporating them into their literary culture. On the one hand, they
loaded images with complex ideas to raise them above the level of mere
representations or symbols with simple correspondences to become
charged with abstract meaning; hence they elaborated emblems, imprese, hieroglyphs, and other such devices whose highly compressed
complexity revealed "a higher reality whose very presence exerted its
mysterious effects."[75] On the other hand, the recognition of the power
of the visual image to convince and to impress itself on the mind led
intellectuals to refine the rhetorical device of creating pictorial images
with words to put ideas across to readers and auditors. Following this
course, painting allied itself with literature; and once painting was admitted to this rhetorical culture of the imitative arts deeply steeped in
the classical tradition, the first claims were made for it as a higher
intellectual activity that separated it from the mechanical arts and placed
it as a sister art alongside poetry. The secularization and privatization of
painting opened the way for an infinite range of subject matter and a
corresponding enlargement of its rhetorical possibilities. While the visual arts were thus winning a way into the intellectual's world, artists
themselves began to assert intellectual claims on their own terms. As a
consequence, artists had greater range for innovation, and patrons in
turn enlarged their aesthetic experiences. This venture of Italians into
a seemingly infinite pictorial world thus led to the discovery of art as a
particular realm of human activity, where the mind was elevated to a
new sphere of operation.

When, in the sixteenth century, the cry of iconoclasm began to be
heard north of the Alps, it fell on deaf ears in Italy. The pictorial world,
along with the luxury of the entire liturgical apparatus, was too solidly
in place. Art and the artist had won impressive credentials with the
intellectual and social establishment outside the church. Zwingli's con-
demnation of holy images on the ground that, having been made by
man himself, they are unworthy of his veneration could hardly make
sense in a culture that was venerating them, at least in part, for the very

74. Mary Carruthers, *The Book of Memory: A Study of Memory in Medieval Culture*
(Cambridge, 1990), pp. 221–29.

75. E. H. Gombrich, "*Icones Symbolicae*: Philosophies of Symbolism and Their Bearing
on Art," in his *Symbolic Images: Studies in the Art of the Renaissance* (Chicago, 1972), p. 179.

reason that these things were in fact made by men—men with special, artistic talents. More important, images had worked their way into the very heart of religious practices and sensibilities. Italian writers who rallied to the cause of religious imagery against the attacks from Protestant reformers hardly made a defense at all, largely ignoring the iconoclasts' arguments, so much did they take it for granted that imagery had made an indelible impression on the Italian subconscious. Images, according to Bishop Paleotti, the author of the most celebrated tract on the subject, were "the strongest, most efficient instrument" for dominating, even ravishing, the senses; for the Jesuits, images inspired mystical contemplation and thereby enhanced spirituality. To remove them would have threatened the stability of the social order.[76]

It has been too little observed that the iconoclasm of the Protestant north was part of a larger program to rid the church not only of images but of the entire material culture of luxury that had grown up around the liturgy and to redirect that wealth to the poor. The iconoclasts' objections to much of the traditional liturgical apparatus was that it was sensuous in its luxury, it absorbed too much church wealth, and it deprived the poor of needed sustenance. Reformers were concerned about the monetary value of liturgical utensils, including candles as well as pictures; and in clearing out their churches of all these things, they were often explicit that money saved should go to the poor. As Zwingli saw it, man himself, especially the poor, should be the proper object of veneration, since people are made in God's image.[77]

The success of the Protestants' policy against the traditional material culture of the liturgy, and the little attention the Counter Reformation church in the north seemingly gave to the subject—to judge from recent studies of Speyer and the Palatinate, of Lyon and its environs, and of Champagne—indicate rather different traditions in the north and in Italy. In any case, in Italy, for all the Tridentine sumptuary legislation directed against luxury in the personal lives of the clergy, there could hardly be any pulling back from the use of luxury to enhance the entire liturgical apparatus and from the further development of the pictorial arts to appeal to religious sensibilities. The material culture of worship built on the propositions that God needs to be venerated and admired and that the visible convinces was too embedded in tradition. Reform orders such as the Capuchins and the Jesuits who, like the Cistercians, Franciscans, and a host of others before them, had originally wanted

76. This is the theme of Giuseppe Scavizzi, "La teologia cattolica e le immagini durante il XVI secolo," *Storia dell'arte*, no. 21 (1974), 171–212.

77. Lee Palmer Wandel, "The Reform of the Images: New Visualizations of the Christian Community at Zürich," *Archiv für Reformationsgeschichte* 80 (1989), 105–24.

severely stark churches eventually found themselves operating in rich and sumptuous places. That most zealous of reforming prelates, Carlo Borromeo, did not hesitate to call for marble and other precious objects in his instructions for endowing churches with the splendor and decorum proper to holy places. The Baroque church, presenting itself as a completely orchestrated program of extravagantly rich decoration and profuse imagery extending throughout the entire space, was a logical outcome in the history of the material culture of Christianity. By this time a veritable consumerism in the religious sphere had been defined and fully endorsed by the church itself.

Italians, therefore, made little of the argument that the wealth incorporated in the liturgical apparatus could be better used to help the poor. Some church thinkers, confronted with mounting cries from reformers for charity to the poor, defended extravagant expenditures on the grounds that, quite simply, God comes first.[78]

MICHELANGELO FELT THAT THE "most noble science" of painting came from heaven and that, although it therefore belonged to no country, it in fact just happened to be Italian. A powerful tradition of romanticized notions subsequently grew up to place art more firmly in the Italian character; and many would agree with Martin Wackernagel that a "deeply underlying fact" of Italian civilization was "the powerful need to look at images that was alive in all levels of the population; . . . the directly artistic aspect of the work of art, of form's powers of aesthetic stimulation and attraction [figures] only in the last place [as almost a] side effect, and not always an absolutely necessary one."[79] To explain this "need for art" and why the Italian artistic tradition is so extraordinary in comparison with that of other European countries, however, it is not enough to postulate, with Wackernagel and so many others, "an elemental instinctive drive." Instead, if Italians underwent some kind of profound transformation in their basic modes of perception, it was because they were engulfed in images and luxury; the "need for art" was the result of a historical process in which the changing world of material goods conditioned the modes of perception of an entire population.

78. Scavizzi, "Teologia cattolica," pp. 201–4.

79. Martin Wackernagel, *The World of the Florentine Renaissance Artist: Projects and Patrons, Workshop and Art Market* (Princeton, 1981), pp. 7–8.

# Demand in
# the Secular World

**ITALY AND TRADITIONAL
CONSUMPTION HABITS**

The Feudal Model

The Model in Italy

**URBAN FOUNDATIONS OF NEW
CONSUMPTION HABITS**

The Civic World of Architecture

Concepts of Nobility

Attitudes toward Wealth

**THE CULTURE OF CONSUMPTION**

Architecture

Domestic Furnishings

**CONSUMPTION AND THE GENERATION
OF CULTURE**

I N THE HISTORY OF EUROPEAN SECULAR ART, the Italian Renaissance marked a much bigger break than it did in the history of religious art. Whereas in the religious realm material culture changed less in kind than in quantity and artistic elaboration, in the secular realm the production of art was stimulated by major changes in basic consumption habits that brought into existence a new world of goods. Secular architecture came into its own, especially with the house, or palace, and its wider spatial setting, the city as a whole; and with the country house, or villa, and its wider spatial setting, the garden. Sculpture broadened its range to take in everything from miniatures and medals to equestrian monuments for the adornment of all these places, both inside in palaces and villas and outside in city squares and gardens. Above all, furnishings of every kind, from pottery and beds to paintings and frescoes, proliferated to fill up interior domestic space. A fundamental proposition about the history of Italian art in the secular realm is the vast enlargement of the Italians' world of goods along with the invention of new forms and the seemingly infinite expansion of the variety of goods.

Why did Italians want these things, and why were they prepared to spend the extra money needed to endow them with artistic quality? The following discussion deals with how this demand arose. First, however, medieval consumption habits in the secular sphere of life are surveyed so as to have a backdrop against which to see what is distinctive about Italian spending habits. The discussion then turns to the areas of Italian life in which different attitudes about spending arose—the public world of the city, the social world of the upper classes, and the economic world of the marketplace. Next, the nature of consumption is described as centering on architecture and on household furnishings; and finally, some concluding remarks attempt to assess the cultural significance of the new consumption habits.

## ITALY AND TRADITIONAL CONSUMPTION HABITS

### The Feudal Model

The history of luxury consumption in medieval Europe is different from what it had been in the ancient Mediterranean world and from what it was in the contemporary Islamic world. Europeans almost from the beginning developed a taste for particular forms of luxury; and the growth of trade and manufacture stimulated by their very different consumption habits largely accounts for the extraordinary economic development of the medieval West in contrast to the stagnation and eventual decline of the economies of both ancient Rome and contemporary Islam. Neither the fabulous wealth of the great Roman senatorial families—not to mention the seemingly optimum conditions for economic development that obtained during the unity and peace provided by the Empire—nor the enormous quantities of gold and silver that flowed into the Levant during the Middle Ages made enough impact in the market for durable goods in either area to sustain economic growth through trade and manufacture. The difference in medieval Europe was the emergence of a distinctive material culture.

In the barbarian West the luxury object par excellence was something splendid to behold, both rich in its inherent materials and elaborate in its manufacture. It consisted above all of gold, silver, jewels, and other precious and semiprecious materials. A taste for such showy things is common enough among archaic societies, but the marked indulgence in these materials by Germanic tribes in contrast to other peoples at a comparable level of development owed much to both their geographical location and their history. They had entered the Iron Age and developed the techniques of metalworking in an area where both gold and silver were to be found, the latter in plentiful quantities. Moreover, these kingdoms grew up on the fringes of the older Mediterranean civilizations, where a great treasure of precious materials had been accumulating ever since the birth of civilization in the Near East, especially after the opening of direct trade with the Far East during the Hellenistic period; and since during the Roman period some of this wealth was drained off to Rome, once the Empire lay in ruins this vast treasure was exposed to plunder by the barbarians.

With this taste for precious materials, a king considered his treasure the glory and center of his government. But it was not just a storehouse. There was no idea that treasure should remain a raw material to be hoarded; it was, rather, to be worked into wondrous objects to be displayed. When the sixth-century Burgundian king Gunthram, inspired by a dream, found a treasure of gold, he had it made into a bejeweled canopy for a saint's tomb; treasure thus remained treasure, but it was now reworked to enhance the precious materials and put on display.[1] The king's treasury was therefore a center of production, where the best craftsmen were gathered and where an artistic tradition

---

1. L. Little, *Religious Poverty in the Profit Economy in Medieval Europe* (Ithaca, N.Y., 1978), pp. 3–6.

took root that flowered in the finest expression of the culture of these Germanic peoples.

It is significant also that Gunthram made a gift of his newly found treasure, for the taste of these people for display was conditioned by the habits of a gift society. Although it is mostly the pillaging rampages of the barbarian kings that history has recorded, the counterpart of their despoiling was the gift: if they took, they also gave. Tribute was paid by the vanquished, but exchanges on a more equal basis were continually arranged between kingdoms to assure stability and peace, and in any case the ruler's booty from whatever source was expected to be shared as gifts both to his warriors and to his gods. And one gift called for another in return. When King Aethelbert of Kent sent a silver-gilded cup and two woolen cloths to Boniface in Germany, he fully expected something in return and did not hesitate to say what it was he wanted— a pair of falcons of a type rare in his part of the world. For men whose mentality was dominated by the habit of pillaging and the obsession with offerings, the gift symbolized values that gave some structure to a highly fluid society not yet underpinned by a solid institutional framework. If strength and courage were the supreme political-military virtues that justified the accumulation of wealth, liberality and generosity were the supreme social virtues that determined its redistribution. In such a social system the exchange of goods was much more a matter of the complementary actions of taking and giving than that characteristic of the market. As Georges Duby has argued, "every gathering around a ruler appears as the high point of a regular system of free exchange, permeating the whole social fabric and making kingship the real regulator of the economy in general."[2]

The mentality of a gift culture, with its marked emphasis on the symbolic value of luxury display, became deeply embedded in social traditions that eventually developed into feudalism. In part, feudalism regularized this exchange by incorporating it into a coherent political, social, and cultural system. In a highly decentralized political society with little sense of public authority, in which the structure of relations among an elite who possessed land and men was built on the feudal contract, symbols such as the scepter, the rod, the ring, the glove, and the gift of whatever sort on special occasions were needed to make agreements among men visible and hence objectify their relations, impressing on participants the values that held the system together. Since

2. See Duby's discussion in *The Early Growth of the European Economy: Warriors and Peasants from the Seventh to the Twelfth Century* (London, 1973), pp. 48–57; and also Aron Ja. Gurevič, *Le origini del feudalesimo* (Bari, 1982), pp. 59–77.

government, too, was largely a matter of communications, "ceremonies and their gestures [to quote Karl Leyser] made visible and therefore understandable, abstract ideas about the higher ends of human governance to unread and illiterate multitudes, including nobles: ideas of justice, equity, mercy, the protection of the weak."[3] Display, therefore, was at the center of feudal culture, and it took the forms of gift exchange, elaborate ceremonies, and personal adornment. It was a world where goods, services, and simple courtesies were exchanged in order to gain good will and secure loyalties, and where ostentation and ritual were the means of asserting one's social status as well as the essential instrument of the exercise of government. Marc Bloch commented on how wealth in such a society was meant to be spent as the assertion of status; and generosity, luxury, and sheer extravagance constituted its proper use.[4]

Three basic facts of life determined the display that characterized the material culture of the noble. The first was his activity as a soldier and a member of a military elite with a fully developed ethos. Given the nature of military technology, the knight had to be continually in training; and the games he played to do this—the hunt, the joust, the tournament, the enterprise of arms—were important occasions for ceremony and display as expressions of the chivalric code. Training in arms was expensive, for it required continual exercise and outlays for horses and equipment. The very appearance of a knight, clad in armor and accompanied by attendants decked out with the symbols of status, was a spectacle; and the ritual that accompanied these occasions incorporated a program for the expression of feudal ideology in all of its political, social, and cultural aspects.

Ceremonial display was also a primary function of the second kind of luxury goods that dominated aristocratic expenditures—what has here been called the liturgical apparatus. The church sanctioned both the military ethos and the class status of the noble, and he asserted his special relation with religious authority in the manorial church to serve his tenants, the private chapel of his castle, and the monastic house associated with his family. These places were often furnished with an astounding abundance of gold and silver liturgical utensils and the other items of the liturgical apparatus that fill our museums today; and probably more expensive than these were the priestly garments, numerous and various enough to accommodate the exigencies of an extremely

---

3. K. J. Leyser, "The Tenth-Century Condition," in his *Medieval Germany and Its Neighbours, 900–1200* (London, 1982), p. 5.
4. Marc Bloch, *Feudal Society* (Chicago, 1961), p. 311.

intricate liturgical year.[5] In addition, the noble possessed many other religious objects—rosary beads, portable altars, devotional books—that accompanied his own person and therefore had to have the appropriate attributes of luxury.

The third category of expenditures consisted of those with which a landlord asserted his status in the eyes of tenants and a noble his place in an elite hierarchically structured around a system of mutual obligations. His stage was not the city or, except rarely, the court but his country seat amidst the possessions that constituted his wealth. His household, therefore, was the center of his attention, where he received both his peasants and his peers. The fifteenth-century Burgundian court historian Georges Chastellain observed that "after the deeds and exploits of war, which are claims to glory, the household is the first thing that strikes the eye, and which is, therefore, most necessary to conduct and arrange well." For it was, above all, hospitality that marked the noble way of life. Largess was the supreme medieval aristocratic virtue, with strong Christian overtones; by opening his house to all comers—friends, followers, and even persons unknown to him—and offering them food, drink, and accommodation, the noble lived up to the highest expectation of his class. Lesser nobles attended the households of greater lords and appeared in their retinue on specific occasions wearing their livery and badges; and the poor noble found honor even in the most personal and intimate service in the lord's household. In England well into modern times the young were sent to great households for their "education." As for the nobles' tenants, peasants, and laborers, they too found the great house a place of hospitality on festive occasions and the scene of the lord's beneficence. The survival in England of expansive hospitality well into the seventeenth century marks how deeply the aristocratic mentality was rooted in the culture of gift exchange.

This gregarious life centered on the great hall of the lord's house and was highly ritualized by elaborate ceremony. Consumption was directed to the rounding out of this scenario for the assertion of status. Nobles concentrated expenditures on their personal appearance and on retinues of liveried servants, dependents, and clients. In his role as lord of the manor and host in his castle, or as guest in another's, it was self-adornment that counted, now in a mode different from that of the knight. Luxury cloths for personal attire dominated expenditures, and the demand for them was a major stimulus to the growth of the medi-

5. Penelope Eames, *Furniture in England, France, and the Netherlands from the Twelfth to the Fifteenth Century* (London, 1977), p. xxiii n.

eval economy. In addition, most of the precious objects now considered typical art forms of the period had the function of ceremonial display. They were associated with the noble's person and were largely portable to accommodate a style of life that saw him frequently on the move. Gold, silver, ivory, bone, rare woods, enamels, and jewels were elaborately worked into small objects: toilette accessories such as combs, mirrors, and caskets; gaming devices such as boards, dice, and cards; hunting utensils such as horns and knives—all "condensing pomp and circumstances" (in the words of Duby) to something "which one could clasp in the hand."[6]

For the aristocratic way of life, conspicuous consumption directed to these three major categories of expenditures—military equipment, liturgical apparatus, and household—was an investment in the noble's social position that secured service and paid dividends in the universal recognition of his dignity and status, however much it led to the uneconomic and irrational dissipation of an estate. Consumption habits established nobles' relations with one another and with the rest of society and confirmed the system that held the entire society together; and their world of goods was where life took on its meaning. This is the sense of Huizinga's observation, cited earlier, that in the late Middle Ages artistic life was still enclosed within the forms of social life.

In short, underlying the consumption habits of the landowning class of northern Europe was a coherent social ideology, a concept of nobility that, far from being submerged still inchoate in the subconscious, had long found explicit expression in literary and scholarly writings on chivalry. It incorporated an aristocratic ethos with Christian and military components; it extolled the virtues of service, largess, and pride in ancestry and status; and it organized social life around the expansive household of a rural, landowning class.

THIS FEUDAL MODEL, SYMBOLIZING IN MATERIAL CULTURE the ideology of Europe's dominant class, was remarkably resistant to erosion. It was still intact at the end of the Middle Ages; and, as we shall see, it loomed large in the eyes of the elites who emerged in the cities of Renaissance Italy. However transformed feudalism had become by the time it reached its "bastardized" form in England and its "nonfeudal" form in France at the end of the Middle Ages, it still survived in many forms— in the hierarchical structure of the upper class, in the organization of the

6. Georges Duby, *The Age of the Cathedrals: Art and Society, 980–1420* (Chicago, 1981), p. 204. On the English household, see David Starkey, "The Age of the Household: Politics, Society, and the Arts, c.1350–c.1550," in *The Late Middle Ages*, ed. S. Medcalf (London, 1981), pp. 225–305.

social life of nobles around the households of great magnates, in their military ethos, and in their landed interests. At a time when the traditional bonds of homage were weakening and central monarchical government was generally unstable, common interests drew knights and landowners together in "affinities" or "alliances" under the auspices of a local magnate who offered protection by opening up his household; hence a new system of clientage was devised to hold together the greater and lesser members of the aristocracy in the exchange of service for support and protection. Despite the assertion of monarchical government in the sixteenth century, these men were still in a position to dispense patronage on their lands, in local government, on royal estates, and in the army. The bonds that held these groups together were more monetary self-interest than contractual obligations of a classical feudal kind; but the system was personalized by the cult of lordship with its emphasis on service, fidelity, and obedience, by the military culture of the knight with its sense of honor and independence, and by a sense of class with a heightened feeling for the solidarity of the lineage—all traditional feudal values.[7]

The chivalric code expressed these very values, and it therefore could still be evoked by the upper class as a rationale for its social behavior. Although the number of dubbed knights declined at the end of the Middle Ages, following developments in military technology, the model of the knight had more appeal than ever both for great magnates and kings, who needed to inspire loyalty and military ardor, and for the nobility as a whole, which needed to sharpen the definition of itself at a time when its ranks were becoming increasingly diversified and its privileges threatened. That the late medieval affinity was no longer primarily military did not weaken the appeal of the chivalric code; as Maurice Keen has argued, the greater emphasis that came to be put on nobility of blood rather than on the actual taking of knighthood "clearly did not, in any significant degree, undermine the conception of the essential role of the secular aristocracy as being a martial one."[8] The

7. P. S. Lewis, "Decayed and Non-feudalism in Later Medieval France," *Bulletin of the Institute of Historical Research* 37 (1964), 157–84; idem, *Later Medieval France: The Polity* (New York, 1968), pp. 175–208; Christine Carpenter, "The Beauchamp Affinity: A Study of Bastard Feudalism at Work," *English Historical Review* 95 (1980), 514–32; G. L. Harriss, in the introduction to *England in the Fifteenth Century: The Collected Papers of K. B. McFarlane* (London, 1981); J. Russell Major, "'Bastard Feudalism' and the Kiss: Changing Social Mores in Late Medieval and Early Modern France," *Journal of Interdisciplinary History* 17 (1987), 509–35; Kristen B. Neuschel, *Word of Honor: Interpreting Noble Culture in Sixteenth-Century France* (Ithaca, N.Y., 1989), pp. 4–5 and passim.

8. Maurice Keen, *Chivalry* (Oxford, 1984), pp. 152–53. Keen's notes are guides to the literature on chivalry especially for the later Middle Ages; and his view about the impor-

resurgence of chivalry at the end of the Middle Ages is reflected in the formal organization of heralds, the institutionalization of rules and codes, and the proliferation of orders (monarchical, confraternal, fraternal, cliental, honorific).[9] Hence, for Keen and other scholars who have recently been attracted to the subject, this was not, as Huizinga regarded it, an attempt to escape the harsh realities of life into a dream world of play and fantasy. There was no divorce between dream and reality; if anything, chivalry was at its height in the fourteenth and fifteenth centuries, never stronger as a force shaping attitudes and behavior, because it represented a powerful traditional ideal that aroused men's nostalgia for a model of corporate class behavior they could still cling to as relevant to their lives in a period of rapid social and political change.

Despite the introduction into northern Europe of literary notions about nobility during the Renaissance, the landed class clung to military ideals. In England, in fact, the gentry continued to play a real military role well into the Tudor period. In France, after the nobility had lost much of its military functions at the end of the sixteenth century, it nevertheless held tenaciously to the military stereotype; and nobles were successful in projecting that image of themselves on the rest of society. Until the formation of the court in the seventeenth century, they had, in fact, no other model to follow. However bastardized feudalism had become, loyalty, service, and courage were still the essential cement holding aristocratic society together.[10]

The model of the noble as rural landlord, exercising power over his tenants, offering hospitality to his peers, and juggling his position in the larger network of patron-client relations, also survived into the sixteenth century. In a letter to the urban patrician Willibald Pirckheimer (1518), Ulrich von Hutten grimly—and with all rhetorical license—

tance of chivalry at that time is reiterated in the review by Georges Duby in the *Times Literary Supplement* of 29 June 1984, p. 720.

9. These are the categories of D'Arcy Jonathan Dacre Boulton, *The Knights of the Crown: The Monarchical Orders of Knighthood in Later Medieval Europe, 1325–1520* (New York, 1984), pp. xvii–xxi.

10. Davis Bitton, *The French Nobility in Crisis, 1560–1640* (Stanford, 1969), pp. 29–39; Ellery Schalk, *From Valor to Pedigree: Ideas of Nobility in France in the Sixteenth and Seventeenth Centuries* (Princeton, 1986); J. P. Cooper, "Ideas of Gentility in Early Modern England," in his *Lord, Men, and Beliefs: Studies in Early-Modern History* (London, 1983), pp. 43–77; G. W. Bernard, *The Power of the Early Tudor Nobility: A Study of the Fourth and Fifth Earls of Shrewsbury* (Totowa, N.J., 1985), pp. 185–97. The recent literature is surveyed by Diego Venturino, "L'ideologia nobiliare nella Francia di antico regime: Note sul dibattito storiografico recente," *Studi storici* 29 (1988), 61–101.

cautioned against a romanticized view of the German knight's life in the country. To meet the ever-present threat of violence, von Hutten argued, a knight had to seek the protection of a lord, fit himself out with an equipage of horses, arms, and followers, and go about in arms to hunt and fish or simply to inspect the countryside; to keep harmony among the people on his own estates, he was forever involved in the settlement of endless quarrels among neighbors, retainers, and relatives, including his own household staff and even his brothers; his estates and the well-being of the people on them required constant vigilance, especially in view of the vicissitudes of the weather; and his doors had to be kept open to all comers, including strangers.[11] In an anonymous dialogue written later in the century on the relative merits of rural and urban life in England, the participant who defends rural living comes up with all the old values—the virtues of love and charity, as expressed in hospitality and largess; power, exercised through local political authority; prestige, demonstrated in servants and retinues of followers; and, in this period of the rapidly growing market in London, the greater economy of life in the country, where there was less need for money.[12] The land continued to keep its hold on the nobility of northern Europe into early modern times not simply because of economic interest but because of the attractiveness of the seigneurial way of life. Although an increasing number of nobles took up residence in the city, attracted by the court and the growing bureaucracy, their urban residences were usually little more than a pied-à-terre that took a secondary position to a country establishment—and this was true well into the eighteenth century.[13]

The traditional model of knight and landlord hence survived with all the old values, and this is why traditional material culture embracing war, liturgical apparatus, and household remained intact: nothing had changed in the noble's basic way of life that made new functional demands on the things he surrounded himself with. For all the flamboyance and exaggeration that characterized the aristocratic world of goods at the end of the Middle Ages, nobles were spending their wealth in essentially traditional ways.

11. Hajo Holborn, *Ulrich Von Hutten and the German Reformation*, trans. R. H. Bainton (New Haven, 1937), pp. 18–19.

12. "Cyvile and Uncyvile Life" (London, 1579), reprinted in *Inedited Tracts Illustrating the Manners, Opinions, and Occupations of Englishmen during the Sixteenth and Seventeenth Centuries*, ed. W. C. Hazlitt (London, 1868).

13. Philippe Contamine, "La noblesse et les villes dans la France de la fin du moyen âge," *Bullettino dell'Istituto Storico Italiano per il Medio Evo e Archivio Muratoriano* 90 (1984), 467–89.

## The Model in Italy

As the expression of the ideology of a European-wide elite, which had in addition the full sanction of the church, chivalric culture also took root in Italy, even though feudalism as a legal and political system was stunted in its growth in much of the peninsula by the emergence of towns as the centers of political and economic power. Feudalism had its focus in the person of the German emperor, the nominal overlord of much of Italy, and in the sequence of royal houses that ruled the south; and nobles who were attracted into towns did not lose sight of the chivalric model. Indeed, in the potentially threatening environment of urban life they may have looked to it all the more intensely to maintain their class identity as landowners who clung to their independence, as knights who fought for the commune, and as an elite who found strength in family unity and a sense of lineage. Nevertheless, nobles inevitably entered into the life of the city, investing and participating in capitalist enterprise, marrying into the new entrepreneurial class, and joining with others in political affairs; and it became increasingly difficult to identify them in economic and social terms. In their behavior, however, they retained some of their distinctive ways as an aristocracy, and in this they founded a role model for the newer men of urban origins with whom they were being assimilated.

The aristocratic model demonstrated extraordinary appeal even in the foremost centers of capitalist growth. In Siena Europe's first generation of great international merchant-bankers at the end of the thirteenth century succumbed almost completely to it, largely because the city lost its preeminence as a financial capital after the turn of the next century, before a distinct urban elite of wealthy entrepreneurs became entrenched. These Sienese entrepreneurs, who had risen through the ranks within the city, focused their social ambitions on the traditional nobility, in a sense retreating from the city without, however, actually abandoning it. They invested in rural estates complete with seigniorial rights and appropriated the older noble values; and they were not followed by a second generation that might have gone on—as in Florence—to develop an urban alternative. In contrast to both Siena and Florence, Genoa remained a major center of capitalist expansion from the Commercial Revolution in the eleventh century well into the modern period, yet its elite continued to behave in many of the ways of a landed aristocracy. Many of the nobles who came into the city and entered the business world were long in pulling up their roots in the mountains that ring the city where they maintained autonomous seats of power, complete with fortified residence and private army. This independence from the city provided the basis for the notorious "individualism" that precluded the formation of an effective and stable central government in Genoa until well into the sixteenth century. Nor was the Venetian nobility, which, at the other extreme, was entirely urban and mercantile in formation, with no roots in the countryside, immune to the appeal of the model. It included men such as Marco di Pietro Ziani (d. 1253), who kept a company of fighting men, built a "palace," and sought status abroad, seemingly driven by ambitions to achieve a special presence in the city for himself. For all the fame of their corporate sense of the state, the spirit of militarism, independence, and recalcitrance bred violence in the ranks of the Venetian nobles well into the fourteenth century.[14]

Amidst the rough-and-tumble of communal political life of the thirteenth and early fourteenth centuries, the Italian urban elite (in sharp contrast to those in the rest of Europe), whatever its origin, established corporate groups of relatives, followers, and hangers-on—the *consorterie* and tower societies in Florence, the *alberghi* in Genoa, the *squadre* or *classi* in Piacenza—that were probably not very different, except in scale, from the affinities and *alliances* so characteristic of bastard feudalism in northern Europe. They directed their conspicuous consumption to the assertion of their public presence and to the maintenance of their tight networks of relations and clients. Hardly any of the documentary materials that survive from the earlier period, however, throw much direct light on the matter of their private expenditures; as rich as they were, we do not know much about the durable goods men such as the Bardi and the Peruzzi bought. Imposing buildings of a fierce military nature—crenelated residences, dominating towers, and family compounds—expressed their power on the urban scene just as castles functioned in the countryside; family chapels in prominent churches established their credentials with the religious authorities; loggias provided the public stage for their private ceremonies; the spectacle of great family festivals and celebrations drew together their clients and supporters; and luxurious personal attire defined their social rank for the general public. In short, they directed their consumption to satisfying

14. Giuliano Pinto, "'Honour' and 'Profit': Landed Property and Trade in Medieval Siena," in *City and Countryside in Late Medieval and Renaissance Italy: Essays Presented to Philip Jones*, ed. T. Dean and C. Wickham (London, 1990), pp. 81–91; Juergen Schulz, "Wealth in Medieval Venice: The Houses of the Ziani," in *Interpretazioni veneziane: Studi di storia dell'arte in onore di Michelangelo Muraro*, ed. David Rosand (Venice, 1984), pp. 29–37; Guido Ruggiero, *Violence in Early Renaissance Venice* (New Brunswick, N.J., 1980), ch. 5. For Florence, see Carol Lansing, *The Florentine Magnates: Lineage and Faction in a Medieval Commune* (Princeton, 1991), pp. 158–61.

their gregarious instincts as public figures, both as heads of family clans and client groups and as magnates deeply imbued with the strong spirit of faction.

Thus, with the assimilation of the nobility into urban life, the feudal model—precisely because it was the only fully legitimated model for secular behavior—continued to have its appeal also to the wealthy and powerful of nonfeudal origin. The rich tradition of chivalric literature in the Italian towns testifies to the fascination noble culture had for common city dwellers.[15] That fascination found an outlet in real life, for example, on the occasion of civic funerals, with the caparisoned horse accompanied by an honor guard and by grooms and pages bearing weapons and other knightly trappings.[16] One might argue that public spectacles of a chivalric nature—war games, triumphant entries, ritualistic ceremonies—were all the more popular in Italy because towns provided the urban aristocracy with a permanent captive audience ever ready to be amused—if not politically distracted—by such displays.

FOR ALL THE APPEAL OF THE FEUDAL MODEL, the values and attitudes associated with it nevertheless became increasingly remote from the realities of life for the urbanized elites of late medieval Italy. On the one hand, the older nobility saw its independent basis of power in the countryside slowly eroded by the extension of the authority of the commune over the countryside; meanwhile, it had no feudal authority around which to rally outside the city once it was clear the imperial cause was lost. Within the city, on the other hand, nobles had to confront the fact that urban residence required adjustments in their way of life. As a sense of public authority gradually asserted itself against the amorphous corporatism of the earlier commune, the nobility found its room for independent behavior constricted and its idiosyncratic ways curbed. Moreover, social assimilation with the newer mercantile elite led inevitably to compromise. In Florence, where by the end of the fifteenth century this process of assimilation had gone as far as it had anywhere else, magnate status was little more than a category of old families excluded from political affairs, hardly referring anymore to a social elite with traditional rights and a distinctive lifestyle. Traditional forms of the public display of status were no longer appropriate to city

15. Philip Jones, *Economia e società nell'Italia medievale* (Turin, 1980), pp. 88, 153, with further bibliographical references; see also Marina Beer, *Romanzi di cavalleria: Il "Furioso" e il romanzo italiano del primo Cinquecento* (Rome, 1987), pp. 227–46 (on the wide readership of early editions).

16. See Sharon Strocchia, *Death and Ritual in Renaissance Florence* (Baltimore, 1992), pp. 31–39, 75–82.

life. The dismantling of private towers of the great families and the proliferation of antimagnate and sumptuary legislation were symptomatic of the growing disenchantment. This class was thus circumscribed and isolated and so encouraged to give up its old ways and to integrate itself into civil society; and others were discouraged from imitation of its behavior and its taste for display, particularly on occasion of great family ceremonies celebrating weddings and funerals.[17]

In addition, the nobility eventually lost what had been its unique contribution to urban life once the commune began to have recourse to professional soldiers in the fourteenth century. Hence, the professionalization of war further weakened the military ethos of urban elites. As a result, military service was not a matter of communal obligation on the part of residents but simply a business contract with outsiders. Moreover, many of these military leaders physically removed themselves from the communal state to establish political independence in their own states, mostly in small towns in remote areas. By the fifteenth century knighthood in most towns in central and northern Italy was a civic honor that brought certain privileges, including the right to carry a sword and to take precedence on certain public occasions, but did not necessarily have anything to do with military service. "Some of our officials and other citizens," observed one of the participants in Poggio Bracciolini's dialogue *On Nobility*, "wear a gold pin in token of knighthood, although perhaps they don't have a horse and know nothing of warfare. Their lives," he adds perceptively, "are unrelated to their splendid dress." It was not unusual for an urban patrician who represented his government at the imperial court to be presented with a patent of count palatine; but the honor meant little once he was back home, where it most likely ended up forgotten in the family archives.

So too expenditure of the urban classes for ostentatious military gear declined notably. It is prominent in Florentine inventories well into the fifteenth century; for example, the 1418 inventory of the Medici household lists a full complement of armor in the young Cosimo's chamber; and some men were still prepared to pay handsomely for parade gear on ceremonial occasions. By the end of the century, however, account books do not record many new acquisitions, and to judge from later inventories, older inherited equipment of this kind was not kept around. Public office in republican Florence, moreover, did not require personal outlay for spectacle. Florentines called into highest govern-

17. The antiaristocratic bias in Italian sumptuary legislation, in contrast to that of the north, is suggested by Diane Owen Hughes, "Sumptuary Law and Social Relations in Renaissance Italy," in *Disputes and Settlements: Law and Human Relations in the West*, ed. J. Bossy (Cambridge, 1983).

ment service on the Signoria wore the same simple garb and lived in dormitories within the confines of the government palace for the tenure of their office, one of them being made responsible for keeping accounts of their daily expenditures for food. If a Florentine took an office in the countryside, as a vicar, captain, or podestà, where he had to make a ceremonial entry as the representative of central government and keep up a conspicuous presence, he took along a helmet, shield, sword, standard, and other such trappings of office; but many men did not personally possess such objects and so had to borrow them from someone who did, apparently unbothered by riding into town to take charge of a new post decked out in borrowed gear bearing the arms of another family. That in Italy one could rent horses without compromising his gentleman's status surprised Montaigne—a reaction occasioned by a highway encounter with no one less than a Medici prince and his train, all riding on hired horses.[18]

Elites of the great commercial centers still enjoyed incorporating much of the spectacle of the traditional knightly class into their own lives whenever they could, from the ceremonies of investiture on receiving a benefice to the trappings of arms and horses in funeral processions. They had a passion for chivalric military games, and the subtle relation between play and reality had political overtones for a dominant elite in a tradition that associated the state with military power. In Florence the Guelf Party was an official sponsor of such events, and some men paid dearly for the sake of putting up a good appearance at it.[19] It remains to be shown, however, how many of these men were in fact prepared to bear the cost of real armor and the attendant expenses of maintaining the staff and stable required to play the real game—not to mention the time they would have needed to keep fit through continual exercise. What they played must have been a far cry from a real war game—as the condottiere Federico da Montefeltro intimated when, responding to a request from Lorenzo de' Medici in 1468 for a man to participate in a Florentine joust, he apologized for not having anyone in his employ who was really handy with "arms" of this type.[20] Venetian

18. *The Diary of Montaigne's Journey to Italy in 1580 and 1581*, ed. E. J. Trechmann (London, 1929), pp. 92, 94. Ugolino di Niccolò Martelli, *Ricordanze dal 1433 al 1483*, ed. F. Pezzarossa (Rome, 1989), of the mid-fifteenth century is just one of many *ricordanze* that register repeated loans of family military equipment to others for their use while in office.

19. Alison Brown, "The Guelf Party in Fifteenth Century Florence: The Transition from Communal to Medicean State," *Rinascimento* 20 (1980), 44, 46, 48.

20. Paolo Viti, "Lettere familiari di Federico da Montefeltro ai Medici," in *Federico di Montefeltro: Lo stato*, ed. G. Cerboni Baiardi, G. Chittolini, and P. Floriani (Rome, 1986), p. 480.

nobles enjoyed jousting and tournaments as much—but as a spectacle organized by their professional military captains, which they watched from a safe distance and without incurring the personal expense of participation.[21] Military games at the courts of the Italian despots, as compared with the violence one encounters in the chronicles of contemporary Burgundy, seem to have been tame affairs—such as the tournament organized by Cardinal Antonio de Beatis in Milan in 1518, which he described as "more notable for pageantry than for prowess [there not being] a single casualty or wound, nor any honourable thrust."[22] By the end of the Middle Ages, when in the north the chivalric tradition enjoyed a highly romanticized—and expensive—resurgence, the "bastardization" of feudalism notwithstanding, it was receding from costly real life in the streets of urban Italy into the realm of popular entertainment and literary fantasy. How much it actually entered into the reality of the social life of the upper classes is a subject that has yet to be studied.[23]

The upper classes of Italy were perhaps only somewhat less prone to personal violence by the very nature of their residence in cities, since most cities sought to maintain internal peace. Blood feuds among the nonmagnate families, however, were certainly not unknown. Still, in early fifteenth-century Florence, men of magnate status could show a marked tendency for violence—like Buonaccorso Pitti, who, traveling around Europe, felt quite at home with knights and monarchs, gambling and playing military games with them and sometimes engaging in real combat; and like Luca di Matteo da Panzano, of an old noble family but orphaned and put out as an apprentice in a silk shop, who took time off before finally setting himself up in business on his own to go off to Naples to avenge the murder of his father some twenty years earlier.[24]

A century later, however, such behavior was much less common in most Italian cities. In the Veneto (and above all in Vicenza), where many nobles were registered soldiers and could legally carry arms, the tradi-

21. Michael Mallett, *Mercenaries and Their Masters: Warfare in Renaissance Italy* (Totowa, N.J., 1974), pp. 214–15.

22. *The Travel Journal of Antonio de Beatis*, ed. J. R. Hale (London, 1979), p. 182.

23. For example, the recent volume of the proceedings of a symposium, *La società in costume: Giostre e tornei nell'Italia di antico regime* (Foligno, 1986), has much material about the chivalric tradition as ideology, as ritual and spectacle, and as the subject of treatises but hardly anything about its social foundation.

24. Pitti's chronicle has been translated in *Two Memoirs of Renaissance Florence: The Diaries of Buonaccorso Pitti and Gregorio Dati*, ed. G. Brucker (New York, 1967); da Panzano's record book (1400–1434) is published in *Archivio storico italiano*, 5th ser., 4 (1889), 149–53. For Venice, see Ruggiero, *Violence in Early Renaissance Venice*, ch. 5.

tion of violence continued well into the sixteenth century in the occasional confrontations with one another on the streets and organized banditry in the countryside.[25] Genoa remained one of the most violent cities well into the sixteenth century because the nobility held on tenaciously to its independent base of power in the hills outside the city. Sixteenth-century legislation forbid anyone from carrying offensive arms and from going through the city on horseback with more than two servants, and it limited groups going about at night to no more than four persons and required that they carry a lantern. Nevertheless, the frequent violence in the streets recorded in the Pallavicino chronicle in the 1580s—like much of the violence in other Italian towns at the time—does not appear to have been of the characteristically aristocratic kind erupting as either challenges to personal honor or as family vendettas and rivalries, and it is not clear in the chronicles whether nobles or mere ruffians were involved.[26] In any event, personal violence among Italians seems to have been "little encumbered with niceties" derived from the chivalric ethos.[27]

The duel, too, has a somewhat different history in Renaissance Italy. In the sixteenth century, when Italian elites were obsessed with a desire to define just exactly what honor meant both to set themselves apart from the rest of society and to protect themselves from the absolutism of princes, the duel came in for considerable attention in the light of the concept of honor around which new ideas about the nature of nobility were coalescing. Toward midcentury an extraordinary number of treatises appear on the duel, some of which went through many editions. This theoretical writing by both jurists and literary figures flourished in an effort to give the subject of honor some underpinnings in philosophy, religion, and law. In effect, these writers attempted to tame the duel, depriving it of its chivalric content and subjecting it to another system of values, in a sense (as François Billacois comments) sublimating it by writing about these values. In any case, practically all of them assume that it pertained only to military men, or at the most courtiers, who constituted only a minuscule part of the Italian nobility. As Francesco Erspamer

25. Howard Burns, *Andrea Palladio, 1508–1580: The Portico and the Farmyard* (London, 1975), pp. 10, 20; James S. Grubb, "Catalysts for Organized Violence in the Early Venetian Territorial State," in *Bande armate, banditi, banditismo, e repressione di giustizia negli stati europei di antico regime*, ed. G. Ortalli (Rome, 1986). Cf. Gio Battista Zanazzo, "Bravi e signorotti in Vicenza e nel Vicentino nei secoli XVI e XVII," *Odeo olimpico* 5 (1964–65), 97–138; 6 (1966–67), 259–79; 8 (1969–70), 187–225.

26. *Inventione di Giulio Pallavicino di scriver tutte le cose accadute alli tempi suoi (1583–1589)*, ed. Edoardo Grendi (Genoa, 1975).

27. V. G. Kiernan, *The Duel in European History* (Oxford, 1988), p. 70.

has put it, much more ink than blood was spilled over the matter.

The subject became largely an academic issue, however, once the Council of Trent, in 1563, threatened excommunication for anyone involved in the practice; and the writing and publication of treatises on the subject fell off sharply after enjoying a fad that had lasted hardly a generation. The success of the decree, however, is probably to be attributed less to ecclesiastical sanctions than to lack of a real interest in the subject. By the end of the century the duel had become largely extinct in most of Italy (Piedmont and parts of the Veneto were notable exceptions). Meanwhile, in France the duel gained popularity with the marked rise in the level of personal violence among the nobility, including also feuds and vendettas. Henry IV tried to get a grip on a bad situation in his kingdom by punishing duelists by the thousands, perhaps without realizing that he could not deal peremptorily with a value so central to the culture of the upper class. The duel derived its appeal from the military ethos of the landed aristocrat, and its continuing—indeed, mounting—popularity in early modern Europe on the other side of the Alps marked the extent to which that ethos still dominated the upper classes, both the threatened military class that took refuge in activities such as the duel and the upwardly mobile class that aped the ways of those on whom it set its social ambitions. Italy lacked the social foundations to nourish a practice that was such "a shrill, extreme claim to honor" in its violence.[28]

Sixteenth-century travelers to Italy, like Montaigne, were impressed that Italians did not carry swords—"for the Italians in our age . . . ," observed Fynes Moryson at the end of the century, "are not given in their nature to undergo dangerous and equal combats, howsoever honourable." Likewise, Italians abroad, from Guicciardini in early sixteenth-century Spain to Giambattista Marino a century later in France, were struck by how everyone seemed to carry swords.[29] In the

28. Francesco Erspamer, *La biblioteca di don Ferrante: Duello e onore nella cultura del Cinquecento* (Rome, 1982), esp. pp. 70–73 and ch. 4; Frederick R. Bryson, *The Sixteenth-Century Italian Duel: A Study of Renaissance Social History* (Chicago, 1938); François Billacois, *The Duel: Its Rise and Fall in Early Modern France* (New Haven, 1990), pp. 40–46. For the social psychology of the practice, see Kiernan, *Duel in European History*, esp. chs. 5–6. For France, see Robert R. Harding, *Anatomy of a Power Elite: The Provincial Governors of Early Modern France* (New Haven and London, 1978), pp. 77–78; Billacois, *The Duel*; Neuschel, *Word of Honor*, p. 206. For Spain, see Raffaele Puddu, *Il soldato gentiluomo. Autoritratto d'una società guerriera: La Spagna del Cinquecento* (Bologna, 1982), pp. 177–78.

29. Francesco Guicciardini, *Diario del viaggio in Spagna*, ed. Paolo Guicciardini (Florence, 1932), p. 53; Marino is cited by Fernand Braudel, "L'Italia fuori d'Italia," in the Einaudi *Storia d'Italia*, vol. 2, pt. 2 (Turin, 1974), p. 2202. See also *Travel Journal of Antonio de Beatis*, p. 165 (on France).

mid-seventeenth century a Florentine diarist, remarking on a brief fad that broke out in the early part of that century in Florence for carrying swords, adds that no one, including ducal employees, carries them anymore.[30]

There is no question that what has been called the military courtier had a lively presence on the Italian scene in the sixteenth and seventeenth centuries. One has the impression, however, that the writers who extolled his virtues were rallying around a phantom; in any case, their work has a strong polemical tone to it. After the stabilization of the political order the professional military man could not find much of an outlet for his ambitions without going abroad to fight for a foreign prince, and he was therefore all the more sensitive to his image at home. In his polemical treatise *Il cavaliere* (1589), Domenico Mora, a soldier who made his career in the north of Europe, desperately protested the situation in his native country, where men esteemed letters more than chivalry and where, in fact, they had shamefully forgotten, if not indeed rejected, their chivalric origins. Castiglione was not the only Italian to comment on the incapacity of his countrymen for fighting. "So," in the opinion of a foreigner, David Hume, over two centuries later (talking "of Refinement of the Arts"), "the modern Italians are the only civilized people, among Europeans, that ever wanted courage and a martial spirit."[31]

Whatever the so-called refeudalization of Italy's upper classes meant in the sixteenth century, it certainly did not mean that they spent any more money for these knightly pursuits. The only knightly order founded by an Italian prince, the Order of Santo Stefano, set up by the Medici duke in 1561, was a religious, not a monarchical, order. Although it defined an "honorable" lifestyle as the prerequisite for membership and its members took up the military life, the order did not immediately attract many of the older families within Tuscany itself. It won attention, however, for the social ambitions of upwardly mobile men from the business and industrial world—including even sons of brickmakers—and from provincial towns who could hardly have

---

30. Tommaso Rinuccini, "Considerazioni sopra l'usanze mutate nel passato secolo del 1600," in Filippo di Cino Rinuccini, *Ricordi storici*, ed. G. Aiazzi (Florence, 1840), p. 276.

31. Claudio Donati, "L'evoluzione della coscienza nobiliare," in *Patriziati e aristocrazie nobiliari*, ed. C. Mozzarelli and Pierangelo Schiera (Trent, 1978), pp. 13–36; Giancarlo Angelozzi, "Cultura dell'onore, codici di comportamento nobiliare e Stato nella Bologna pontificia: Un'ipotesi di lavoro," *Annali dell'Istituto Storico Italo-Germanico in Trento* 8 (1982), 305–24; Erspamer, *Biblioteca di don Ferrante*. See also the comments of Rinuccini, "Considerazioni," p. 276.

known anything about the military ethos. Moreover, membership did not involve an intimate association with the prince—one of the real social benefits, and functions, of monarchical orders in the more traditional feudal courts. By 1600 the order was more popular with the older families as a status symbol in the new regime, especially for younger sons of men who themselves nevertheless continued to be active in the business world.[32]

Not even the nobles of Verona, who more than any others in Italy "kept faith with their ancient feudal and knightly pretensions,"[33] were really prepared to pay the cost of belonging to the military academy they set up in the sixteenth century to get themselves in shape to play military games; and eventually it could not compete for their attention with another academy—the first ever—founded to promote interest in music, an art that in its taming sociability could hardly have been more remote from war—and one that perhaps cost as much in time if not in money. Elsewhere in the Veneto in the late sixteenth and early seventeenth centuries, military academies were organized here and there; but the best indication that the noble's heart was not really in this activity was his unwillingness to pay the relatively insignificant cost of operating them. These academies were able to open only after the Venetian Senate was prevailed on to grant them subsidies (which it did out of its concern for the state's defenses); and they all degenerated into finishing schools and social clubs within a generation of their founding.[34]

These attitudes of the Italians are no more clearly manifest than in their use of heraldry, the very language of chivalry. By the fourteenth century both merchant and noble were caught up in the European passion for coats of arms; they put these visual symbols of status on banners and military equipment (to the extent they had these things) and mounted them on permanent public display in their family chapels. Florentine merchants eagerly accepted heraldic privileges conferred on them by foreign princes: Francesco Datini added the Angevin fleur-de-lis to his coat of arms, the Medici decorated one of their heraldic balls with the fleur-de-lis of the French king, and Giovanni Rucellai had the

32. F. Angiolini and P. Malanima, "Problemi della mobilità sociale a Firenze tra la metà del Cinquecento e i primi decenni del Seicento," *Società e storia*, no. 4 (1979), 17–47; R. Burr Litchfield, *Emergence of a Bureaucracy: The Florentine Patricians, 1530–1790* (Princeton, 1986), p. 37.

33. Marino Berengo, "Patriziato e nobiltà: Il caso veronese," in *Potere e società negli stati regionali italiani fra '500 e '600*, ed. E. Fasano Guarini (Bologna, 1978), p. 196.

34. John R. Hale, "Military Academies on the Venetian Terraferma in the Early Seventeenth Century," *Studi veneziani* 15 (1973), 273–95; see also Angelo Ventura, *Nobiltà e popolo nella società veneta del '400 e '500* (Bari, 1964), pp. 338–43.

diamond-ring motif granted by the d'Este as a personal insignia carved into the spandrels on the façade of his palace. The idea of working heraldic symbols into the fabric of a building originated in Florence, when Cosimo de' Medici had not only his arms but also his personal insignia built into the family palace and the churches he sponsored; and other Florentine patricians quickly followed suit. No other people in Europe so surrounded themselves with these symbols of personal and familial status as the Florentines; they put them on many of their possessions, working them into the fabric of their buildings and into the decoration of their furniture, pottery, and silverware.

Yet, all this exuberance was utterly uncontrolled by any regulation in the interest of caste definition. Italian heraldry does not symbolize vassalage and subordination; and there seems to have been no authority whatsoever that granted the privilege of using arms, either in Florence or in any other Italian town. They could be adopted by anyone, including the lower classes. The virtual anarchy of the situation in Italy precluded the evolution of the science of heraldry that developed in the rest of Europe precisely at this time as a language with its own grammar and law of arms, subject to legislation and regulation through hierarchically structured corporations of heralds chartered by royal authority. At Italian funerals no heralds showed up to supervise the proper display of arms for the assertion of hierarchy and status and to assure a correct symbolic expression of the transfer of titles and power. Moreover, arms were not divided and quartered according to the complex genealogical rules worked out in the kingdoms of the north. Nowhere in Italy does one find the elaborate display of arms to be found on English sepulchral monuments, where the familial ancestry of the deceased through generations of converging lineages can be taken in with a glance by the knowledgeable observer. Italian treatises on nobility offered no instruction in the matter such as that Thomas Peacham included in his manual for the complete English gentleman (1622). Rather than preoccupy themselves with the elaboration and control of these public badges of social status, the Italians were more inclined to invent highly personal insignias, or imprese, with the fantasy of a recondite and often impenetrable intellectualism.[35]

35. Italian heraldry is surveyed by Hannelore Zug Tucci, "Un linguaggio feudale: L'araldica," in the Einaudi *Storia d'Italia: Annali*, vol. 1 (Turin, 1978) pp. 811–77. On Tuscan usage, see idem, "Istituzioni araldiche e pararaldiche nella vita toscana del Duecento," in *Nobiltà e ceti dirigenti in Toscana nei secoli XI–XIII: Strutture e concetti* (Florence, 1982), pp. 65–79; Franco Cardini, "Concetto di cavalleria e mentalità cavalleresca nei romanzi e nei cantari fiorentini," in *I ceti dirigenti nella Toscana tardo comunale* (Florence, 1983), pp. 163–67; and Michel Pastoureau, "Mutamenti sociali e cambiamenti di arme

Surveying the map of Italy, one is impressed by the number of places with weak traditions of military service as a strong political value even after they passed from the communal stage to the despotic or oligarchical one. In Florence the Medici established their peculiar brand of princely power in the fifteenth century without assuming the role of military rulers; they scrupulously maintained their image as merchant-bankers and enhanced it with cultural, not military, attributes. In Venice the nobles fought at sea but assumed no military function in landed warfare; and so the elites of Verona, Vicenza, Treviso, Padua, Brescia, Bergamo, and smaller towns that came under the rule of Venice with the expansion of the state throughout the terraferma in the fifteenth century found themselves subjects of a state that offered them no aristocratic model of military service. Moreover, with the general pacification of Italy that came with the final establishment of the commanding presence of Spanish power in the sixteenth century, the occasion rarely offered itself for urban elites, including those in princely capitals (with the notable exception of Naples), to move into military service on a large scale. Thus, in the sixteenth century, militarism subsided in Italy and the spell of the military ethos lost much of its power—just at a time when northern Europe was still racked by war and nobles everywhere found a new lease on life. Indeed, the great exploits of the age—the Portuguese explorations, the French invasion of Italy, and the Spanish conquest of the New World—have been partly explained as military ventures purposely organized as external escape valves for the potentially destructive restlessness of the nobility in the kingdoms beyond the Alps.

THINGS WERE SOMEWHAT DIFFERENT in what has been called "the other Italy," that of northern Italian princes in towns at the periphery of the world of capitalistic urban development—but not so very much. Ceremony was obviously more elaborate than in merchants' homes, and much of it had a knightly gloss to it. Many of these men were, after all, military men, and what other model was there to follow? However much they may appear to have been Realpolitiker, these Italian princes wanted the legitimacy that a feudal title could nominally confer. They

---

nella Firenze del XIV secolo," in *L'araldica: Fonti e metodi* (acts of a symposium; Florence, 1989), esp. pp. 35–39. The heraldic funeral in England is discussed by Clare Gittings, *Death, Burial, and the Individual in Early Modern England* (London, 1984), ch. 8. See also Malcolm Vale, *War and Chivalry: Warfare and Aristocratic Culture in England, France and Burgundy at the End of the Middle Ages* (Athens, Ga., 1981), pp. 88ff; and Cooper, "Ideas of Gentility."

sedulously cultivated relations with kings and especially with their nominal overlords, the emperors, and eagerly flaunted the honors and emblems received in return. Their courts had all the trappings of feudal rites and ritual. Inside their palaces despots like the Gonzaga, d'Este, Della Scala, and Visconti surrounded themselves with tapestries and frescoes depicting scenes from courtly romances, chivalric heroes, and the aristocratic pleasures in general. As Julius von Schlosser showed, much of their secular art, at least in the fourteenth and fifteenth centuries, falls entirely in line with the European pattern—except, of course, for style: love, arms, and the hunt were the three great themes in princely life no less in the Renaissance than they were in the Middle Ages.[36]

The Italian courts, however, differed significantly from their northern counterparts in several ways. First, in that rough-and-tumble political world so brilliantly described by Burckhardt, the feudal model could hardly have maintained the legitimatizing force it had in the north, where monarchs were vigorously resisted in their efforts to extend authority over vassals but seldom challenged about their right to their crowns. How successful could feudal ceremony be in holding a state together which, like that of the Visconti, Gonzaga, or d'Este, stayed afloat on mutual-defense pacts drawn up in terms of sheer power, not claims of tradition or legitimacy; in which local lords held their distance and resisted being absorbed into the court life of the ruler; in which claims of family—the strongest of feudal bonds—were continually answered by violence or rejected in favor of illegitimacy? In the fifteenth century many princes of the minuscule states in Emilia jealously guarded their autonomy from the Milanese dukes; they sought to circumvent their traditional overlord by appealing to imperial authority for recognition, by following a policy of marriage and appointments to ecclesiastical benefices that extended beyond the Visconti-Sforza lands, and by selling their military services anywhere on the Italian political scene. Many resisted too much personal involvement at the courts of the dukes and indeed zealously built up their own minuscule courts as propaganda for their autonomy. For all the fawning protestations of devotion to the dukes, their attitude was conditioned by a subtle sense of the realities of power in the relation between the obvious superiority of the prince and their own lack of complete autonomy; they were not inspired by a traditional feudal ethos.[37]

In the d'Este state, fiefs had long ceased to have any military function

---

36. Julius von Schlosser, *L'arte di corte nel secolo decimoquarto* (Pisa, 1965).

37. Giorgio Chittolini, "Il particolarismo signorile e feudale in Emilia fra Quattro e Cinquecento," in *Il Rinascimento nelle corte padane: Società e cultura* (Bari, 1977), pp. 23–52.

and carried little involvement in ceremonies, oaths, and acts of fealty, and for the most part vassals did not include the local nobility. Moreover, military clients tended to be "foreigners" or at any rate to come from outside the local nobility, entering service to the prince through nonfeudal contracts in return for fees or pensions, contracts more of privilege than of subjugation. Although these contracts resemble the arrangements associated with bastard feudalism in England and France, they did not involve the participants in the same kind of social life associated with the large households of northern lords, organized around traditional feudal customs; and a apparently few Ferraresi numbered among the knights. In the present state of our knowledge, the nobility that surrounded the dukes cannot be altogether understood as evolving from territorial vassals into a courtly class along the model of northern Europe; in any case, their urban residence must certainly have made a difference in their behavior that has hardly been noted.[38]

A distinct feature of the Italian court was in fact its location in towns. Many of these princes emerged as strongmen out of the anarchy of communal factional politics. With a fixed location in an urban residence instead of an itinerant life in the countryside going from one fortified rural place to another, they developed different consumption habits— and the following sections on the taste for architecture and for furnishings will deal with this implication of their residential habits. The household of an Italian prince was more a purely private affair, and feudal ceremony was less of a cement holding it together. Even if, like the d'Este, they required their military clients to take up residence in the capital, these men were likely to establish their own residences; they did not become part of the prince's household in a literal sense. Nor was the local nobility in the larger capitals necessarily absorbed into court. The Florentine patriciate, for example, was hardly involved in the social life of the first grand dukes, for all the antiquity of the Medici family. We cannot impose on the Italian court of the Renaissance the later Baroque model laid down by Louis XIV at Versailles.[39]

38. Isabella Lazzarini, "Un'Italia di feudi e di città? Alcune considerazioni intorno al caso ferrarese," *Società e storia* 14 (1991), 149–50; cf. Trevor Dean, "Lords, Vassals, and Clients in Renaissance Ferrara," *English Historical Review* 100 (1985), 106–19; idem, *Land and Power in Late Medieval Ferrara: The Rule of the Este, 1350–1450* (Cambridge, 1988), pp. 146–49.

39. Samuel Berner, "The Florentine Patriciate in the Transition from Republic to Principato," *Studies in Medieval and Renaissance History* 9 (1972), 3–15; Litchfield, *Emergence of a Bureaucracy*, pp. 34–35, 48–49, 77–83. The lack of sociological study of the Renaissance court, however, has been noted in the survey of the recent literature on courts by Elena Fasano Guarini, "Modellistica e ricerca storica: Alcuni recenti studi sulle corti padane del Rinascimento," *Rivista di letteratura italiana* 1 (1983), 605–34; Pierpaolo Mer-

Moreover, since so much of the Italian political order was founded on illegitimacy, princes were perhaps more anxious than their northern European counterparts to establish their credentials by propaganda. They did this, as we have seen, by promoting something like a state church and, as we shall see, by sponsoring architectural projects in their capitals. They also viewed the court as a public relations agency. Since Italian princes were in effect sovereign rulers, their staffs included administrators, financiers, secretaries, ambassadors, and other officials who formed a solid bureaucratic core to the household; and many of these being neither vassals nor clients in the feudal sense but often men of education with a different type of personal dependence on the prince, they gave a distinctive flavor to the cultural life that emerged at these courts.[40] With their interest in learning, letters, and the arts, all rooted in the culture of antiquity, the humanists introduced new legitimating values into courtly culture. Scholar, poet, and artist produced the propaganda that glorified and commemorated the prince in terms now of classical history and mythology.

Even his prowess at arms, for all the fascination the literature of chivalric romance held for these men, was often presented in classical garb as a model of ancient military virtue rather than in the chivalric guise of the northern European military traditions of his own times; and a body of literature on warfare grew up in Italy that had little to do with the chivalric tradition.[41] The highest praise that the age was able to give a leader was the union of military skills and *humanae litterae*, a combination that was first exemplified, in the eyes of many contemporaries (and of many observers still today), by Federico da Montefeltro, Duke of Urbino. By the time of Castiglione it was taken for granted that letters went along with arms as the essential interests of a prince. Italian princes, including the pettiest of condottieri, seized on the patronage of learning and the collection of antiquities with a real passion. The style of a Renaissance despotism, to use Werner Gundersheimer's formulation

---

lin, "Il tema della corte nella storiografia italiana ed europea," *Studi storici* 27 (1986), 240. See also the comments of Giorgio Chittolini, "Stati padani, 'Stato del Rinascimento': Problemi di ricerca," in *Persistenze feudali e autonomie comunitative in stati padani fra Cinque e Settecento*, ed. G. Tocci (Bologna, 1988), esp. p. 21.

40. Cesari Vasoli, *La cultura delle corti* (Florence and Bologna, 1980), pp. 64–87; Sergio Bertelli, *Le corti italiane del Rinascimento* (Milan, 1985), pp. 28–33.

41. See Raffaele Puddu, "Lettere ed armi: Il ritratto del guerriero tra Quattro e Cinquecento," in *Federico di Montefeltro*; Pier Giorgio Pasini, *I Malatesta e l'arte* (Bologna, 1983), p. 75. A good survey of the military literature is Aldo A. Settia, "*De re militari*: Cultura bellica nelle corti emiliane prima di Leonardo e di Machiavelli," in *L'epoca delle signorie: Le corti*, in the series *Le sedi della cultura nell'Emilia Romagna* (Milan, 1985), pp. 65–89.

for his study of fifteenth-century Ferrara, was something different from the traditional feudal mode. The introduction of the Burgundian-Spanish model into Lombardy by Charles V exposed the difference between two mentalities, one formed by the chivalric sense of the state as an embodiment of personal relations among military men around a dynastic tradition, the other based in a tradition of administrators that had bred a possessive, elitist, and highly institutionalized sense of office.[42]

Under these circumstances traditional feudal consumption habits could not altogether satisfy the exigencies of the actual social situation. "Yet no doubt," observed Fynes Moryson, who came from a country where the household of a member of the peerage and episcopacy easily numbered well over one hundred, "they of all Nations can worst judge what it is to keepe a plentifull house, or a Princes Court and Trayne." In Florence, the seat of one of the most splendid courts in Italy, Moryson "saw nothing in the trayne, or Tables of the Court, wherein many of our Earles and Barons doe not equal it," an observation seconded by Robert Dallington, who asserted that no more than twenty-four servants were among those who ate at the ducal palace in Florence. Moryson found the court of Mantua "after the Italian manner, faire for building but solitary for trayne of Courtiers."[43] Castiglione's literary portrait of the court, for all its fame outside Italy as a model, is not something very relevant to court life there: other than the few functionaries who only occasionally move onto the scene, the idealized court at Urbino is a private affair, made up of close personal friends and relatives representing the international society of princely families (some of the participants in the conversation themselves became princes), not the local aristocracy and an inner circle of court advisors, dependents, and hangers-on.

Finally, the courts of Italy must always be seen in a perspective that is not distorted by the splendor of the patronage at many of them. In many respects they were a temporary and marginal phenomenon: outside Naples and the Piedmont, dynastic courts came into existence only in the fourteenth century, they proliferated rapidly and then most disappeared by the later sixteenth century, many were located in minuscule towns, and with few exceptions all were in the economic backwaters.

42. Federico Chabod, *Lo Stato di Milano nell'impero di Carlo V* (Rome, 1934), pp. 166–83.

43. *Shakespeare's Europe*, ed. C. Hughes (Manchester, 1902), pp. 106–7, 117–18; Robert Dallington, *A Survey of the Great Dukes State of Tuscany* [1591] (London, 1605), p. 38. See also Kate Mertes, *The English Noble Household, 1250–1600* (Oxford, 1988), pp. 187, 218.

The most striking feature about them, perhaps, is how few urban elites fell within their ambit.

The elites of most major city-states were in fact not organized around a princely court. Some of the largest and wealthiest cities, such as Venice and Genoa, were, of course, oligarchies with no formal court at all. Florence, too, was long an oligarchy; and when in the sixteenth century the Medici consolidated their control over the city as dukes, their court in the early years remained largely a private affair, with much of the older upper class not socially involved in it at all. In other places that on first glance appear to be organized on the monarchical principle, closer inspection reveals that the court did not dominate social life in the traditional way. The papal court at Rome, though monarchical in its political organization, was more oligarchical in its social structure, with the courts of some of the cardinals, not to mention those of the great financiers, at times being able to hold their own independently of the curia; and the oligarchy itself was highly fluid and largely non-Roman. The courts at Milan and Naples—two of the largest cities in Italy—were in the hands of foreign surrogates; and the viceroys and governors, who came and went with great frequency and without any familial continuity, were hardly able to impose their courts on local social life in the way an independent prince might have done. The same situation obtained for papal Bologna. In all these situations the upper class was largely left to its own devices. Consumption habits were not dominated by a concern to play a role in court, and a court did not therefore shape and direct demand as it did in the more traditional feudal-type monarchies. For all the splendor of the patronage of some courts, the vast majority of rich Italians were relatively uninvolved in the life of a court and not indoctrinated in courtly ideology of the northern European kind.

NORTHERN TRAVELERS TO ITALY at the end of the sixteenth century and the beginning of the seventeenth felt the distance Italy had traveled from the feudal world that still survived in their homelands at this late date. In the north, chivalric culture was still alive, however transformed; travelers to Italy were struck by the lack of a military ethos symbolized by the carrying of swords, by the lack of aristocratic magnanimity expressed in gregarious hospitality, and by the lack of social presence in large retinues of liveried servants. By this time—the beginning of the seventeenth century—things were changing in the north: the nobility no longer had a personal military function in the feudal sense, and the age of spectacular public tournaments was certainly over; the great hall, the former center of aristocratic life, was being abandoned for smaller quarters where the family could enjoy the pleasures of privacy; the attraction of the court and the capital city weakened the local collectivities of the later Middle Ages; and a growing sense of civil society and the rule of law eroded the older system of personal allegiances. Yet, despite these changes, the older values were not to be put aside so easily, and they lingered on. The considerable confusion about noble status in the changing conditions of their existence generated a more intense class consciousness to preserve their identity along the lines of the older values.[44] Travelers made their observations about Italy with an eye on the threats to the old ways back home. They did not find in Italy the material culture the feudal model for consumption had generated in the north.

## URBAN FOUNDATIONS OF NEW CONSUMPTION HABITS

If the feudal model never became deeply entrenched in Italy, it was primarily because the city was not the most fertile soil for it. Whether taken into the city by the rural nobility or adopted by the capitalist class therein, the feudal model found a less solid foundation in the realities of Italian urban life than elsewhere in Europe. In the Italian city it lacked the legitimacy of feudal authority, and it was functionally irrelevant—if not contradictory—to an acceptable code of behavior. With the assertion of their autonomy as territorial states, Italian cities freed themselves from the ideological grip of their nominal imperial overlord; and to the extent they absorbed the rural nobility, they eradicated the chivalric ideal in the immediate vicinity. In a real sense urban elites in late medieval Italy had no focus for their social ambitions outside the city—unlike merchants in Tudor London, who were always ready to abandon their counting houses and the city for country estates and the social move into the rural gentry, and unlike the patricians of German cities, who, while less likely to abandon urban residence, were nevertheless ready to improve their social credentials by accepting vassalage as imperial officials and owners of rural fiefs.

Moreover, the violent internal factionalism that so characterized life in the early communal period utterly failed to appropriate traditional ideologies to local causes: Guelfism and Ghibellinism transferred to the urban arena as rallying cries for pope and emperor largely lost their original meanings to become little more than party tags in local political

44. This theme is developed by Bitton, *French Nobility in Crisis*; and by Felicity Heal, "The Idea of Hospitality in Early Modern England," *Past and Present*, no. 102 (1984), 65–93.

strife. In fact, except in Venice and, to a lesser extent, in Florence, urban values never congealed into a fully developed political ideology based on communal or constitutional institutions that was able to deal with internal instability by appropriating the terms of factional discord and that therefore was strong enough to resist despotism. Nevertheless, the full evolution of a thoroughly urbanized way of life eventually conferred on the Italian upper classes a new concept of culture that gained momentum more as a stimulus for opening up the search for more realistic and congenial alternatives than as a countervailing force against the attraction of the feudal model.

Both Italians and northerners were aware of the fundamental difference in the social foundations of their respective nobilities. *Civile* is the word Italians at the time used in describing what these northern rural nobles were not—and by that they meant everything that is implied by residence outside a city, something that struck all Italian observers as peculiar about the northern nobility, just as the Italian nobility's residence in the city impressed northern travelers well into the seventeenth century. "Nobility," Poggio Bracciolini has Niccolò Niccoli say in his dialogue on the subject, "is gained and exercised best in cities, among people, and less easily among wild beasts in solitude or in dealings with farmers . . . [it] is not something peculiar to country estates, as the French and English think, or set among mountains and busy with robbery, as the Germans believe."[45] According to an old Tuscan proverb, already cited by Paolo da Certaldo in the late fourteenth century, only animals lived in the country; and in the words of a Florentine exile a century later, to be sent away from the city was to be expelled from *civiltà*.[46]

As the residence of the dominant groups within society—both merchants and landlords—the city became the unchallenged center of culture in Italian life; and as they slowly worked out a higher sense of public authority, the city itself came into clearer ideological focus.[47] New aesthetic, social, and economic values arose in the urban context that impinged on consumption habits in three ways: first, communal

45. R. N. Watkins, *Humanism and Liberty: Writings on Freedom from Fifteenth-Century Florence* (Columbia, S.C., 1978), p. 132.

46. D. V. and F. W. Kent, *Neighbours and Neighbourhood in Renaissance Florence: The District of the Red Lion in the Fifteenth Century* (Locust Valley, N.Y., 1982), p. 29.

47. Sergio Bertelli, *Il potere oligarchico nello stato-città medievale* (Florence, 1978), pp. 149–64; Maria Consiglia De Matteis, "Societas christiana e funzionalità ideologica della città in Italia: Linee di uno sviluppo," in *La città in Italia e in Germania nel Medioevo: Cultura, istituzioni, vita religiosa,* ed. R. Elze and G. Fasoli (Bologna, 1981). See also Giulio Carlo Argan and Maurizio Fagiolo, "Premessa all'arte italiana," in the Einaudi *Storia d'Italia,* vol. 1 (Turin, 1972), pp. 734–36.

embellishment of the physical world of the city served an educational function by arousing people's appreciation of their architectural environment; second, a new concept of nobility enlarged (if it did not undermine) the feudal consumption model and redirected the spending habits of the upper classes to set themselves off from ordinary people; third, a reevaluation of wealth in a commercial society created a new intellectual and moral atmosphere for the very act of spending money.

## The Civic World of Architecture

Nothing indicates more clearly how life in the city conditioned values and behavior than the way people collectively spent their money. Life in the city meant, above all, subordination to a more complex and demanding collectivity, to a fluid society based more on monetary arrangements than on status. One direct cost urban life carried was self-taxation, a burden Italian urban elites were more prepared to accept—albeit still disguised as forced loans—than most northern European nobles because the greater autonomy of the city as a territorial state and the relative political instability in Italy imposed on them a correspondingly greater responsibility for security. The history of the taxation of recalcitrant nobles in feudal kingdoms points up, by contrast, the importance of the different kind of socialized consciousness among urban upper classes.

This sense of collectivity among urban elites also expressed itself, in a more private and voluntary way, in the forms of their charity. The feudal noble dispensed charity in a characteristically personal gesture, literally handing it out in an act of hospitality on his own premises; or he simply made blanket gifts to the church as intermediary between the social orders, in a sense abdicating any direct responsibility for society at large.[48] Life in the city, however, raised more pressing problems of social control; and the mendicants offered a new ethic of philanthropy based on urban economic foundations. Urban elites assumed the responsibility for dealing with the general welfare through donations and testamentary bequests to orphanages, hospitals, confraternities, and other institutions dedicated to the distribution of alms. Men's willingness to support both the fisc and charitable institutions indicates how the city—and not only the Italian city—came to represent a discrete social organization with its own system of values that slowly took

48. Joel T. Rosenthal, *The Purchase of Paradise: Gift-Giving and the Aristocracy, 1307–1485* (London, 1972), pp. 130–31; Felicity Heal, *Hospitality in Early Modern England* (Oxford, 1990), pp. 122–40.

possession of urban elites, setting them off from the rural nobility of feudal Europe.

The most obvious physical expression of this cultural outlook was the city itself; and the proof of the real loyalties it could inspire was that disposition so notable among Italians to spend their money collectively on urban monuments. As Peter Brown has shown, a strong sense of civic patriotism arose already in late antiquity around the cult of local saints, taking its vigor from the need for refocusing loyalties and collective feelings in a disintegrating imperial system; and in the later Middle Ages, as we have seen, new saints kept coming forward in towns and cities throughout Italy in contrast to northern Europe, where the popular saints were less parochial.

In Italian cities, too, the local clerical elite did not stand apart detached from urban society as in the north; city and church were more strongly integrated.[49] Civic patriotism inspired both official and private spending for the church's physical plant to a much more impressive extent in Italian cities than in northern ones. The great cathedrals of Italy, to take the example of the most conspicuous monument in most medieval cities, were public projects sponsored and managed by communal governments, whereas many a famous Gothic cathedral in northern Europe was put up by an ecclesiastical authority, usually a noble-dominated cathedral chapter, which often explicitly limited the participation of local burghers in the enterprise.[50] One of the most distinctive features of the urban scene in many Italian towns is a gigantic free-standing baptistery, and it too is a civic monument marking the place where all the city's residents were inducted into a common society. The aesthetic sensibility that was aroused by such concerns became one of the most forceful components of civic ideology: it nourished a vigorous tradition of civic patronage of art, and in time this tradition created an environment conducive to private patronage of architecture, the most public of the arts.

The history of the secular patronage of art in Italy begins with the determination of communes to find a physical expression for their nascent political and ideological autonomy. This effort got under way in the expanding towns of northern Italy, especially in the Po Valley, where economic growth was accompanied by political struggle for freedom from imperial control, and in the great maritime republics of

49. Giorgio Chittolini, "Stati regionali e istituzioni ecclesiastiche nell'Italia centrosettentrionale del Quattrocento," in the Einaudi *Storia d'Italia: Annali*, vol. 9 (Turin, 1986), p. 181.

50. W. H. Vroom, *De financiering van de kathedraalbouw in de middeleeuwen in het bijzonder van de dom van Utrecht* (Maarssen, 1981), pp. 106–8.

Venice, Genoa, and Pisa. Already in the twelfth century these towns were erecting cathedrals and public halls as monumental symbols of their autonomy; and although in other respects the vigorous tradition of urban improvements in these cities was more notable for the serviceability of public works than for the elaboration of an urban architectural aesthetic, this patronage gave rise to a strong tradition of civic art. In sculptural decoration on cathedral façades and in frescoed walls within public halls, religious, historical, and chivalric themes associated with traditional ideas of justice were incorporated into programs of local historical significance in order to legitimate communal authority. The taste for such sculptural and painted programs emerged in northern towns as they began to assert independence in the twelfth century, and it appeared also in central Italy. In many places, despots who took over in the fourteenth century somewhat dampened this enthusiasm for public monuments or appropriated it for themselves; but civic art flourished in those centers (above all, in the Tuscan hinterland) where economic development remained strong and where internal constitutional arrangements continued to evolve, thereby strengthening the confidence of the ruling classes at a time when they were also expanding the territorial state. Siena, Florence, and Venice are perhaps the first places that come to mind, but Perugia, Bologna, and many others deserve mention in the continuing story of communal art toward the end of the Middle Ages.

In these towns the desire to heighten and refine the physical presence of the city eventually, around 1300, brought a genuine urban aesthetic into focus. This aesthetic consisted in the monumentality of enlarged or new cathedrals, civic halls, and other public buildings; and each town also sought to give to its projects distinctive stylistic qualities. The civic aesthetic consisted, too, in the organizing principles of spaciousness, regularity, orthogonality, symmetry, and centrality. These principles were reflected in legislation directed to tame the medieval welter of private buildings and maze of streets but more successfully realized in the laying out of streets and squares both in new suburbs designed to accommodate population growth of the twelfth century, such as the "*città nuova*" at Massa Marittima, and in new towns founded in expanding territorial states, such as those established by Florence in the early fourteenth century at Firenzuola, Scarperia, San Giovanni, Terranuova, and Castelfranco. Finally, in the painted and sculptural decoration of public buildings, both inside and out, and in the subsidies for ecclesiastical projects of major importance to the life of the city, especially those of the mendicants, communal governments pressed religious art into public service. All this gave an impetus to the patronage of monumental architecture and sculpture; and to the extent a capital city like Florence in the fourteenth century and Venice in the sixteenth replicated its public monuments and squares in subject towns, architecture became an instrument of state building.

Such patronage was directed to expressing the power and glory of the city-state, to strengthening the regime, and to providing political and ethical instruction to its citizens. The city, therefore, often singled out a work of art—and the artist—for special honors. The Sienese paraded Duccio's *Maestà* through the streets before its installation in the cathedral to replace an earlier picture commemorating a great victory a half-century earlier; and the Florentines heaped high praise on Giotto on his selection as supervisor at the cathedral works, asserting that "in the whole world no-one can be found who is more capable." Such attention, especially in the context of the intense rivalries with other city-states, was bound to heighten the public's appreciation of urban monuments and open the way for viewing them for qualities apart from their political or religious content. Communal documents on these matters are replete with evidence of the concern for beauty, and such expectations on the part of the public surely stimulated the creative impulse of artists and sharpened the competition among them. The perception of the civic role of the artist in Florence from Giotto onward greatly contributed to that process by which he and his work—within a generation after his death—came to be elevated into that realm of greatness that today is called art.[51]

The city most notable for its tradition of communal art at the end of the Middle Ages is, in fact, Florence. From the end of the thirteenth century through the first third of the fifteenth century, it engaged in the most ambitious building program undertaken by any city since ancient times, notable for both the sheer monumentality of some of the projects and the originality of their stylistic features. The Palazzo dei Signori (now known as the Palazzo Vecchio), built at the end of the thirteenth century, has been called one of the most important buildings in the history of Italian architecture for the influence its centralized plan, symmetrical façade, and articulated rustication had on the evolution of domestic architecture in the Renaissance, not to mention also its distinctive tower. The grand scale on which the commune continued to build throughout the fourteenth century is manifest in the cathedral

---

51. Helene Wieruszowski, "Art and the Commune in the Time of Dante," *Speculum* 19 (1944), 14–33. The importance of the communes as patrons of art is the central theme of John Larner, *Culture and Society in Italy, 1290–1420* (London, 1971). For general remarks on the earlier communal period, see Jonathan B. Riess, *Political Ideals in Medieval Italian Art: The Frescoes in the Palazzo dei Priori, Perugia (1297)* (Ann Arbor, 1981), ch. 9.

complex, the grain market at Orsanmichele, and the loggia in the Piazza della Signoria where the city fathers addressed the public; and many of these public buildings (in the judgment of Marvin Trachtenberg) "were not the products of an evolutionary process (like the French cathedrals), but of highly imaginative, self-conscious, and individualistic acts of design that drew freely on eclectic sources."[52] Most impressive of all, of course, is the cathedral. Begun in 1296, the project was enlarged in 1331 with the discovery of the bones of the city's patron saint, Saint Zanobius; and the plans were modified once again in the 1360s to project what was to become the largest church in Christendom. The cupola that eventually covered the crossing is one of the great engineering feats of the period.

The plan to tie these buildings together with a widened street lined with uniform façades and to set them off with open spaces indicates the sophisticated notions of Florentines about urban design. Furthermore, at the beginning of the fifteenth century they began to deck out these buildings with an abundance of monumental public sculpture, some of it charged with civic ideology; and they erected monumental tombs for the city's great humanist chancellors and, on a more modest scale, for notable military captains as well as the two artists, Giotto and Brunelleschi, who had most contributed to the fame of the glorious artistic tradition the city had come to enjoy abroad. The persistence with which the city went forward with these projects, notwithstanding the devastating loss of population as a result of the plagues from the mid-fourteenth century onward and the severe fiscal pressures as a result of the military threats at the turn of the next century and again in the 1420s, bespeaks the extraordinary civic spirit that lay behind communal patronage.

With this tradition it is hardly surprising that by the fifteenth century Florentines took it for granted that architectural monuments were an essential qualification for the greatness of a city. Leonardo Bruni (departing from both his classical model and the medieval tradition of urban panegyrics) opens his *Laudatio* (1403–4) with praise for the site of Florence and for the beauty of the city itself, that is, its buildings, including private palaces; he becomes so carried away with the subject that he feels the need to apologize for his enthusiasm. In his *Dialogues for Pier Paolo Vergerio* Bruni has Salutati begin his praise of Florence with a reference to his own (Bruni's) keen appreciation of the beauty and

52. Marvin Trachtenberg, "Archaeology, Merriment, and Murder: The First Cortile of the Palazzo Vecchio and Its Transformations in the Late Florentine Republic," *Art Bulletin* 71 (1989), 581.

elegance of the city, unsurpassed even by ancient cities. In the 1420s Goro Dati—an unlettered Florentine merchant, not a humanist following a classical model—for the first time in the history of Europe wrote about looking out on a specific urban scene with a genuinely aesthetic sensitivity to the spatial setting of buildings and the materials out of which they were made. And it was another Florentine, Leon Battista Alberti, who a few years later first theorized on the beauty of the ideal city as a collection of buildings related to the whole and reflecting the rational organization of its political structure.

During the fourteenth century perhaps no other city underwent such an extensive renewal as Florence. Others, however, had comparably ambitious schemes for their cathedrals as symbols of civic pride. Siena planned an enlargement that would have almost doubled the size of its cathedral, but the project was cut short by the fall in population brought about by the Black Death. Other cities, however, that had suffered similarly heavy population losses at this time nevertheless went ahead with greatly enlarging their principal churches: in 1386 Milan began a new cathedral that is still one of the largest in Christendom, over 500 feet in length; a few years later Bologna, a much smaller place, followed suit with San Petronio, which was projected to be about as large. Venice never undertook to replace San Marco; but its ongoing policy of concentrating major public buildings around it and in a single space opening on the port itself—the Doge's Palace housing all the elected councils and offices of the state, the buildings of the powerful procurators, the library, the mint—eventually, by the sixteenth century, resulted in one of the most remarkable squares to evolve in any commune and one of the most notable exemplifications of the humanist ideal of a focused plan in the history of urban development.[53]

THE CITY-STATE WAS FIRMLY ENTRENCHED in the culture of Italians. It had emerged out of the ferment of communal politics to find an ideological identity in the medieval world otherwise occupied by popes, emperors, and kings; and this urban tradition reached its culmination in Renaissance notions of the ideal city. As Eugenio Garin has written, the "moderns" saw their birth in the autonomy of the small city-state, for the city was the incarnation of the totality of human functions.[54] That totality included its buildings. When, therefore, men began to think

53. Juergen Schulz, "Urbanism in Medieval Venice," in *City States in Classical Antiquity and Medieval Italy*, ed. A. Molho, K. Raaflaub, and J. Emlen (Stuttgart, 1991), pp. 419–42, who cites the literature on the earlier communal period.

54. Eugenio Garin, "La città ideale," in his *Scienza e vita civile nel Rinascimento italiano* (Bari, 1965), pp. 33–56.

also about the physical form of the ideal city, the intellectual climate in which they did so was marked by concern with viable projects, not with evasion of reality into the realm of intellectual fantasy. Bruni's praise of the beauty of Florence was simply the extension to its physical presence of the rational principles by which life in the city was organized; and with Alberti the idea of the monumental city reached its maturity in a conception linking political structure and architectural design that has no precedence in the ancient and medieval literature on cities.

The city, moreover, was not an idea that was tied to any particular form of government. If it had emerged in the communal world, it survived the failure of communal governments in many places to remain the basic fact of political and cultural life. Any government could therefore appropriate this tradition in the attempt to justify itself in the eyes of the urban residents it sought to rule. It was thus natural for Italian despots to regard the city as the symbol of their political position; the basis of their power, after all, derived more from the authority originally invested in them by the commune than from conferment of imperial and papal titles. The first to undertake public works to legitimize his power and to give his state some focus seems to have been Azzone Visconti, the new lord of Milan in 1329, whose program was articulated by the Dominican historian Galvano Fiamma. Azzone established his palace in the center of the city next to the cathedral, and that the prince's residence did not have a primarily military function has been noted by Louis Green as an important innovation.[55] In the fourteenth century other despots established their residences in cities and announced that fact by making them conspicuous fortified places, often in a central location, as at Ferrara; and, like the later Visconti in Milan, they might well throw their support behind the rebuilding of a cathedral or some other such prestigious urban project. In his letter of 1373 to the Carrara lord of Padua, Petrarch defined the patronage characterizing a great prince as including also civic buildings, churches, and public works.

In the fifteenth century, description and praise of cities were rhetorical exercises that often had nothing to do with older communal values.[56] Giovanni Conversino, taking up the attack against Bruni's defense of republics cited above, defends princes in precisely Bruni's terms by asserting that they are more enlightened than republics as patrons of public works and urban beautification in general. At the end

55. Louis Green, "Galvano Fiamma, Azzone Visconti, and the Revival of the Classical Theory of Magnificence," *Journal of the Warburg and Courtauld Institutes* 53 (1990), 98–113.

56. Gina Fasoli, "La coscienza civica nelle 'laudes civitatum,'" in *La coscienza cittadina nei comuni italiani del Duecento* (Perugia, 1973), p. 11.

of the century Giovanni Sabadino degli Arienti, in his tract praising the virtues of Ercole d'Este, engages in a description of the beauty of Ferrara as evidence of the sense of justice with which Ercole governed his state. The architectural theorists, too, worked out their ideas about urban architecture fully aware of the political realities of Italy: Alberti allowed for either a republic or a prince in his discussion of the ideal city, and Filarete's Sforzinda—the fictional town that is the subject of his architectural treatise—was in fact the residential capital of a prince.

Ambitious schemes of urban renewal associated with the lord's presence began to appear in the second half of the fifteenth century. By this time some despots were sufficiently well established in their towns to want to reinforce their dynastic claims with more tangible evidence of their presence. After the Peace of Lodi in 1454, which signaled the stabilization of the Italian state system by balance-of-power politics, they had more money to build, since reduced military commitments released funds for other kinds of expenditures.

Nicholas V (1447–55) is generally regarded as the first prince to have had extensive plans for the renovation of his capital city. Presumably influenced by the ideas of Alberti, Nicholas built to accommodate the presence of the renewed papal power in the aftermath of the conciliar movement and to articulate the cultural roots of the city as visible in ancient monuments; and with him begins the long list of popes whose projects added up eventually to the greatest rebuilding any city underwent during the Renaissance. In the 1460s Lodovico Gonzaga, Marquis of Mantua, extensively remodeled the central market and political square of his capital, including the rebuilding of the church of Sant'Andrea on a design by Alberti. The first genuine model of the princely city, however, was established with the rebuilding of Pienza by Pius II in the early 1470s. The place being nothing more than a village, which the pope wanted to commemorate as his birthplace, he could for all practical purposes plan a new town. Here the palace of the prince is a completely civilian building opening on a public square that it shares with the cathedral, the bishop's palace, and the town hall. The scheme, in other words, appropriated religious and civic traditions into the new princely arrangements; and the plan called for reorganizing the entire town around this nucleus, although Pius's death ended further work in such a remote place with no economic viability.

Elsewhere, in older and larger centers, it was not so easy for princes to rebuild their capitals, but the efforts they made follow this urban model. At Urbino, Federico da Montefeltro (d. 1482) integrated the fortified residence of his family at the edge of the town into urban space by giving it a completely civilian façade and opening up a large square in front across which he projected a new cathedral. Not only did the town within become reoriented around this space, but the new project for the palace took advantage of its site above this hill town in such a way as to give the princely capital a commanding presence in the surrounding countryside. Proceeding in the same fashion at Mantua with their castle of San Giorgio on the edge of the city, the Gonzaga added a large new palace wing that extended into the square of the cathedral, which they eventually, in the sixteenth century, rebuilt. At Vigevano, the small capital rebuilt in 1492–94 by Lodovico Sforza (before he became duke of Milan), the castle at the edge of town was given access from the central square by a large ramp, and the square was then surrounded by a uniform portico tying this monumental entrance to his residence, the cathedral, and the town hall into a coherent space—the first example of such planned uniformity imposed on a square since antiquity. At Carpi in the Emilian plain Alberto III Pio (d. 1531), whose family castle was also at the edge of town, turned outward instead of inward to take advantage of the available unbuilt space beyond: he opened up an immense new square in front, complete with a new collegiate church, and laid out two new suburbs, thereby reorienting the town around the new public space dominated by its prince's residence. All these projects tamed the former fortified and detached residence of the local lord by integrating it into the town, giving it a civilian presence, and incorporating it into a monumental public space that embraced civic and religious functions, thereby reorienting the town around the prince. In short, Italian princes transformed the symbol of their physical presence from a detached fortification into the city itself.

Princes of other towns who abandoned their castles on the fortified perimeter to take up residence in the town center envisaged a similar restructuring of older public space to integrate their residence and other public buildings into it—or, rather, to organize older space around their new residence. For example, in Faenza, where the Manfredi lords inhabited the former communal Palazzo del Popolo, Carlo II started construction (in the 1470s) of an impressive double loggia on its façade planned to be continued eventually around the public square; and his brother, the bishop, complemented the project by rebuilding the cathedral.

One of the grandest schemes to assert princely presence in an older urban center was devised for Florence by the first Medici dukes. Cosimo I gathered together all the guilds and some major magistracies into a single bureaucratic center, the Uffizi, built on a loggia around its own square. From one end of the building an elevated passageway extended along the river over an open arcade, crossed the bridge, and cut through the jumbled urban scene to arrive at the new ducal residence, the Pitti Palace; and vague schemes existed for extending the plan of the Uffizi at the other end by unifying the numerous buildings on the adjacent public square—the Piazza della Signoria—with a grandiose loggia running around the entire space. Moreover, these great public spaces were to be the stage where a host of sculptures played out their propagandistic roles—great Florentines in the pillars around the Uffizi, and, in the main square, the Neptune fountain symbolizing the maritime ambitions of the new state, the gigantic equestrian monument of the grand duke himself, and other figures in front of the Palazzo Vecchio and under the Loggia dei Lanzi. The Medici were second only to the popes in the extravagance of their plans for asserting a princely presence through the reorganization of urban space.

The ideal solution, presumably, would have been to lay out an altogether new city. Italian rulers, however, had emerged within the world of communal politics, and they could not so easily detach themselves, either politically or psychologically, from their original capitals—if, indeed, they ever thought about such a move. Pienza, after all, was by no means a capital city but more a resort for occasional visits, and it obviously had no political future whatsoever. It would have made no sense to these Italians to do what many a German territorial prince was to do in the eighteenth century, following the model of Versailles—lay out a completely new city, obviously on a symmetrical and centralized geometrical scheme, and then establish a bureaucratic and courtly capital there in splendid isolation from their subjects. A few of these Italian despots, however, finding themselves lords of altogether new but utterly minuscule states with no towns to settle down in, regarded the first order of business the foundation of a minicapital—the notable examples being Cortemaggiore, founded in 1479 by Gianlodovico Pallavicino, who had to divide his father's state of Busseto with his brother; and Sabbioneta and Guastalla, where cadet branches of the Gonzaga established seats in the mid-sixteenth century.[57]

A different kind of urban rebuilding program is represented in one of the most famous projects undertaken by a Renaissance prince—the Herculean Addition begun in 1492 in Ferrara by Ercole d'Este. This was an entirely new suburb designed partly to extend the defensive network of city walls, but it in no way changed the monumental center of the city, nor did it include any major public buildings. Instead, the new area

---

57. For a survey of some of these projects, see Enrico Guidone, "L'urbanistica dei centri signorili," in the volume *L'epoca delle signorie: Le corti*, in the series *Le sedi della cultura nell'Emilia Romagna*, pp. 91–115.

incorporated into the city served primarily a residential function for a number of important men attached to the court who built palaces there. A few years earlier Lorenzo de' Medici considered similar plans for the suburban extension of undeveloped land still within the city walls of Florence, to be laid out around a suburban villa he hoped to build in the area. Oligarchs, too, shared in what Enrico Guidone has called "la cultura delle addizioni." In the third quarter of the sixteenth century the government of Genoa, now firmly in the hands of the nobility, supported the project of five families to lay out their own neighborhood with ten palaces along the Strada Nuova, thereby creating what has been called a "distinctively new type of urban space—the residential palace street or linear piazza—to legitimize and enhance the authority of a ruling elite."[58]

Indeed, urban renewal in Italy was not exclusively a princely activity. Oligarchs as well as princes viewed the city as the natural setting for the physical expression of their authority once they were securely ensconced in their positions. Local elites everywhere in Italy profited from the stabilization of the political system after the mid-fifteenth century, when new regimes confirmed their status; and in many older cities that had seen few major projects since the earlier communal period, this situation gave rise to a second—Renaissance—phase of civic building. Urban renewal was a way to celebrate the consolidation of power by the local oligarchy, even if under the auspices of an outside government. In these places where the establishment of "foreign" rule, far from uprooting the power structure, stabilized the local political scene by ending factionalism and by assuring a certain protection from abroad, oligarchies now confirmed their authority in architectural projects. The establishment of the Venetian state in the later fifteenth century was the occasion for celebration by local elites; and the ruling class in Vicenza, Brescia, Bergamo, and other towns found an appropriate expression of the new arrangements in public building, often in imitation of Venetian models.

In Lombardy two of the most impressive (if incomplete) urban renewal schemes got under way in Cremona and Pavia at the end of the fifteenth century, once their oligarchies found themselves deeply entrenched and their local autonomy assured by the new Sforza dukes in a way that it had never been under the Visconti. In 1488 the city fathers of Pavia undertook to build an entirely new cathedral, a project that in-

58. See the conference paper by George L. Gorse, "A Classical Stage for the Old Nobility: The *Strada Nuova* and Sixteenth-Century Genoa," to be published in a volume edited by R. B. Litchfield.

volved extensive demolition of the center of the city, tearing down the two Romanesque cathedrals, the baptistery, the bishop's and canons' palaces, and a monastery; and the new centralized structure with its highly intellectual plan represents one of the most innovative experiments in monumental architecture at the time. In 1491 the Cremonesi began a largely new façade on the cathedral that included a monumental two-story portico linking it to the campanile on one side and intended to embrace the baptistery on the other, a vast scheme envisaged to complement improvements on the public hall opposite. Some two decades later they commissioned a fresco cycle for the inside façade and nave of the cathedral that was one of the most ambitious undertaken anywhere in Italy up to that time; and in 1525 work began on an equally grandiose sculptural monument to the patron saints of the city, to be 6 meters wide and 11 high, sustained by four angels and twelve columns and adorned with six life-sized statues and seventeen figures on top. Neither of these Lombard cities was able to see these great projects to completion; but with remarkable persistence they kept them going through the tumultuous 1520s, despite two invasions by the French, the exile of the Sforza, and, for Cremona, a long occupation by the Venetians.

BY THE SIXTEENTH CENTURY it was second nature for the Italian ruling class to regard urban renewal of capital cities as an expression of power. In northern Europe, in contrast, princes had their roots in the rural nobility and tended to avoid cities. Their states were vastly larger, the landed elites were widely distributed throughout, and itinerancy was required if effective control was to be maintained. When a late medieval prince like the Duke of Burgundy took up residence in a town, his living quarters were great fortified structures dominating the local scene rather than being integrated into it.[59] Not even in the sixteenth century, with the consolidation of political power, the enlargement of centralized bureaucracy, and the formation of the court, did the new Valois, Tudor, and Hapsburg monarchs establish themselves on the urban scene in their capital cities. Francis I built his great chateaux all around Paris and a healthy distance away, just as Henry VII and Henry VIII took up residence at Richmond, Hampton Court, and Windsor and Philip II at the Escorial a good distance from Madrid. The city therefore did not figure into the calculations of these princes, as it did for the Italians, about the use of architecture as an expression of power. Although the building activity of Henry IV in Paris at the beginning of

---

59. See, for example, Patrick M. De Winter, "Castles and Town Residences of Philip the Bold, Duke of Burgundy (1364–1404)," *Artibus et Historiae* 8 (1983), 95–118.

the seventeenth century went far beyond anything his predecessors had done and was not to be exceeded in scale until the nineteenth century, his enlargement of the Louvre was directed to an interior space, not the exterior urban scene; and his other urban projects lacked any touch of monumentality and could hardly be characterized as "aristocratic, honorific, and grandiose."[60] When, finally, monarchs turned to building their great Baroque capitals as centers of court and government, it was in a different spirit than that of the communal traditions that inspired so much public building in Renaissance and Baroque Italy.

IT IS HARDLY SURPRISING THAT AMONG URBAN ELITES the desire for publicity and the need for public approval eventually converged in building in the private as well as in the public sector. Architecture, as Alberti observed, is preeminently an urban art form; and, writing in the fifteenth century, he takes it as a given that anyone with the means will want to build something. Earlier, in the days of the commune, rich and powerful men, driven no less than their counterparts in the countryside to assert their presence in impressive buildings, erected great fortified residences in the city marked by protruding towers and often grouped into enclosed compounds; but for the most part their buildings signaled military strength or the size of the clan rather than a taste for what can properly be called a developed architectural style. In few towns before the fourteenth century did domestic architecture assert itself in ways that broke with this medieval tradition, even when these buildings lost something of their military character as magnates became tamed to more civil behavior. Pisa and Venice, both great maritime emporiums, are among the notable exceptions: the private palace there showed signs of embellishment and monumentality apart from sheer mass and defensive strength. In Florence, too, the distinctive palace style that emerged in the early Renaissance, including the refinement of rustication and the symmetry and articulation of façades, can be shown to have had a slow evolution going back to the model represented by the Palazzo Vecchio built at the end of the thirteenth century, although a full-blown palace architectural style does not emerge until well into the fifteenth century.[61] In general, however, the communal phase of civic architecture

60. Hilary Ballon, *The Paris of Henri IV: Architecture and Urbanism* (Cambridge, Mass., 1991), p. 255.

61. F. Redi, "Dalla torre al palazzo: Forme abitative signorili e organizzazione dello spazio urbano a Pisa dall'XI al XV secolo," in *I ceti dirigenti nella Toscana tardo comunale*, pp. 271–96; Schulz, "Wealth in Medieval Venice"; Brenda Preyer, "Two Cerchi Palaces in Florence," in *Renaissance Studies in Honor of Craig Hugh Smyth*, ed. A. Morough et al. (Florence, 1985), 2:613–25.

and urban renewal did not include private residences.

By the fifteenth century, however, a boom in the building and re-building of private homes for the rich got under way throughout Italy unlike anything Europe had ever experienced before. In the process, domestic architecture emerged as a distinctive art form, including not only the urban palace but also the rural villa with its attached garden. The timing of palace building varied from city to city and depended largely on local conditions. In general, it can be said that this private phase of the architectural history of Renaissance Italy got under way once local elites felt secure enough in the control of political affairs that the large outlay of capital required to build appeared as a solid invest-ment in the future of their family as members of the ruling class. Thus the early closure of the nobility of Venice explains the older tradition of domestic architecture in that city. In Florence the great period of palace building begins after 1434, when the Medici established a regime that coopted much of the patriciate and largely ended the factionalism that had long disturbed civic harmony.

In the rest of Italy conditions for building improved with the stabili-zation of the general political order brought about first by the balance of power established in the second half of the fifteenth century and then by the foreign domination imposed by the Hapsburgs in the early six-teenth century. In the cities of the Veneto and of Lombardy, palace building dates from the end of the fifteenth century, by which time these places had been absorbed into larger, more stable territorial states and at the same time confirmed in their local autonomy. Palaces went up in Rome, Bologna, and the smaller cities of the papal states once the papacy proved it could govern effectively. Despite the economic vitality that Genoa experienced in the sixteenth century, it was one of the last cities to see much palace building, because it was only toward the end of the century that its long history of internal discord and instability gave way to a new regime based on general political accord among the upper class.

With this boom in private building architecture entered into the game of social competition among urban patricians as it had among princes. The embellishment of buildings offered a new standard for conspicuous consumption and for the expression of status by rich and powerful men who, having been won over to a civic ethos and absorbed into a fairly coherent ruling class secure in its position, found the tradi-tional feudal forms of competition, including the quasi-military charac-ter of their earlier homes as well as private violence in the streets, no longer appropriate. The civic tradition of building informed private behavior by providing men with an architectural education, and it also provided a rationale for conspicuous private building. Civic monuments aroused interest in architecture and constituted a context that set new terms for social competition. In northern Europe it was not until the seventeenth century that the town house became a notable architectural form for rich burghers: for all of his civic patronage and his Italian inspiration, the German architect Elias Holl, working in Augsburg at the beginning of the century, was still producing domestic architecture for the rich that was more notable for its functional forms than its beauty and monumentality.[62] Meanwhile, the Italians had added a completely new chapter to the history of architectural forms as well as to the history of style.

## Concepts of Nobility

The social history of Italian urban elites has been written around the evolving relations between the traditional rural nobility and the new mercantile classes in the context of the nascent commune, where they met one another on common ground; and the emphasis has been on the eventual outcome of the ensuing dialectic, with its themes of the "betrayal of the bourgeoisie," its "aristocratization," and, finally, in the sixteenth century, "the return to the land," "ruralization," and "refeudalization"—to use the slogans of the argument as it has been formulated in the recent literature. The history of the upper class has therefore been written according to a sociological law Georges Duby regards as one of the animating forces in the development of medieval culture in general—the popularization of aristocratic values in a slow, descending movement as the immediately inferior class, fascinated by the power and prestige of the elite, sought to imitate its ways. A repeated theme in the social history of Europe well into early modern times is this irresistible attraction of the bourgeoisie to the aristocracy, including the literal abandonment of the city by merchants who could afford to move into the countryside and in a variety of other means buy their way into the landed gentry. This thesis is modified for Italy—going back to the older sociological interpretation of Alfred von Martin—only in the sense that some have posited the independent evolution of a fully developed bourgeois culture—hence, the Renaissance—that, however, eventually gave way to the aristocratic ethos. The traditional view thus leaves the urban residence of Italian elites as a mere transitional stage in the long history of a dialectical process through which the traditional noble

---

62. Bernd Roeck, *Elias Holl: Architeckt einer europäischen Stadt* (Regensburg, 1985), p. 63; for contemporary Paris, see Barbara Diefendorf, *Paris City Councillors in the Sixteenth Century: The Politics of Patrimony* (Princeton, 1983), pp. 62–64.

values kept the upper hand by eventually winning over the emerging bourgeoisie. This social process has been generally considered as being so complete that Fernand Braudel explained Italy's decline as "the betrayal of the bourgeoisie," and Philip Jones has gone so far as to wonder provocatively whether the very notion of the bourgeoisie in Renaissance Italy was not a "myth" in the first place.[63]

Things did not go quite this way in Italy, however. The city was, rather, the stage for the evolution of a new kind of nobility, where the class dialectic resulted in a synthesis that was ongoing from the moment that the rural nobility and the new men of the commercial and financial world confronted one another in an urban environment—something that did not happen in northern Europe. If, as some would have it, the bourgeoisie somehow betrayed its mission, the nobility for its part had to give much ground to accommodate itself to city life. By the sixteenth century in most cities—in sharp contrast to northern Europe—it is difficult to make distinctions between magnates or feudal nobles on the one hand and patricians or the bourgeoisie on the other. Ruling groups had for the most part fused into a distinct aristocratic class that consciously sought to consolidate its social position around an elitist mentality but within the urban context. As Marino Berengo has insisted, it was in Italy—not in Flanders or Germany or Castile—that the urban elite succeeded in asserting itself and absorbing the older nobility without leaving anything behind.[64]

In some places—Vicenza and Verona in the Veneto, for instance—men on ruling councils regardless of origins were already calling themselves nobles by the fifteenth century. Ruling groups of many cities legally defined themselves as such, ending the long evolution of communal government by formally closing their ranks to all others through the so-called *serrata* or by assuring their hereditary dominance of major

63. Philip Jones, "Economia e società nell'Italia medievale: Il mito della borghesia," in his *Economia e società*, pp. 3–189; Alfred von Martin, *Sociology of the Renaissance* (New York, 1963). A criticism of this historiographical tradition, with special reference to the recent literature on the communal period, can be found in Renato Bordone, "Tema cittadino e 'ritorno alla terra' nella storiografia comunale recente," *Quaderni storici* 52 (1983), 255–77; and a more recent survey of the literature on the sixteenth century is in Paola Lanaro Sartori, *Un'oligarchia urbana nel Cinquecento veneto: Istituzioni, economia, società* (Turin, 1992), pp. 193–200.

64. Marino Berengo, "La città di antico regime," *Quaderni storici* 26 (1974), 668–71; the exception made by Berengo for Lucca and Verona has been challenged by James S. Grubb, *Firstborn of Venice: Vicenza in the Early Renaissance State* (Baltimore, 1988), ch. 8; and by A. A. Smith, "Il successo sociale e culturale di una famiglia veronese nel '500," in *Civis* 8 (1984), 299–318. Giorgio Borelli, "Il patrizio e la villa," *Nuova rivista storica* 74 (1990), esp. 385–93, is a recent statement on the fusion of nobility and patriciate.

city councils. By so identifying themselves on enrollment lists and limiting access to newcomers, they gained a privileged position in the highest echelons of city government; and in many places they were confirmed in their position of local power by the prince's or the central government's recognition of their prerogatives. Moreover, the general stabilization of the Italian political scene after the mid-sixteenth century tended to freeze such arrangements. In Florence, where the ducal government eliminated the political foundation of elite status, everyone nevertheless knew that many old families without titles, magnate status, or feudal origins but with a history of service in the republican period were noble long before the Austrians codified their status in the eighteenth century.[65]

By the sixteenth century these elites were strengthening their image in other ways as well. They eschewed ignoble economic activities, namely the crafts and trades. Looking to the future, they invested heavily in landed estates to transform the family patrimony into a permanent dynastic possession for all time; and to assure that objective, they bound this patrimony with fideicommissa to prevent alienation and practiced primogeniture, if not in legal fact at least through the custom of limiting marriages to oldest sons. Another sign of their heightened self-consciousness as an exclusive elite was the inflation of dowries, a mechanism by which they bound themselves together through alliances within their own ranks. In some places—the Veneto, for instance (but not in Venice)— there was also increased use of noble titles, the most obvious effort at self-definition; but in other places, such as Florence, these signs of status did not appear until well into the seventeenth century.[66]

All these practices have often been noted as the marks of aristocracy that measure the extent to which the urban elites of late Renaissance Italy fell into line with the traditional nobility. Yet, for all their accumulation of estates, titles, and even feudal rights, these men did not reorganize their lives around their rural possessions. Italians did not incorporate rural names associated with their estates into their very names, as did the French and the Germans; and the titles of nobility that came into greater use in the later Renaissance seldom made reference to the bearer's estates. Nor, for all their passion for villa building at the time, did the rich give up "living miserably in [their] houses and dwelling all in the Citie . . . so the whole country is emptie"—as a disapprov-

65. Litchfield, *Emergence of a Bureaucracy*, pp. 35–36.
66. Claudio Donati, *L'idea di nobiltà in Italia, secoli XIV–XVIII* (Bari, 1988), pp. 280–81 (for Italy in general); Rinuccini, "Considerazioni," pp. 273–74 (for Florence).

ing James I of England put it.[67] The Neapolitan nobility, the most traditional in Italy, also dug its roots deeply in the capital city, to the extent in fact that many—like older urban elites elsewhere in Italy—preferred burial there rather than on their feudal estates (at least during the Spanish period).[68] These urban landowners, in short, never entered into the spirit of country living that pervaded the aristocracy of northern Europe. As one Englishman observed in the mid-sixteenth century, their "fair houses" in the country were "made only for the owners' pastime against the heat of the summer."[69] They did not organize the lives of peasants around their personal presence in the countryside; and it is highly doubtful that they knew much about the expansive sociability of the country life of a northern European landed aristocrat isolated from his peers and surrounded with peasants, tenants, and other dependents.[70]

Villa life did not take on what Lawrence Stone has called the "old country ways" of the rural nobles of northern Europe, who maintained hoards of servants and a large kitchen so that they could, in the words of one late sixteenth-century English writer, "keep open houses for all comers and goers," to the point of often receiving guests who were completely unknown to the host.[71] Still, at the end of the sixteenth century, great Elizabethan country houses were being built to accommodate a daily life of hospitality, ritual, and knightly service; and the great household, organized around a vast staff of servants and operating according to the elaborate customs that Felicity Heal has incorporated into a veritable law of hospitality, was a living institution well into the seventeenth century. Heal has suggested that by the seventeenth century in England the tradition of hospitality, if no longer a social reality, was still strong enough to be utilized as a "rhetorical weapon" wielded to evoke a mythical past against the encroachments of the marketplace on traditional values. In sixteenth-century France hospitality seems not

67. Cited in Alison Brown, *The Renaissance* (London, 1988), p. 116.

68. Maria Antonietta Visceglia, "Corpo e sepoltura nei testamenti della nobiltà napoletana (XVI–XVIII secolo)," *Quaderni storici* 17 (1982), 597, 602.

69. William Thomas, *The History of Italy*, ed. G. B. Parks (Ithaca, N.Y., 1963), p. 15.

70. Giorgio Chittolini, "Feudatari e comunità rurali nell'Italia centrosettentrionale (secoli XV–XVII)," *Studi storici Luigi Simeoni* 36 (1986), 11–28; Burns, *Andrea Palladio*, p. 163.

71. The quote is from Fynes Moryson, *An Itinerary* (Glasgow, 1907–8), 4:94–95; one specific and contemporary instance of the receiving of unknown guests is confirmed by Mary Finch, *The Wealth of Five Northamptonshire Families, 1540–1640* (Oxford, 1956), pp. 80–81. The similar situation in France is remarked by Kristen B. Neuschel, "Noble Households in the Sixteenth Century: Material Settings and Human Communities," *French Historical Studies* 15 (1988), 605–6.

to have surfaced in contemporary comment on social values as it did in England, but nevertheless it is regarded as having been deeply embedded in the social practice of the rural nobility.[72]

In urban Italy there was not such a mythical past to appeal to. It is important, therefore, to regard the new consumption habits of the Italians as emerging in the characteristic context that must always be insisted on in dealing with their behavior—the city. Italians could hardly have conducted their lives in the style of the traditional feudal nobility, which required retinues of servants and hangers-on, lavish hospitality, public spectacle, and other habits of the expansive social life of a rural landlord. All of this would have been exorbitantly expensive in the city, where everything had to be paid for in cash.

In the city, expenditures of the rich tended to be redirected to durable goods rather than personal service; and to the extent demand for goods is heightened by the game of social competition, consumption was all the more intense in Italy because of the urban residence there of the upper classes. As Giovanni Botero observed in his analysis of cities at the end of the sixteenth century, the closer proximity of nobles in the city, where they are continually on view by one another, breeds a keener sense of competition and changes the terms of that competition, so that the urban nobility spends more lavishly than the rural nobility, and this leads "necessarily" (says Botero) to more building and the multiplication of crafts.[73] An anonymous contemporary of Botero's in England, the writer of the dialogue already cited on the relative merits of the "Cyvile and Uncyvile Life," written at a time when the city of London was beginning to have its appeal to the nobility, threatening the old country ways, made the same point in defending the older values of country life on the grounds that there the noble has fewer expenses (and hence greater profit). In fact, once nobles in the north began moving into the city in the seventeenth century, they too found themselves drawn into the market of durable goods. Thus French nobles who had been content to reside in ancestral country seats that were sparsely furnished became passionate consumers once they took up residence in Paris, even if (as was often the case) they only rented their premises and frequently moved from one to another; and for all the building of great country houses in England, it was in London (at least before the later

---

72. Heal, *Hospitality*; Alice T. Friedman, *House and Household in Elizabethan England: Wollaton Hall and the Willoughby Family* (Chicago, 1989), p. 51; Neuschel, *Word of Honor*, pp. 4–5, 85, 170; Mark Motley, *Becoming a French Aristocrat: The Education of the Court Nobility, 1580–1715* (Princeton, 1990), pp. 37–38.

73. Giovanni Botero, "Delle cause della grandezza e magnificenza delle città," in his *Della ragion di stato*, ed. L. Firpo (Turin, 1948), bk. 2, ch. 12.

eighteenth century) that the great landed aristocrat kept his prized possessions.[74] The city, yet once again, accounts for much of what is distinctive in Italian behavior.

ANOTHER POINT TO BE MADE about Italian elites is their social and
cultural independence from courts—at least before the seventeenth century. One of the corollaries to the traditional notion of the aristocratization of Italian society in the later Renaissance is the emergence of the
court as a major institution, a development that is seen as bringing Italy
more into line with northern feudal traditions. Much of the recent
attention to the subject, in fact, has been inspired by renewed interest in
the court culture of northern Europe. The tendency is to regard the
northern court model as having been built on Castiglione's prescrip-
tions and then to impose the pattern of its subsequent evolution there,
culminating in Versailles (as described by Norbert Elias, for example),
on the Italian experience. Apart from the relevance of Castiglione to
court life in Italy (as observed above) and the dubious enterprise of
reading backward in time from one place to another, this view of Italian
courts oversimplifies what in fact was a complex situation in Italy,
where courts were a mixed bag, hardly any fitting the northern model,
and where many urban elites lived outside the orbit of court culture.

The largest courts—in Rome, Naples, and Milan—were not dynastic. The papal court lacked the social continuity and cohesiveness of a
dynastic enterprise; and the city had the atmosphere of an oligarchy,
where some of the courts of cardinals, for all their provisional nature,
could at times rival those of the princely capitals. Likewise, Naples and
Milan, with the frequent coming and going of viceroys and governors
representing a foreign state, lacked a dynastic court properly speaking.
The grand-ducal court in Florence perhaps came the closest to fitting
the northern model, being located in a large city and ruling a sizeable
territorial state; and yet, although the Medici had deep roots in the
patrician class, the court of the first grand dukes was very much a
private affair that did not command the lives of many of the older
families by reaching out to embrace them in an expansive court life.

74. Jean-Pierre Labatut, *Les ducs et pairs de France au XVII siècle* (Paris, 1972), ch. 5;
Francis Haskell, "The British as Collectors," in *The Treasure Houses of Britain: Five Hundred Years of Private Patronage and Art Collecting*, ed. G. Jackson-Stops (Washington, 1985),
p. 51. On the urban as opposed to the feudal quality of Baroque culture, see José Antonio
Maravall, *La cultura del barocco* (Bologna, 1985), esp. ch. 4. On mobility of residence by
nobles living in Paris, see Natacha Coquery, "Les hôtels parisiens du XVIIIe siècle: Une
approche des modes d'habiter," *Revue d'histoire moderne et contemporaine* 38 (1991), 205–
30.

Significantly, at Florence the definition of nobility did not center on service to a prince as it did in the smaller princely capitals with weaker bourgeois traditions. Many of the other truly dynastic courts—those of the d'Este in Ferrara (and later in Modena) and the Gonzaga in Mantua, not to mention the host of smaller ones in Emilia—were minuscule, located in towns that in effect had no significant elite outside the court circle of government employees, dependents, and hangers-on. Moreover, most of these dynastic courts were relatively closed, sometimes not offering room and board to courtiers (as Moryson observed in Florence and Mantua, invidiously—and correctly—contrasting these courts to the great households of any number of peers in England).

Some of the most important and largest Italian cities were oligarchies with no princely or dynastic courts at all, including Genoa, Venice, and (until the sixteenth century) Florence. Elites in many other places with their own communal traditions but incorporated into larger states felt little pull from the capital city, whether it was a courtly center or not, although individual nobles in provincial cities—particularly in the Veneto—sought careers in nearby courts. Venice left the elites of its subject cities—Verona, Padua, Brescia, and others—alone; and the Spanish government in Milan exercised little attraction for the local elites of Pavia and Cremona. The rich and powerful from all over the peninsula certainly crowded into Rome, with the largest and, in effect, most national court in Italy; but most of these men exploited the occasion of a temporary residence to reinforce their families back in their native cities. Naples was the most successful of these capitals in attracting the provincial nobility into it, but that was largely because the rural feudal class throughout a kingdom lacking real cities had no other urban associations.

The urban elites of late Renaissance Italy as a whole, however, were not drawn into the orbit of court culture. In many cities a proud and autonomous patriciate developed its own institutions—above all, the academy—for the vigorous pursuit of its interests in education, literature, music, and the arts. Italian opera, originating as a court activity and traditionally considered one of the most courtly of the arts, nevertheless took on its characteristic form in the seventeenth century in the process of evolving as a commercial venture directed to the entertainment of urban patricians.[75] Because of the prominence of individual princely patrons, the courts have given a high gloss to our picture of Italian life in the sixteenth century, but the substance of

75. Lorenzo Bianconi, *Il Seicento*, vol. 4 of *Storia della musica*, ed. Società Italiana di Musicologia (Turin, 1982), pp. 163ff.

much late Renaissance culture is more patrician or aristocratic than courtly.

THE COMPLEXITY OF THE ITALIAN SITUATION is reflected in the efforts to define nobility.[76] In northern Europe the nobility took itself—and was taken by everyone else—for granted, at least up to the end of the sixteenth century, when it had to confront new ideas about nobility (primarily from Italy) and real social and political threats to its assumptions. But until then almost no one debated its position or discussed the nature of nobility. It was otherwise in Italy, where an interest in definitions surfaces in Dante and in the writings of fourteenth-century jurists addressing problems of a communal society confronted with the presence of imperial and communal knights, magnates, and other kinds of feudal nobles, and in the writings of humanists anxious to establish the nobility of their own activities in the eyes of their patrician and princely patrons. The subject became all the more compelling as urban patriciates tightened their hold on government and sought to buttress their power by establishing their social credentials. There was much thrashing about to define nobility; and already in the fifteenth century so many ideas were being bandied about in discussions of the concept, ranging from strictly legal definitions based on titles and investiture by monarch, bishop, or commune to ethereal notions of individual virtue, that one could have it just about any way he wanted it. Generally speaking, however, the argument got shifted from the nature of nobility to the behavior of the noble; and along the way, most of the essential elements of the traditional definition—arms, service, virtue, blood, economic activities—were qualified.

Hardly anyone in Italy disputed the nobility of arms; and perhaps taking it for granted, few elaborated on it. It is not difficult, however, to find lists of famous men drawn up by communal writers that include jurists, scholars, poets, and even artists (as in Florence) but no military men; and when local historians wrote about their cities in the sixteenth century, few could dredge up military heroes in the grand tradition of feudal historiography.[77] Some writers sought to enlarge the traditional concepts of honor and virtue associated with arms to a more universal

76. The treatises on the subject have been exhaustively surveyed, albeit somewhat outside their broader social context, by Donati, *L'idea di nobiltà*. For a discussion of the legal realities in one place, see Grubb, *Firstborn of Venice*, pp. 86–93; also Joanne Ferraro, "Oligarchs, Protestors, and the Republic of Venice: The 'Revolution of the Discontents' in Brescia, 1644–1645," *Journal of Modern History* 60 (1988), 627–53.

77. For example, Cremona: Eric W. Cochrane, *Historians and Historiography in the Italian Renaissance* (Chicago, 1981), p. 217.

application. The idea of service was an especially keen preoccupation, but by it was meant corporate activity in the councils of urban government rather than personal attendance at a princely court. In the many cities where the upper class continued to run local affairs, service brought with it the satisfaction of virtuous performance as well as the political privilege of a closed oligarchy. It also, incidentally, engendered a strong sense of collective responsibility and a certain spirit of cooperation within the ranks of the ruling class, however much these urban oligarchies sacrificed the wider vision of the civic world that had been the glory of the Italian communal tradition to their own selfish interests. This highly structured political cooperation was a socializing experience that was largely unknown to the traditional nobility of other places; it was another aspect of urban residence—as already observed above with reference to their willingness to tax themselves and their disposition to sponsor public welfare programs—that accounts for the different behavior of Italian elites.

By the sixteenth century the rich and powerful, in defining nobility to set themselves off from others, became more conscious than ever of the quality of ancestry. Their concern with hereditary rank was, in fact, a growing preoccupation also of the aristocracy in northern Europe, which had heretofore taken ancestry for granted but which in the course of the sixteenth century found its status threatened by social and religious upheavals and by the formation of the great royal courts. In the north the concern arose in response to threats from outside the ranks of the traditional nobility, which may explain why its defense could take extreme forms such as the quasi-racist theories of class that grew up in France. In Italy, however, the concern was to formulate an ideological confirmation of a class that in fact had finally consolidated its position in society once and for all and yet did not have the tangible evidence of status that the northern feudal nobility could take for granted—familial estates, seigneurial jurisdiction, privileges, titles. On the one hand, they sought to establish their credentials by demonstrating the antiquity of their family tradition in public service or simply the antiquity of their eligibility for public office. Florentines, for example, established their credentials by fervently compiling an endless number of the so-called *prioristi* listing holders of the highest office of the by-then defunct republic throughout its entire history; and these documents, often organized by family and embellished with coats of arms, were in effect "golden books" of nobility. On the other hand, these urban elites sought to guarantee credentials for descendants by building family monuments—above all, the town palace; and they also devised dynastic policies to avoid partible inheritance in order to keep their property forever intact, binding it with ties of inalienability and limiting the number of younger sons and the proliferation of cadet branches.

Another difference in the Italian discussions of nobility lies in economic assumptions. These discussions rarely put any emphasis on the ownership of land. Literary writers alone, reflecting a stronger influence of classical ideas, tend to praise rural life; but what they found in the country is a far cry from the life of the grand landed seigneur in the northern sense. In later sixteenth-century Siena a noble was required to have some income from land, but this was balanced by the additional requirement that he in fact live in town and in an appropriate house.[78] If nobility was not rooted in the land, neither was it incompatible with the city. The Italians rarely denied their urban economic traditions, although the nobility who lived in towns with only modest capitalist development—Ferrara, for instance, and places in the Marches—or with militaristic traditions—Verona and other places in the Veneto—could be condescending about involvement in business even at the highest levels;[79] and into the seventeenth century northern visitors continued to be struck by how Italian nobles not only lived in cities but engaged in business.[80] In jurists' statements, in treatises on nobility, and in practice, one finds little denial of the propriety of engaging in large-scale commerce and finance. Sixteenth-century religious thinkers who addressed economic issues reveal no inherent aversion to commercial wealth, nor do they recognize any hierarchy in the acquisition of wealth.[81] Strong prejudices were expressed against manual labor, craft activities, and retail trade; but even in this area one can find a surprising open-mindedness—for instance, at Genoa, where still in the late sixteenth century someone from the working class could in fact qualify for noble status on the condition that he abandon his former means of

78. Danilo Marrara, *Riseduti e nobiltà: Profilo storico-istituzionale di un'oligarchia toscana nei secoli XVI–XVII* (Pisa, 1976), pp. 113–15.

79. Marino Berengo, *Nobili e mercanti nella Lucca del Cinquecento* (Turin, 1965), pp. 256–57; B. G. Zenobi, "Politica del diritto e deroga dallo status nobiliare nella città dei domìni pontifici dal XVI al XVIII secolo," *Ricerche storiche* 19 (1989), 305; Lanaro Sartori, *Un'oligarchia urbana*, pp. 58–61.

80. Thomas, *History of Italy*, p. 14; Otto Brunner, *Vita nobiliare e cultura europea* (Bologna, 1982), p. 103. For other comment on the subject, see Brian Pullan, "The Occupations and Investments of the Venetian Nobility in the Middle and Late Sixteenth Century," in *Renaissance Venice*, ed. J. R. Hale (Totowa, N.J., 1973), p. 386 (cf. Ugo Tucci in the same volume, pp. 347–48); Giorgio Politi, *Aristocrazia e potere politico nella Cremona di Filippo II* (Milan, 1976), pp. 448–551; Giovanni Vigo, *Fisco e società nella Lombardia del Cinquecento* (Bologna, 1979), p. 193; Daniela Frigo, *Il padre di famiglia: Governo della casa e governo civile nella tradizione dell'"economica" fra Cinque e Seicento* (Rome, 1985), pp. 169–71.

81. Gino Barbieri, *Ideali economici degli italiani all'inizio dell'età moderna* (Milan, 1940), pp. 52, 61, 139–60, 169.

livelihood; and at Florence, where men far down the social scale were not excluded from the grand-ducal Order of Santo Stefano.[82]

In at least one respect the Italian definition of nobility included ideas that had nothing to do with the northern tradition—the nobility of letters. Although there was a tradition of humanist thought on the subject going back at least as far as Petrarch, the notion was not confined to the isolated world of intellectuals. Indeed, as recent studies have shown, already in the fifteenth century most humanists and literary figures either came themselves from the upper class or managed to enter its ranks. Such was the prestige of letters and of learning in general that upstart professional military men—the condottieri—grasped at the symbols of books, libraries, and learned courtiers at least as enthusiastically as they toyed with chivalric notions.[83] Federico da Montefeltro made this clear in the study of his palace at Urbino, where he surrounded himself with depictions of musical and scientific instruments in wood inlay, with twenty-eight portraits of philosophers, poets, and jurists from all ages, and with a picture of himself reading at a lectern. In the fifteenth century Vespasiano da Bisticci, the unlettered biographer of eminent contemporaries, praises one after another of his subjects for their love of culture. By this time literary studies, alongside more traditional aristocratic pursuits, were taken for granted in discussions of education; and in the sixteenth century, at a time when only a handful of aristocrats in the north can be associated with letters and learning, literary and musical academies sprang up everywhere in Italy under the auspices of local elites. In their assimilation of the world of letters as well as the world of capitalism, the Italians enlarged the concept of nobility much beyond its traditional confines—and much beyond anything conceivable in northern Europe.

After all is said and done about legal distinctions, political privileges, and social and cultural notions, the ultimate definition of nobility came down to behavior: one was noble because he lived the life of a noble. In this respect the upper classes in Italian cities were fairly homogeneous by the later Renaissance, despite their geopolitical fragmentation and different urban traditions, and whether or not their origins were in the remote feudal past, in the business world of the city, or in service at court. Perhaps the most important feature distinguishing them from urban elites everywhere else in Europe was the absence in the immediacy of their everyday lives of the model of nobility rooted in feudal

82. Mario Nicora, "La nobiltà genovese dal 1528 al 1700," *Miscellanea storica ligure* 2 (1961), 273; for Florence, see note 32 above.
83. Puddu, "Lettere ed armi," esp. pp. 489–94.

traditions that dominated other societies, providing a clear target for one's social ambitions. In sixteenth-century England the tendency of the richest London merchants to move into the rural gentry worked against the formation of commercial dynasties beyond three generations. In France the emerging *noblesse de robe* tried to gain recognition as an established social class between the traditional feudal nobility and the bourgeoisie, and indeed the things they cultivated—learned interests, leisure, rural *otium* without abandoning the city—resemble the interests of Italians at the time; but they could never quite remove the ambiguity about their status within the contemporary hierarchy of social values.[84]

The proof of the proposition about the homogeneity of the Italian upper classes is in their consumption habits. There is no doubt, of course, that the older consumption and behavioral model, in the absence of any other, held a great fascination for these urban elites; but, as we have seen, they were constrained in their imitation of it by the conditions of urban life. As attractive as the feudal-chivalric model looked to urban dwellers, the exigencies of urban life eroded much of its relevance and practicality. In Italy the nobility did not remain aloof in the countryside to maintain the reality and prestige of the model. When it came right down to it, as Antonio de Beatis observed in the early sixteenth century, "very few Italians in fact live the life of true gentlemen, even if they have the manner and style of a gentleman."[85] The way was thus prepared for another model, which gained its authority from values bred in the city itself. It is not that the older model was altogether replaced; rather, that model was in part weakened by the erosion of older values and in part transformed by the emergence of new values.

By the sixteenth century a new consumption model was emerging that contrasted with the rural, feudal traditions of the north. It was at once urban in its emphasis on the architectural grandeur of the noble's residence and private in the exclusiveness of life within: these were the values that informed the new consumption habits. The new material culture created by the Italian upper classes expressed their sense of what constituted noble status; their spending habits arose from what is perhaps the universal desire of the rich to utilize wealth to set themselves off from ordinary people. The divergence of these habits from the traditional ways of the aristocracy in spending one's money is the mark of how Italians had redefined the traditional concept of nobility.

84. George Huppert, *Les Bourgeois Gentilhommes: An Essay on the Definition of Elites in Renaissance France* (Chicago, 1977), esp. ch. 8; on mobility in England, see Sylvia Thrupp, *The Merchant Class of Medieval London (1300–1500)* (Ann Arbor, 1962), pp. 222–24.
85. *Travel Journal of Antonio de Beatis*, p. 166.

## Attitudes toward Wealth

Urban residents of the medieval city brought other considerations to bear on conspicuous consumption. Botero, in the later sixteenth century, could take lavish spending for consumer durables for granted as the way one played the game of social competition; but such behavior was the result of an enormous change in attitudes about the uses of wealth that had evolved over the preceding two centuries. In the fourteenth century a monetary economy was already highly developed in Italian towns, but consumer mentality had not kept pace with market developments. There were still some effective cultural brakes on the spending of money.

One brake on consumption was the religious suspicion of the profit economy. Private wealth posed particular problems in the prosperous towns of medieval Italy, where the economy was largely monetized and the market presented greater temptations for consumption. Serious religious thinkers, of course, recognized the essential functions of urban economic activities, and some were prepared to approve the possession of riches; but they had doubts about the motivations and behavior of economic man, about his avaricious instincts, about his attachment to goods of this world, and above all about his outright illicit financial activities involving usurious contracts. Luxury was considered something sinful in its violation of nature and reason. In the eyes of popular preachers, conspicuous consumption tended to confirm these natural suspicions about the moral pitfalls awaiting the rich. Moreover, with the rise of the Franciscan movement in the thirteenth century, a strong reaction set in against the wealth of this world. The friars vigorously promoted the ideal of poverty not so much out of commiseration for the poor as to provide a rationale for the proper uses of wealth. In the cities of Italy around 1300 the popular suspicion of the psychology of avarice far overshadowed the more rational approach of the scholastics. Medieval religion, in short, exhorted capitalists to charity, which was the denial of consumption; and it circumscribed any urges they might have had to use wealth for consumption in the secular world. With its own notions of the validity of wealth for the expression of power, as described earlier, the church did not hesitate to preempt for itself any desire the lay person might have for conspicuous consumption.

The other brake on consumption was social pressure. In the factious politics of the commune, where rivalry, jealousy, and envy were always coming into play—for instance, in procedures for fixing tax assessments—it behooved a person below the status of a great magnate not to display wealth too conspicuously. Later fourteenth-century Florentine merchant-writers, such as Paolo da Certaldo and Giovanni Morelli, repeatedly advised against advertising one's wealth and counseled deception in matters of investment. Sumptuary legislation proliferated in Italian cities to keep the powerful from stepping too far out of line and disturbing political harmony. In short, urban patricians of either mercantile or magnate origin, far from having a consumption model to follow, found their spending habits bound in by their own doubts and fears about wealth if not by the law itself.

By the fifteenth century attitudes about wealth were undergoing a change. The thrust of the older suspicions of wealth had begun to lose its force. Merchants became increasingly cynical about the opinions of churchmen, who kept compromising themselves on the usury doctrine in order to accommodate certain business practices the economic legitimacy of which they could not deny. Urban elites also felt less inhibited by social and religious suspicions of wealth as they became more stable and more clearly defined in their social status, either because they had a firmer grip on local governments or because they were able to entrench themselves with the support of the despots who rose to power in many towns. While on the one hand the older suspicions about wealth were thus losing their force, on the other hand the potential power of wealth was increasingly manifest to Italians. In late fourteenth-century Florence a man of middling status, Paolo da Certaldo, advised people not to keep cash idle,[86] and it has already been noted how this attitude precluded the hoarding of wealth in the conspicuous forms so characteristic of the more traditional societies of northern Europe. In an urban economy where the market was thoroughly monetized, where money was being freed from cultural restraints, and where the rich—and not only the rich—were becoming richer, the very fluidity of wealth caught people up in its inexorable flow to the marketplace. The question was: how to spend one's money?

OBVIOUSLY, BEHIND THE IMPULSE TO CONSUME lay a confidence about wealth and a freedom about using it for purely private purposes. Not many intellectuals showed much awareness of this new attitude about wealth that was emerging in their midst. On the whole, the humanists did not take up economic themes, but perhaps it is significant that they in fact took the economic system for granted and were not at all interested in the problems that had so preoccupied the scholastics regarding the legitimacy of how money is made. Nevertheless, some of the Flor-

---

86. Paolo da Certaldo, *Libro di buoni costumi*, ed. A. Schiaffini (Florence, 1944), p. 227 (n. 356).

entine humanists in the early fifteenth century perceived a growing social and psychological need to find a rationale for the proper uses of wealth.

Their forbears, Petrarch and the first generation of his followers at the end of the fourteenth century who upheld the model of the contemplative life, had embraced the ideal of poverty, inspired no doubt by Franciscan spirituality but also by the Stoic doctrine of indifference to material things found in some Roman writers. When they faced the real world of civic affairs, it was in the spirit of what Hans Baron has called the "political romanticism" of those Romans who extolled the republican virtue of simplicity in political leaders. The next generation of humanists, however, had very different ideas, especially those Florentines who addressed themselves not so much to other intellectuals as to a public of wealthy entrepreneurs. They discovered a different side of Aristotle—above all, in the pseudo-Aristotelian *Economics*, translated and edited by Leonardo Bruni—that opposed poverty and reevaluated the importance of private wealth for both the well-being of society and the self-fulfillment of the individual. Bruni, Alberti, and Matteo Palmieri, far from condemning wealth, or being suspicious of it, now extolled it as a necessary condition for the exercise of virtue in the active life. Wealth presents a moral challenge because it puts virtue to the test in ways not experienced by the person who is not burdened by the encumbrances of material possessions. These Florentine writers assumed an active involvement in civic life, where the rich have a special role to play; and they recognized both the reputation and the special authority the rich enjoy among their fellows. What these intellectuals were in fact doing was establishing the nobility of a wealthy upper class that had no cultural traditions to appeal to for underpinning its status: its only credential was wealth and what wealth could buy—political power and social status. The discussion of such notions in the vernacular testifies to the wider audience these writers sought to reach.[87]

The central problem that had to be addressed was the proper use of wealth. The humanists considered the problem entirely in secular terms, although their reliance on classical sources, above all Aristotle, who had exercised so much influence throughout the Middle Ages, gave their arguments a familiar ring. For them wealth does indeed have a usefulness beyond the traditional claims on it by charity and good works, and this usefulness can be entirely a matter of private advantage

---

87. The change in the attitude about wealth is documented by Hans Baron, in three chapters on civic wealth in his collected and revised essays, *In Search of Florentine Civic Humanism: Essays on the Transition from Medieval to Modern Thought* (Princeton, 1988), 1:158–257.

and pleasure. Although they thrash about trying to find the happy medium between avarice and prodigality, they come down clearly in support of possessiveness. To an extent they defined the usefulness of wealth in the traditional aristocratic terms of glory seeking, albeit now in a civic context; but the consumption model the humanists came up with was not the traditional one of the feudal nobility. It reflected the new habits of spending that possessed Italians at the time: it centered on architecture. As indicated in the previous section, the quality of magnificence associated with architecture was highly touted throughout the fifteenth century by numerous writers.

Magnificence is the key term in the discussion by the humanists of the positive uses of wealth. In dealing with the subject they of course referred to classical authorities; but at the same time they were also appropriating a medieval notion associated with the uses of wealth by princes. Feudal princes became more self-conscious about magnificence when they began to lead a more settled existence. The concept involved the splendor with which they sought to endow their presence with the authority of their position in the feudal hierarchy, but it also called for generosity in the spirit of virtuous liberality. Medieval discussions of liberality, largely inspired by Aristotle, focused on the right uses of wealth: liberality was the mean between the extremes of the vices of prodigality and avarice. It was, however, a princely virtue involving those gestures of spectacle, feasts, gifts, and charity by which a prince asserted a public presence. The late thirteenth-century writer Egidio Colonna had this essential function in mind when, for all of his concern about avarice and wasteful luxury, he argued that in fact a prince could hardly ever be guilty of prodigality. Magnificence, in a sense, was a rationalization for luxury, which was otherwise condemned as sinful and unnatural. In the courtly literature of England, which has been carefully combed for usage of the term, magnificence was synonymous with magnanimity and was inextricably associated with the Christian concept of nobility; and it was demonstrated in generous and splendid hospitality on a grand public scale. This sense of the term continues to find expression in the literary tradition through the Renaissance and into the seventeenth century. It is in light of this medieval expectation about princely behavior that Machiavelli's exhortation to parsimony must have been shocking for its unconventionality if not for its forthright honesty about good management of a prince's finances.[88]

88. Allan H. Gilbert, *Machiavelli's "Prince" and Its Forerunners: "The Prince" as a Typical Book "de Regimine Principum"* (1938; reprint, New York, 1968), pp. 84–97, 177; Margaret

In Italy the term underwent a redefinition to fit a nonfeudal society. The basic meaning remained the same: magnificence is the use of wealth in a way that manifests those qualities that express one's innate dignity, thereby establishing one's reputation by arousing the esteem and admiration of others. But it is now distinct from princely magnanimity and largely deprived of its overtone of Christian charity. It becomes associated with that greatness of spirit so characteristic of the humanists' notion of the civic nature of man. True to the Aristotelian idea, however, it is regarded as a social concept, involving a grand gesture made toward the collectivity of society if for no other reason than it provided a spectacle on the public stage.

Also truer to the original discussion of the concept in Aristotle, the Italians explicitly associate magnificence with the proper use of wealth and money in general and not just by princes in particular; it is a virtue that only the rich can possess. Filelfo is explicit in assigning this virtue to the rich, and for Paolo Cortesi and Giovanni Sabadino degli Arienti its prerequisite is wealth. Giovanni Pontano, who takes up the subject in a tract written on just those social virtues that involve the spending of money, opens his discussion calling magnificence the "fruit" of wealth. Although magnificence involves an extraordinary manifestation of wealth and luxury, these writers shift the emphasis from expenditures for the public good to private expenditures to establish one's public reputation or simply to give one pleasure. Aristotle had emphasized the public-spirited nature of magnificence and only in passing allowed for its application also to the furnishing of the rich man's house as a suitable use of his wealth. Alberti, however, elaborates on how such possessions, by enhancing a man's reputation and fame, strengthen the public image of his family and help build those networks of friends that were so important in urban public life. Pontano, too, shows how magnificence can consist of private possessions as well as extravagant expenditures for ceremonies, feasts, hospitality, gifts, and the other gregarious activities of an expansive social life. Thus a classical notion with all its added feudal overtones was detached from claims of feudal legitimacy and power and appropriated to serve an elite in a society with different foundations.

The preoccupation with wealth emerges most clearly in the five tracts on the social virtues written by the Neapolitan Pontano at the end of the fifteenth century. Pontano's work, in fact, is the only systematic effort to build up a consumption model, the earlier comments of the

---

Greaves, *The Blazon of Honour: A Study in Renaissance Magnanimity* (New York, 1964); Heal, *Hospitality*, pp. 24–28, 188–91.

Florentine "civic humanists" being for the most part scattered about in more general discussions. Pontano's objective is to treat only those virtues linked to that part of ethics that presupposes the spending of money; and the singling out of this particular economic activity for moral analysis—especially by a man who lived not in the midst of a capitalist oligarchy but in Naples, the most feudal court in Italy— indicates in itself the tenor of the times throughout the peninsula, even in its economically more backward area, in contrast to much of the rest of Europe. In many ways Pontano's model is traditional: it assumes an aristocratic and courtly society in which largess is an appropriate way to excite admiration, although his conscious models were derived from classical sources. But in his discussion of the five virtues he proceeds, almost step by step—or rather, virtue by virtue— from the public and expansive social world of the familiar virtues of "liberality" and "beneficence" to a private world of "magnificence," "conviviality," and "splendor." Pontano's view of magnificence, which has been cited above, was entirely in line with a long tradition of humanist comment on the subject: it consists of those kinds of expenditures—above all, architecture—that establish one's public presence but serve a purely private function. The last two of Pontano's categories, however, were in effect brand-new "virtues": splendor is the quality one gains through personal possessions, and conviviality consists in dining and companionship at table. Despite the traditional courtly nature of much of what Pontano has to say, the essential thrust of his discussion, here and elsewhere, pointed to a new sense of urbanity in human relations, including the pleasures of material culture now raised to a level of ethical dignity. The pursuit of these ends lies behind much of the demand that brought into existence the Renaissance world of goods.[89]

The thrust of the economic thinking of these Italian intellectuals was toward the proper uses of wealth. Otherwise, however, they were no more interested in the nature of the economic system than had been the scholastics. They did not engage in economic analysis in any proper sense of that term, and the value of productive economic activity in and of itself was of no concern to them except in the most general terms. In other words, the humanists made no step whatsoever toward a theoretical formulation that might have given a moral or philosophical rationale to the entrepreneur; that was not to happen, of course, until the

---

89. Giovanni Pontano, *I trattati delle virtù sociali*, ed. Francesco Tateo (Rome, 1965); these tracts are discussed by Tateo in his *Umanesimo etico di Giovanni Pontano* (Lecce, 1972). See also Charles Trinkaus, "Themes for a Renaissance Anthropology," in *The Renaissance: Essays in Interpretation* (essays dedicated to Eugenio Garin; London and New York, 1982), p. 85.

advent of the classical economic thinkers of the eighteenth century. It was the spending of money, not the getting of it, that preoccupied these Italian thinkers; and where they broke with tradition was in their consideration of consumption as a purely secular activity and in their effort to endow it with a moral quality. In fact, Florentine account books, justly famous for their detail and organization, tell us much more about what men bought than how much they earned: in many of the ledgers where accumulative expenditures over a lifetime are broken down into various categories and can be read off at a glance, no amount of digging around in the accounts—including those dedicated only to business activities—will reveal how much money they were earning. These documents are above all monuments to the spirit of possessiveness that came over men as they found themselves drawn into the growing consumer market. As the wealthy merchant and enlightened patron of architecture Giovanni Rucellai put it in the mid-fifteenth century, there was something more honorable and more satisfying about spending money than making it.[90]

By the sixteenth century most commentators on economic matters, religious as well as secular, took it for granted that wealth was an instrument for displaying the virtues of magnificence and liberality and hence the means to achieve fame and glory. As Gino Barbieri concluded, in his study of economic thought in late Renaissance Italy, "the love of glory, fame and luxury . . . constitute very important phenomena for understanding the economic spirit of Italians at the beginning of the modern era."[91]

ONE PLACE WHERE ECONOMIC CONCERNS indicative of new consumption habits come in for systematic consideration is the treatise dedicated to household management. These appear throughout Italy in the sixteenth century; and, as in so many aspects of Italian culture at the time, Florentines led the way, for it was in Florence that Xenophon's treatise on household management inspired, within a few years of its discovery in 1427, its first modern imitation with the well-known third book of Alberti's *Della famiglia*. Alberti includes a discussion of the importance of household goods as family possessions, and his redefinition of the word he uses—*masserizia*—reveals his desire to elevate material possessions to a spiritual realm. Originally *masserizia* meant "savings," referring to money stored away, perhaps even hoarded—reflecting what has been called a bourgeois value in opposition to the feudal notion of

90. Giovanni Rucellai, *Il zibaldone quaresimale*, ed. A. Perosa (London, 1960), p. 118.
91. Barbieri, *Ideali economici*, p. 170; also pp. 130, 168–72.

liberality; but by the fifteenth century it comes to indicate things, objects, and most especially household furnishings. Alberti, in his tract on the family, charges the term with high moral value: *masserizia* is a form of wealth that is to be preserved and is therefore central to household management, as if the household possessions of a family were the material core of its identity and existence, the foundation of the reputation of the family; it consists not of money but of those material goods that assure the solidarity of affection and the bonds of blood, honor, and virtue. The word came to signify wealth with two specific qualities: first, it is constituted by material possessions; and secondly, these possessions have a strong moral quality about them. Household goods, in short, were a form of capital that represented family solidarity and honor. Here is a full justification for new consumer habits.[92]

Alberti's redefinition of this word was not just the wishful thinking of an intellectual. In his will, drawn up in 1462, about the time Alberti was writing, the merchant Palla Strozzi gives specific instruction for the disposition of what he calls his *masserizia*, which includes silver, tableware, and several items of furniture—an armoire and a number of chests, simple enough forms but all presumably made with some attention to detail and therefore items of some prestige. Strozzi clearly separates these things from his clothing: the clothing, he says, can be sold but the *masserizia* is to be preserved in the family.[93] For all its monetary value and ceremonial importance, not to mention the durability of rich stuffs that in this period lasted well beyond one generation, clothing did not have the personal meaning of a few pieces of relatively simple furniture. Strozzi was not alone in this view of things, for it is precisely at this time—around the mid-fifteenth century—that Florentines began opening accounts in their ledgers for the specific purpose of keeping track of their household furnishings. The word they universally used to identify this account is *masserizia*, which hence entered into the accounting jargon of the times as a mark of how consumption moved to the center of economic activity.

By the sixteenth century a large body of literature on "economics," or household management, and the internal life of the family established the subject as a proper one for discourse along with manners, ethics, and politics.[94] Honor consisted in knowing how to spend wealth

---

92. Daniele Bonamore, *Prolegomeni all'economia politica nella lingua italiana del Quattrocento* (Bologna, 1974), pp. 37–43; see also R. Romano and A. Tenenti, in their edition of Alberti's *I libri della famiglia* (Turin, 1972), pp. xiii–xxii.

93. Roger Jones, "Palla Strozzi e la sagrestia di Santa Trinita," *Rivista d'arte*, 4th ser., 1 (1984), doc. 140.

94. Frigo, *Padre di famiglia*, surveys this literature.

prudently and appropriately and how to conserve it for one's descendants. Special interest was shown for the site of the house, its comfort, and its arrangements for assuring the privacy of members of the family from one another as well as from servants and guests; and proper household management included expenditures for furnishings. What emerges from this concern for the family and its household and for the lineage and its patrimony is a sense of class based on wealth. In essence these treatises define a noble way of life for the elites in the many Italian cities where they could, finally, take for granted their authority over local government and where they were not absorbed into the life of a court. These treatises, in fact, fix attention almost exclusively on private life and hardly at all on social life beyond the house—neither in the public world of the civic community nor at the court of the prince. They manifest a self-consciousness on the part of wealthy urban classes who heretofore had no real model to follow in order to claim noble status; and, as Daniela Frigo concluded in her study of these treatises, they represent a domestic model with which the Italian urban elites established their cultural and political hegemony. More than anything else a sense of the household gives coherence to the world of goods that came into existence in the Renaissance; the nobility with which people hoped to endow family life explains the deeper impulses that gave rise to the kaleidoscopic changes in the new consumption habits.

## THE CULTURE OF CONSUMPTION

Urban life in Italy saw the emergence of distinctive cultural values that complemented, if not contradicted, traditional feudal notions, including a sharpened aesthetic sensitivity, a modification of ideas about nobility, and new attitudes about wealth; but in addition the exigencies of urban life also eroded the traditional feudal consumption model. Great men in large cities, however much they might have tried to ape the ways of the nobility, could not play out their lives in a style that required military equipment and games, retinues of servants and hangers-on, lavish hospitality, public spectacle, and other habits of the expansive social life of a rural landlord. Not only did the emerging public authority of the commune suppress the unruly independence of the great urban magnates, but the values that sustained the feudal consumption model made less and less sense as urban life evolved. In the fourteenth century powerful and wealthy Italians, contemporaries of Dante and Giotto, like the Bardi and Peruzzi in Florence probably aspired to behave like nobles to the extent that this was possible and practicable, directing much of their consumption to building, clothes, personal adornment, and the liturgical apparatus. For all the written documentation of the economic activities of these men, it is not clear that they spent a significant part of their vast wealth on any other kind of durable goods, nor does the record of surviving artifacts give us reason to think that there was much production of luxury objects for secular use at the time.[95] In the early fourteenth century Florence was hardly a backward and undeveloped place, with its cultural scene dominated by the towering figures of Dante and Giotto and its economy driven by great international merchant-bankers such as the Bardi and Peruzzi; and yet the world of goods was so confined that today it is hardly perceptible.

Architecture was at the center of the model for secular consumption that emerged in Renaissance Italy. The secular culture of architecture, with its roots deep in medieval traditions of communal culture but also taking much of its nourishment from classical ideas resurrected in the fifteenth century by the humanists, was the foundation on which urban elites literally built their claims to status. More than anything else a palace, now embellished as never before, provided its builder with a focus for establishing a public identity. Although obviously a public art, architecture raises questions about the function of interior space. At the least, the heightened aesthetic appreciation of the public presence of one's home would seem to lead naturally to greater concern for interior arrangements, whatever they might be, to bring the interior up to the level of the architecture. Moreover, since Italians had a fixed residence in a single place, conditions were favorable for the accumulation of goods and for the evolution of furnishings as permanent fixtures, whereas in traditional feudal society furnishings were largely transportable to accommodate the itinerancy of great rural households. Finally, if the patrician palace with its great façade was a public assertion of the presence of its builder, his family, and his dynasty, it also closed off a vast inner world behind; and it would be surprising if the passion for palace building were not also related—as either cause or effect—to a concern for the quality of life people wanted to live within these places.

Of the various identities a palace builder might have found inside his palace—through his family and an intimate circle of friends on the one hand, and through his private interests and amusements on the other—the concern here is with his economic role as a consumer and with the material culture he thereby created. The new consumption habits cen-

95. See the discussion of S. L. Peruzzi, *Storia del commercio e dei banchieri di Firenze in tutto il mondo conosciuto dal 1200 al 1345* (Florence, 1868), chs. 3 and 4. The minor arts in the early Trecento are surveyed in *Atti del I Convegno sulle arti minori in Toscana, 1971* (Florence, 1973).

tering on the home were not necessarily contradictory of older ones; they grew up alongside the others and assimilated some of their features. But whereas the feudal model derived its authority from the traditional values, both secular and religious, of medieval culture that were long to survive into early modern times, a new consumption model had to be defined and win its way. Oriented to the filling up of the private world with goods, and to the continual elaboration of that world of goods, this model had enormous implications for the history of the arts; and the values that eventually established its authority constitute much of what Italian culture was all about.

## Architecture

Domestic housing emerged as a distinct architectural genre with its own stylistic credentials in the context of urban building, whether under communal, oligarchical, or despotic auspices. This civic tradition educated people to the nature of public art, and architecture entered into the game of social competition among the upper classes. The timing of this building phenomenon, as already observed, varied according to local political conditions: it can be said to have begun already in the thirteenth century, although not until the later fifteenth century did domestic architecture become a full-blown art form with distinct regional variations that then evolves along its own stylistic trajectory. Style, however, is not the essential matter of this discussion. What is important is that architecture—whatever its style—became an object of consumption as distinct from mere building.

In addition to their own civic traditions Italians were also influenced by the Roman model for building. Once prodded by the humanists to look at the Roman ruins all around them, Italians as no other peoples in Europe found tangible evidence of the grandeur and immortality of architecture. Already in the late fourteenth century Salutati buttressed his patriotic propaganda for Florence with reference to the Roman ruins there, and Giovanni da Prato described the baptistery as an ancient temple of Mars. Observing the inscriptions many of these buildings bore, Italians—like Giovanni Rucellai, on looking at the Pantheon— quite naturally came to regard buildings as representing the fame of the private citizens who had built them. Rucellai undoubtedly had in mind his own building activity when he copied down in his *Zibaldone* Cicero's comment on the great fame a Roman citizen enjoyed after the construction of his palace. The Romans thus provided a model to be followed. In this sense, the new Renaissance architectural style, with its heavy borrowing from classical monuments, came to have profound cultural meaning: it was not just a matter of taste, for style also informed the model with references to the classical past that confirmed people's ideas about magnificence and about their place in history.

Literary evidence, of course, also provided Italians with Roman ideas about building. This material, however, reveals just how wide the gulf in fact was between the built environment of Romans and that of the Italians, for Italians could hardly have found any more inspiration in Roman literature than they did in Roman ruins for the type of buildings they wanted to erect. On the one hand, Roman writers make reference to various public buildings—baths, theaters, sports arenas, aqueducts, porticos, temples—but most of these had no reality in Italian life. On the other hand, they rarely comment on the town house, an exception being a short chapter in Cicero's *Offices* about a palace on the Palatine hill. The private residences Roman writers mostly talk about are villas, Pliny's description being especially notable; but these Roman villas were hardly relevant to Italian rural life. Whenever Romans wrote about private houses, they had in mind places that (as Cicero put it) had to entertain numerous guests and to receive crowds of every sort of people; they had to be above all spacious, since, according to Vitruvius, they were virtually public buildings.[96]

The vast difference between the two ages explains the unreality of Alberti's discussion of domestic housing, in which he treats the town house as little more than a poor urban substitute for the villa. When Pontano argued his case for building with appeals to the Roman model, he could hardly come up with any examples of a private palace from the evidence of ancient literature. Platina had to engage in a little special pleading for private palaces, since he could not cite any ancient authority who talks about them: he argued that if the magnificent citizen is to spend to put up walls, arsenals, aqueducts, theaters, porticos, temples, and all the other types of public buildings Romans expected from prominent men, why should he not also put up a splendid building for his own residence, especially if it too contributes to the beauty of the city? Platina does not add, incidentally, that hardly any of the other kinds of buildings he mentions came within the orbit of Italian patronage. Hence, when the great palace builders of Florence compared themselves to the ancients, they had no real model to follow. They were historically on their own in putting the private residence in the city at the center of their new consumption model.[97]

---

96. Eugene Dwyer, "The Pompeian Atrium House in Theory and in Practice," in *Roman Art in the Private Sphere: New Perspectives on the Architecture and Decor of the Domus, Villa, and Insula*, ed. D. K. Gazda (Ann Arbor, 1991), pp. 33–34.

97. Pontano, *Trattati*; Bartolomeo Sacchi detto Il Platina, *De Optimo Cive*, ed. Felice Battaglia (Bologna, 1944), pp. 260–61. For examples of their classical allusions, see F. W.

Italians concentrated their building efforts in the city on their family residence and chapel (or church). Both were public statements of status. To leave no doubt about the matter, some builders displayed the signs of ownership in the very fabric of the building for all to see. Cosimo de' Medici began the practice—unknown in antiquity—of using his family coat of arms as a decorative motif in capitals and working his personal emblem into the decoration of the façade; and Florentines followed his example with particular enthusiasm and imagination. On the Rucellai palace the personal insignias of Giovanni appear all along the friezes of the string lines and in the spandrels of the windows, and on the Strozzi palace the family crescents appear everywhere—on the windows, on the bronze fixtures attached to exterior walls, and on capitals, corbels, water basins, and fireplaces inside. Builders also put inscriptions on their projects announcing their patronage to the public. Giovanni Rucellai's name can be clearly read high up on the façade of Santa Maria Novella in Florence, and Sigismondo Malatesta's is clearly in evidence on his "temple" in Rimini. The practice became commonplace in the sixteenth century, even in provincial towns such as Orvieto, where some builders repeat inscriptions above doors and windows. Inscriptions commemorate not the architect but the patron, the man who paid the bills (as the *Digest* had long ago legislated). He was the real auctor of a building, as some inscriptions tell us (leaving modern historians wondering whether this does not mean that the patron was in fact also the designer).[98] A frescoed façade was another notable device many owners used to make their palaces into a public statement about themselves, but this remarkably popular art form, to which many notable painters dedicated their major efforts, was not destined to survive the ravages of time and the elements.

Palaces were obviously family, not just individual, monuments. They were usually built in the neighborhood where the family had deep roots, and their builders probably viewed them as a symbol of family traditions and a focus for the loyalties of the wider family collectivity. They also looked to the future, for they were built to accommodate the dynasty that derived from the builder and to give it a prominent physical presence. This obsession reveals itself in builders' testaments. Filippo Strozzi's goes on for pages in his attempt to anticipate all the genealogical possibilities so that his palace would never leave family hands. If Giovanni Rucellai's was more economical in simply ordering

Kent, "Palaces, Politics, and Society in Fifteenth-Century Florence," in *I Tatti Studies* 2 (1987), 51–52.

98. For instance, two inscriptions (1496) on the palazzo Raimondi in Cremona.

that his palace was never to leave the family, he expressed his real concern more explicitly when he added that should the family ever become extinct, the palace was under no condition to pass to another family (it was to go to the commune to be used as a residence for visiting dignitaries). These Florentines rarely show such concern for villas; Francesco Sassetti, in fact, encouraged his sons to sell his great villa at La Pietra if financial troubles arose—but not the home in Florence. As Michelangelo noted in the mid-sixteenth century, "A noble house in the city brings much honor because it is more visible than other possessions"; and nothing preoccupied him more than establishing his family in his native city with an appropriate residence to signify their nobility.[99]

These urban elites also extended their architectural world beyond the city and into the surrounding countryside. This was not, however, a "return to the countryside" accompanied by social and cultural baggage loaded with prejudices about land borrowed from northern European elites. The country house was not an ancestral seat where the noble had an independent basis of power and status. The increased pace of villa building in the sixteenth century accompanied the shift of capital to the countryside, and many of these landlords took an active interest in overseeing and protecting their investments; but the villa did not become the family's principal place of residence, even when it was located—as they often were—where the owner had concentrations of land or where the owner's family had its origins in the remote past. The garden, too, evolved as a new art form not to incorporate the agricultural countryside into the orbit of the villa but instead to extend the rationalized plan of the villa as an outward spatial projection that maintained the marked contrast between the architectural complex and the surrounding countryside. The distinctive literary genre about villa life that arose in the sixteenth century appealed to those who wanted to get away from the city to enjoy the simple pleasures of the countryside. Many villas, in fact, were easily accessible from the city and had nothing to do with landholding interests. Alberti commented that a villa should be within walking distance of the city, and a visitor to Genoa in 1480 observed that in fact merchants went out to their suburban places for lunch before returning to their shops in the city.[100] The villa in Italian life did not represent the refeudalization of the Italian upper classes: their move to the country was, rather, an extension of urban life

99. Richard A. Goldthwaite, "The Florentine Palace as Domestic Architecture," *American Historical Review* 77 (1972), 991–92.

100. Cited by George Gorse, "Genoese Renaissance Villas: A Typological Introduction," *Journal of Garden History* 3 (1983), 256.

into the countryside, and the fetish they made of the *otium* they found there presupposes an urban point of view.[101]

In the fifteenth century the secular princes in Ferrara, Mantua, Florence, and elsewhere built villas across town from their town palaces and others just outside the city walls and yet others somewhat beyond in the more remote countryside; by the sixteenth century many private men who could afford it were doing the same, including above all the great cardinals in Rome. The first grand duke of Tuscany did not spend much time during his long reign in any one place; he was continually on the move going from one villa to another, each place just down the road no more than an hour or so away at the most. Many of these villas—like those of other princes—were not located at the center of great rural estates; they were not in provincial towns, where they might have served to conspicuously remind subjects who the prince was; they were not fortified places strategically located in the defense network of the state. In short, this ceaseless villa hopping that kept these princes ever on the move had a different purpose from the mobility of the itinerant courts of northern Europe.

The importance of the town palace, along with the family chapel, in the establishment of one's social credentials was recognized also by the rural nobility. In the provincial backwashes of the Marches, for instance, they came into town and built palaces and chapels in accordance with the new mode of asserting one's social status. In southern Italy, too, for all their continuing attachment to their fiefs, nobles let their traditional country seats fall into ruin after having abandoned them for residence in Naples; and although many of them frequently changed houses there so that they had much less of an architectural presence in the city than did elites in other cities, they usually chose to be buried in the capital rather than on ancestral estates.[102] The rise of local artistic traditions in Rome, Naples, and Genoa in the sixteenth century was partly determined by the urbanization of rural elites in these places and the consequent change in the spending habits of men in search of a new definition of nobility.

101. James S. Ackerman, *The Villa: Form and Ideology of Country Houses* (Princeton, 1990), ch. 5.

102. Giuseppe Galasso, "Civiltà materiale e vita nobiliare in un inventario calabrese del '500," *Rivista storica italiana* 90 (1978), 754–55, 768; Gérard Labrot, *Baroni in città: Residenze e comportamento dell'aristocrazia napoletana, 1530–1734* (Naples, 1979), esp. pp. 31–36; Maria Antonietta Visceglia, *Il bisogno di eternità: I comportamenti aristocratici a Napoli in età moderna* (Naples, 1988), p. 124. For the Marches, see Bandino Giacomo Zenobi, *Ceti e potere nella Marca pontificia* (Bologna, 1976), pp. 270–71.

AS THE CHIEF TERM THAT REDEFINED the traditional aristocratic concept of magnificence, architecture became one of the most important signs of nobility in Italian society: it presupposed wealth, it signified status, and it could imply special knowledge and taste. Italians, however, sought to elevate their passion for building above the mere desire to express conspicuously their personal and social status. Since medieval moral thought assigned no value to building for secular, private purposes, they had to work out a rationale for building. Some of the values they appealed to in this enterprise reflect the change their culture was undergoing in relation to that of traditional feudal Europe.

Obviously, Italians exploited their civic traditions for this purpose. The heightened consciousness of the built environment could be appropriated to justify their indulgence in conspicuous architecture for their own use. In Florence—and perhaps elsewhere as well—the stylistic evolution of the private palace in fact takes its point of departure from the model established by the new public hall built at the end of the thirteenth century, with its rusticated walls, central courtyard, and symmetrical and carefully articulated north façade; thus stylistic choice was a conscious statement of adherence to a civic ideal. For all the egotism one may want to see in the building activities of both oligarchs and despots ranging from chapels in public places to ambitious urban renewal schemes, of the kind that were not seen in any northern town until much later, we cannot discount altogether the appeal of the arguments made by Alberti, Palmieri, and others, both humanists and architectural theorists, about the contribution of the beauty of such things to the common good and therefore to the fame of the city. The urban tradition provided an ideology that endowed architecture with social as well as personal moral values.

The argument was made, too, that the architectural embellishment of buildings effectively instills in the general population a greater respect for authority. Galvano Fiamma, writing about Azzone Visconti's building program in the early fourteenth century and leaning entirely on Aristotle, stresses how the prince's residence and chapel strike wonder in his subjects.[103] A century later Alberti suggested that the special effect beauty has on the public guarantees buildings against destruction.[104] Paolo Cortesi explicitly recognized the political implications of

103. Green, "Galvano Fiamma."

104. This idea in Alberti is commented on by Jan Bialostocki, "The Power of Beauty: A Utopian Idea in Leone Battista Alberti," in *Studien zum Toskanischen Kunst: Festschrift für Ludwig Heinrich Heydenreich* (Munich, 1964), pp. 13–19; and the higher didactic purpose he assigned to architecture is discussed by Carroll W. Westfall, "Society, Beauty, and the

such a position: in impressing itself on the senses of the uneducated, sumptuous architecture "easily restrains the admiring multitude from doing harm"—and he goes on to mention instances when mobs had destroyed buildings that did not have architectural quality.[105] Architecture can thereby serve as an instrument to confirm the builder's status in society and the constituted authority of the state. Nicholas V, in his alleged deathbed speech, recognized that "noble edifices combining taste and beauty with imposing proportions" could enhance the general public's respect for the church.[106] For Sabadino degli Arienti, the magnificent architecture of a prince expresses his moral authority over his subjects, and the beauty of the city is therefore evidence of good government and justice.

The concept of magnificence was by far the most frequently cited rationale for building in fifteenth-century Italy. The point of departure was Aristotle's notion, found also in Aquinas, that the virtuous use of money consisted in expenditures for religious, public, and private things if they were permanent. Galvano Fiamma defended the various building activities of Azzone Visconti in precisely these terms, although he felt no need to justify other kinds of expenditures.[107] The humanists took full possession of this classical notion that buildings as permanent private monuments adorning public space assured the fame that great and worthy men seek. "Since all agree that we should endeavor to leave a reputation behind us, not only for our wisdom but our power too," asserts Alberti (appealing to the authority of Thucydides), "for this reason we erect great structures, that our posterity may suppose us to have been great persons." Building is therefore an activity that could be rationalized (always echoing classical authors) as the proper expression of one's inner qualities, a moral act as the measure of a man: "the magnificence of a building," according to Alberti, "should be adapted to the dignity of the owner," and for Palmieri "he who would want . . . to build a house resembling the magnificent ones of noble citizens would deserve blame if first he has not reached or excelled their vir-

Humanist Architect in Alberti's *de re aedificatoria*," *Studies in the Renaissance* 16 (1969), 71–79.

105. Kathleen Weil-Garris and John F. D'Amico, "The Renaissance Cardinal's Ideal Palace: A Chapter from Cortesi's *De Cardinalatu*," in *Studies in Italian Art History*, vol. 1 (Rome, 1980), p. 89.

106. Quoted in Peter Partner, *Renaissance Rome, 1500–1559: A Portrait of a Society* (Berkeley, 1976), p. 16.

107. John Onians, "The Last Judgement of Renaissance Architecture," *Journal of the Royal Society of Arts* 128 (1980), 702–3.

tue."[108] Here is an imperative for architectural patronage that all these fifteenth-century Italian writers agree on. Moreover, in emphasizing the architectural component of magnificence, they gave a distinctive Italian sense to a term that traditionally was associated with largess and hospitality; they appropriated a feudal virtue to the urban world.

In Giovanni Sabadino degli Arienti's treatise on the princely virtues of Ercole d'Este, for all of its traditional orientation to religion and to Christian virtue as the organizing principles of the work, Ercole's secular building dominates the chapter on magnificence, which itself constitutes one-third the entire book; other, more traditional courtly activities such as tournaments, jousts, entertainments, spectacles, and sumptuous personal attire barely get mentioned in passing. Giovanni Pontano, too, directed his discussion of magnificence to a feudal court, with all the traditional forms of spectacle that mark a great nobleman; but he endows this traditional feudal value with an overriding aesthetic content, and this manifests itself above all in architecture.[109]

If a potential builder had any doubts about the link between architecture and fame, there were plenty of writers around—lettered and unlettered—to assure them on the matter. In his *Lives* Vespasiano da Bisticci takes it for granted that great and prominent men are patrons of the arts, especially of architecture, although he rarely feels obliged to provide us with any details. Cosimo de' Medici was the first to be widely hailed as a great builder. Contemporaries including Giovanni Rucellai and no one less than the pope himself, Pius II, commented on his zeal for building; and long after he died, writers such as Pontano in Naples and Cortesi in Rome cite him as the first modern exemplar of the model of magnificence. After Martin V, Federico da Montefeltro, and others of this first generation of prominent builders in the mid-fifteenth century, hardly any biographer of a pope or prince fails to mention this kind of patronage if he could. By the end of the century renewal of the architectural environment had become one of the clichés mentioned along with scholarship and the moral quality of life when it came to assessing a man's contribution to the general cultural revival of the times.

108. Alberti and Palmieri citations in Goldthwaite, "Florentine Palace," p. 990.

109. *Art and Life at the Court of Ercole I d'Este: The 'De triumphis religionis' of Giovanni Sabadino degli Arienti*, ed. Werner L. Gundersheimer (Geneva, 1972), pp. 50–79; Francesco Tateo, "Le virtù sociali e l'immanità' nella trattatistica pontaniana," *Rinascimento* 5 (1965), 142–48. On magnificence and building in Florence, see A. D. Fraser Jenkins, "Cosimo de' Medici's Patronage of Architecture and the Theory of Magnificence," *Journal of the Warburg and Courtauld Institutes* 33 (1970), 162–70. A full survey of Italian writers for use of the term in relation to architecture has been made by Georg Weise, *L'ideale eroico del rinascimento e le sue premesse umanistiche* (Naples, 1961), pp. 124–36, 207–8.

Buildings also became significant symbols of greatness in pictorial cycles commissioned by princes to exalt their place in history. In one of the first examples, a ward of the hospital of Santo Spirito in Rome, dating from the second half of the fifteenth century, fresco decorations depict the various construction projects of Innocent VIII and Sixtus IV, both patrons of the hospital. The decoration of the apartments of Leo X in the Palazzo Vecchio in Florence, commissioned by the first Medici duke to celebrate the history of the family, presents a panorama of the architectural patronage of the entire family, from Cosimo il Vecchio through the family popes to Duke Cosimo himself, illustrating through buildings the impact the Medici made on the history of both Florence and Rome. Likewise, Sixtus V had his place in the history of the church and in the history of the world illustrated through building projects in fresco cycles at the Lateran, the Vatican library, and Villa Montalto.

Architecture hence became the principal means by which Italians staked out their claims to grandeur and magnificence; it was certainly the chief luxury they spent their money on; and it was the one art form the upper classes were interested in reading about and showed a passionate intellectual interest in. Alberti wrote his treatise, in Latin, for patrons not for architect-builders; and Lorenzo de' Medici, Ercole d'Este, and other patrons read it. Filarete dedicated his treatise to a prince on the assumption that a building is a product of something like a marriage between architect and patron, so prominent is the latter's involvement in its planning and construction. For Pontano magnificence in a patron implies an aesthetic sensibility to the pleasures as well as knowledge of architecture, including the siting of buildings and the classical vocabulary of their ornamentation. The work of both Alberti and Filarete, who were roughly contemporary to the first two generations of great builders, was a response to the lively interest many of these patrons, in fact, are known to have had in the subject. No wonder that word got around immediately about the great palace Filippo Strozzi planned to build in Florence: abroad no one less than the Duke of Ferrara wanted to see the plans of this merchant's palace.

Interest in architecture could also extend to a creative involvement in artistic planning. Federico da Montefeltro has been credited with a major role in the design of the great palace at Urbino; and it has been claimed that both Lorenzo de' Medici and Ercole d'Este actually made architectural drawings. These men, in any case, kept a close eye on what was going on elsewhere. Lorenzo de' Medici sent for drawings of the palace at Urbino while it was going up, and Federigo Gonzaga also wanted to know about it and consulted with its architect, Francesco di Giorgio, while an extension was being added to his own palace at

Mantua. Ercole d'Este was anxious to have plans and details of the Strozzi palace in Florence. Lodovico Gonzaga's letters to his architect, Luca Fancelli, reveal his interest and knowledge in building and his readiness to criticize.

Standing head and shoulders above all these great fifteenth-century patrons was Lorenzo de' Medici, a man with his own artistic personality as a poet, even if he himself was much less a builder than his grandfather, Cosimo. Lorenzo visited Roman ruins with Alberti, whose treatise he later read. He actively intervened in the planning of some notable churches, including Santa Maria delle Grazie at Prato, Santo Spirito, San Lorenzo, and the hospital of San Gallo; and it was alleged that he did not hesitate to make his ideas known about the private palaces being constructed by other men, including Giuliano Gondi and Filippo Strozzi. He also zealously promoted Florentine architects at the royal court in Naples. Although political motives clearly lay behind much of this interest, there is a growing scholarly consensus that he was knowledgeable about the subject; and, in any case, the very notion of an "architectural policy" indicates the artistic temper of the times. This dilettante tradition continued on in Renaissance and Baroque Italy, where the annals of architecture are replete with amateur architects among the upper class and with patrons whose aggressive and creative—if not also disruptive—involvement in projects fully justified Filarete's assumption that a building is in fact the result of something like a marriage between patron and architect.

IN THE FIRST MODERN THEORETICAL TREATISE on architecture, Alberti took it as a basic assumption that man, having an instinctive desire to build, enjoys a natural proclivity for engaging himself critically in observing architecture. "There are two principal things that men do in this life," wrote his contemporary the Florentine patrician Giovanni Rucellai: "the first is to procreate, the second is to build." Then he added the cautionary note in a traditional mode that building ought not to go beyond necessity; but that caution was itself a recognition that this activity could in fact become an end in itself, an all-consuming passion, or, in the words of Filarete, "a willful pleasure, as when a man is in love." A man as rough-and-ready as the condottiere Andrea Fortebracci, called Braccio da Montone, lord of Perugia (d. 1424), was so obsessed with building that he thought of nothing else while on military expeditions—or so his biographer feels the need to tell us.[110] In a letter of 1507 to his wife, Giovanni II Bentivoglio, who was catching his

110. Puddu, "Lettere ed armi," pp. 501–2.

breath while on the run to escape the mob at Bologna that had thrown him out, concluded his laments about his own fate and about his ignorance of his sons' whereabouts with the hardest of all these blows of fortune—the loss of his great family palace in Bologna.[111] Once such a passion for building found currency in the competitive atmosphere of political life in the Italian city-state system, architecture was bound to flourish.

## Domestic Furnishings

It is not easy to reconstruct the private domestic world of the material culture of Renaissance Italy. The surviving artifacts, in both quantity and quality, are a monumental testimonial to the changes in consumer habits in Italy from the fourteenth to the seventeenth century; and much of the task at hand is to explain how they all fit into patterns of demand. Pictures provide few representations of this new world of goods, of the kind that are so abundant for Dutch life in the seventeenth century; and the record of imaginative literature offers little insight, in contrast to the rich descriptions that can be mined from the literature of ancient Rome. Rhetorical statements at the time about the grandeur of interiors are not very helpful. In his *Laudatio* of the city of Florence, written at the beginning of the fifteenth century, Leonardo Bruni mentions in passing the "beautiful chambers decorated with fine furniture, gold, silver, and brocaded hangings and precious carpets," but without giving any details; and likewise in exalting the greatness of his own times, toward the middle of the century, Giovanni Rucellai observes how houses were furnished better than ever but mentions only wall hangings, wainscoting, and benches.[112] Contemporary praise of the interior of Cosimo de' Medici's great palace singles out its painted and sculptural decoration and the luxury of materials but not its furniture.[113] Alberti, for all his dedication to architecture, seems not to have had much interest in the interior decor of private residences, other than to insist that it should create a spiritual atmosphere suitable for man's highest activities.[114] He hardly mentions furniture and furnishings; and, in fact, his discussion

---

111. Quoted in Andrea Bacchi, "Vicende della pittura nell'età di Giovanni II Bentivoglio," in *Bentivolorum magnificentia: Principe e cultura a Bologna nel Rinascimento*, ed. Bruno Basile (Rome, 1984), p. 285.

112. Bruni's panegyric is translated in *The Earthly Republic: Italian Humanists on Government and Society*, ed. B. Kohl and R. Witt, p. 140; Rucellai, *Zibaldone*, p. 61.

113. Rab Hatfield, "Some Unknown Descriptions of the Medici Palace in 1459," *Art Bulletin* 52 (1970), 232–49.

114. Zygmunt Waźbiński, "La maison idéale selon Alberti," *Acta Historiae Artium* 13 (1967), 13–16.

of the spatial organization of private houses has little to do with the realities of much palace architecture of his own day.

It is significant, too, that humanists such as Bruni and Alberti could not fall back on a Roman model. For all their affectations about imitating ancient Romans, they had little idea how Romans actually furnished their houses. In the famous ninth book of his *Roma trionfante*, Flavio Biondo assembled just about all the evidence anyone could to support his proposition that not one house in the Italy of his time—the mid-Quattrocento—could match the magnificence and splendor of some twenty thousand in ancient Rome; but he talks mostly about villas and, except for richness of materials, could not really say much about the details of furnishings and about functions of town houses in the ancient world. As they went about filling up the enormous spaces within their palaces, Italians were on their own in working out a consumption model.

The only sources for documenting the material culture of the domestic world are inventories and private account books; and, for the early Renaissance, these are abundant only for Florence. The earliest view into the Florentine home we can get from these records dates from around 1400, and there is no reason to think that things had changed much from the time of Dante and Giotto. At this time even large homes with many rooms were sparsely furnished. Besides places with basic support functions, such as the kitchen, pantries, and stables, domestic space seems to have been organized around the chamber of the master of the household that opened out, perhaps through an antechamber, to any number of much larger rooms. The chamber was a small multifunctional space that served primarily as a bedroom but also as an inner sanctum where one could retire into complete privacy for whatever purpose; it was the intimate core of the household, where furnishings and valuables were likely to be concentrated. The other rooms were generalized spaces that were sparsely furnished, although most rooms had beds in them. The typology of furniture does not extend beyond the basic functions of eating, sitting, sleeping, and storage and could hardly be refined by further stylistic categorization; and the analysis of interior domestic space leads only to vague generalizations about the multifunctionality of rooms.

Such arrangements are illustrated by the early fifteenth-century inventories of the very richest men in the city. The 1418 inventory of the household of Giovanni di Bicci de' Medici reveals a house of fewer than thirty rooms; these centered on the three suites of Giovanni and his two sons, Cosimo and Lorenzo, each consisting of a chamber, antechamber, and water closet, and included in addition seven other chambers and three general living spaces (two *sale* and a *saletta*). Almost all the furnishings of importance were concentrated in the chamber and ante-chamber of these private apartments. Of the fifteen religious objects—painted and sculpted pieces—that today would be categorized as works of art, ten were in chambers. The well-known merchant of Prato, Francesco Datini, a man of comparable wealth to his contemporary Giovanni de' Medici, had a much more modest house but one of the same basic type, with simple furniture, a few religious pictures, and several pieces of ceramics, glass, and silver.[115]

In their basic plan of vast, relatively empty spaces on the one hand and the small, richly furnished chamber of the owner on the other, these Florentine houses probably resembled the houses of the rich throughout Europe at the time, whether in town or countryside. A royal household, too, was organized around the king's chamber, the inner sanctum where he both slept and received privately and where the most lavish furnishings centered on the bed of state. Such rooms are depicted in Flemish painting.[116] Other rooms radiating outward from the chamber and serving more elaborate public functions were sparsely furnished. A 1436 inventory of the d'Este castle at Ferrara documents a contemporary example of a princely residence in Italy.[117] The dozens and dozens of rooms are identified not by function (except for essential places such as the kitchen and *guardaroba*) but by the person associated with them or, more frequently, by a particular feature of what was probably their frescoed decoration—the room of the elephants, of the boar, of the crown, and so on. Cloth wall hangings existed in abundance, but furniture was sparse and confined to a few basic types. Everywhere there were benches but no other forms of seating.

The process of change the Florentine world of material goods underwent in the course of the Renaissance can be broken down into several phases: first, in the fifteenth century the chamber evolves as a richly decorated interior space; second, from the later fifteenth century and throughout the sixteenth century the rest of the house begins slowly to

115. The Medici palace has been reconstructed by Howard Saalman and Philip Matox, "The First Medici Palace," *Journal of the Society of Architectural Historians* 44 (1985), 329–45; and its internal arrangements and furnishings are discussed by John Kent Lydecker, "Il patriziato fiorentino e la committenza artistica per la casa," in *I ceti dirigenti nella Toscana del Quattrocento* (Atti del V Convegno, 1982; Florence, 1987), pp. 209–21. Datini's house is described by Iris Origo, *The Merchant of Prato: Francesco di Marco Datini, 1335–1410* (Boston, 1986), pp. 241–63.

116. Craig Harbison, "Sexuality and Social Standing in Jan van Eyck's Arnolfini Double Portrait," *Renaissance Quarterly* 43 (1990), 271–78.

117. Giulio Bertoni and Emilio Vicini, *Il castello di Ferrara ai tempi di Niccolò III* (Bologna, 1907).

fill up with furnishings; third, in this process of accumulation two things happen: furnishings evolve into more highly developed forms, and interior space becomes organized into more specialized functions. This process of accumulation can be measured quantitatively both in the enlargement of this world of goods and in the evolutionary transformation of these goods, and it can be measured qualitatively in the new attitudes it induced about possessions and about goods in general.

THE LOCUS FOR THE FIRST PHASE in this process of accumulation was the chamber. Something of the attitudes of Florentines toward possessions can be inferred from the way they kept track of their increased spending in the account books covering their busy economic lives and carefully kept in double entry. Before the fifteenth century, expenses for furnishings have no particular identity in private accounts; but with the increased consumption in the fifteenth century Florentines took great care to keep records of their acquisitions. The first manifestation is the appearance in many private account books of a separate account just for the furnishing of this one room, the chamber—an account invariably entitled "my chamber" (la camera mia). Some men went further, opening separate accounts for the construction of individual pieces of furniture for their chamber, such as a great chest or a bed, and for the particular artisans who supplied them with household goods. Moreover, it is not at all unusual for them to register the acquisition of important pieces of furniture also in their diaries along with the essential memorable events in their lives, such as births, deaths, marriages, election to public office, and so forth. For instance, Piero Capponi opened an account with Giuliano da Maiano for the construction of furniture with triumphs and a perspective scene in wood inlay and another account with the painter Lorenzo di Piero for the painting of great chests; and after the execution of this work and settlement of accounts, the balancing entries of both these accounts are transferred to Capponi's chamber account. All this yields a full record of the furnishing of Capponi's chamber—who did the detailed work, the terms of the contracts, how long it took, and how much it cost.[118] This detail—summarized on a single chamber account complete with cross references to the more detailed subordinate accounts, kept with the discipline required by double-entry accounting, and entered in the same books of permanent record where he also kept business accounts—reflects an attachment to possessions of a kind that can hardly be documented for an earlier period.

118. Capponi's expenses are recorded in his account book, 1466–75, Biblioteca Nazionale, Firenze: Ginori-Conti 18.

The furnishing and decoration of a chamber were obviously a major economic and social event for these Florentine men, full of significance in the life of its occupant. Such accounts appear at the beginning of the first ledger a youth opened on embarking on his own economic career, even when he in fact remained within his father's house. Not surprisingly, the opening of a chamber account often announced an impending marriage and therefore an independent household. Marriage traditionally required the purchase of the bridal bed by the groom and probably also the outfitting of the nuptial chamber; but such expenses must have mounted considerably in the fifteenth century to merit the attention they get in the accounting record. In any case, these expenses, along with the purchase of the gifts a groom generally presented his wife, could consume a great deal of money, constituting a counterdowry that sometimes mounted to much more than the dowry he received with his bride. For some men the chamber was a one-time expense: it was put together in a relatively short period, and once it was furnished, a man could go through the rest of his life without adding much to it or, indeed, without making many other acquisitions for other rooms in his house. For the young Florentine once on his own and on the verge of marriage, the chamber was a one-time venture into what today might be called the art market to buy major pieces of furniture and artwork; and given the moment in his life when he indulged in this spending spree, he must have considered his chamber highly symbolic as a declaration of independence.[119]

Something of the sense of privacy men felt about their chambers emerges in Alberti's dialogue on the family, in the third book where the domestic economy is treated. There, when Giannozzo describes taking his wife on her first tour of his premises, the chamber is the last room he shows her: on entering, he closes and locks the door behind them and impresses on her the sanctity of the place. He tells us, too, that he kept his most precious things there—his treasury, silver, tapestry, garments, jewels, with each thing having its place, locked up and hidden. He goes on to say that these things gave him pleasure in his privacy. The only things he does not show his wife are his books and records and those of his ancestors: "These my wife not only could not read, she could not ever lay hands on them. I kept my records at all times . . . locked up and arranged in order in my study, almost like sacred and religious objects."[120]

119. Lydecker, "Patriziato fiorentino"; see also Brucia Witthoft, "Marriage Rituals and Marriage Chests in Quattrocento Florence," *Artibus et Historiae* 5 (1982), 52.

120. Renée Neu Watkins, trans., *The Family in Renaissance Florence* (Columbia, S.C., 1969), p. 209.

As the locus for a man's concentration of his most luxurious possessions, the chamber became in the course of the fifteenth century an
elaborate decorative ensemble of furnishings, including some of the
first secular art forms in a domestic setting.[121] It was a relatively small
space furnished with a few major pieces. The principal object was the
bed, which consisted of a sleeping platform placed on a low pedestal
which might contain storage spaces and served also as a seating bench.
Another important piece of furniture was the *lettuccio*, a massive bench
serving also as a bed and containing storage space below. Both the bed
and the *lettuccio* were display pieces of great prestige, made of wood that
could be elaborately carved and decorated in inlay by artists of the
stature of Giuliano and Benedetto da Maiano. Other pieces of furniture
were great chests and benches, massive forms that complemented the
bed and *lettuccio* for their architectonic quality; and the total decorative
ensemble of woodwork was rounded out by wainscoting on the walls
against which these pieces were placed. There were hardly any smaller
pieces of furniture—no chairs, for instance (in the whole of the Medici
house in 1418 there were only six); and luxurious stuffs were not part of
the permanent decorative ensemble but kept in storage, to be brought
out only on an occasion appropriate to their display.

Besides the architectonic quality of the furniture forms and the decorative effect of elaborate woodwork, the other aesthetic feature of the
chamber was the painted picture, and this form, too, was an innovation
in the fifteenth century. Many of these pictures were not framed and
hung on walls but inserted into the wainscoting along the walls and
applied to pieces of furniture as part of the decoration. Cassone (chest)
paintings are the best-known examples of this practice. Botticelli's *Pri-
mavera* was originally part of the back of a *lettuccio*; and Uccello's battle
scenes were probably built into wainscoting in the chamber of Lorenzo
de' Medici. An anecdote in Vasari informs us about an ensemble of
large paintings—twelve of which, by Pontormo, Andrea del Sarto,
Francesco Granacci, and Bacchiacca, survive—in the Borgherini chamber (and the original arrangement has puzzled art historians: one recon-
struction has them built into the bed itself). The chamber also contained
painted portraits, busts, and other works of art that were not built-in, as
well as religious items of the traditional kind but now perhaps somewhat more secular in their ornamentation and feeling; and pictures in
the form of roundels also seem to be another characteristic innovation of

---

121. The following discussion is based on the dissertation (Johns Hopkins University,
1988) of John Kent Lydecker, "The Domestic Setting of the Arts in Renaissance Florence."

these places. Lorenzo de' Medici's chamber included, besides the Uccello battle scenes, a picture by Pesellino and a roundel with an *Adoration of the Magi* by Fra Angelico; and the chamber of another Medici household contained two Botticelli pictures, Michelangelo's statue of Saint John, a roundel by Signorelli, and five other pictures. The chamber of a man of much more modest status, Lorenzo Morelli, had a *Saint George and the Dragon* by Uccello, a picture of Romulus and Remus, and busts of Dante, Petrarch, and the Roman emperor Hadrian. So far as is known, the attention Florentines lavished on their chambers in the fifteenth century far outdid the consumption habits of their ancestors.

ALTHOUGH FOR SOME QUATTROCENTO FLORENTINES significant consumption of household goods was not directed beyond the chamber, in the long run over the fifteenth century the world of goods entered a second phase of change marked by the accelerated accumulation of goods and the filling up of the other rooms in their homes. By the seventeenth century, furnishings were as notable an expenditure in the household of a great family as any of the traditional medieval forms of conspicuous consumption: the outlay for furnishings of the resident of the Strozzi palace equaled that for servants and exceeded all other categories after food and clothing, and the value of these furnishings was three times that of their jewels and silver.

The account books record the process. In fourteenth- and fifteenth-century ledgers most furnishings are found in an account of general expenses, where various household expenses were thrown together indiscriminately, and only the chamber account emerges with its own identity. By the latter part of the fifteenth century, however, as acquisitions and expenditures mounted, various categories of general living expenses are separated out and isolated in entirely separate accounts: for food, for clothing, for "extraordinary expenses," for expenses of specific members of the family, and for *masserizia*—that is, household goods and furnishings. In view of Alberti's redefinition of the word *masserizia* in his discussion of household economy, endowing this form of property with moral and social importance, the appropriation of the word into accounting jargon for household furnishings is suggestive of the importance Florentines attached to the growing quantity of possessions around which the family organized its life.

The *masserizia*, or household account, has two striking features that reveal something about how these Florentines regarded the things they were keeping account of. First is the increased pace of entry and the more hurried nature of the entry, with a corresponding falling-off of the amount of information in it. The pace of accumulation recorded in these accounts reaches an impressive rate. For instance, Bernardo Rinieri, a man of middling rank, began his household account on the third page of his first ledger, opened in the mid-1450s on the occasion of his marriage; the account grew eventually to fill up twenty-nine densely written folios—one-third of the entire ledger. In the earliest of these fifteenth-century household accounts individual entries were not made with great frequency—perhaps not much more than once a month—and they generally included considerable information, either in the entry itself or in its reference to a separate account about the acquisition that was then summarized when a final balancing entry was transferred to the household account. The detail on individual pieces of furniture often recorded on the chamber accounts has already been noted. With the quickened pace of accumulation, however, the growing world of goods got out of the control of the detailed accounting procedures used earlier; by the sixteenth century the accountant was often making entries in the household account with such frequency that he no longer wanted to take the time to record details. If in this process the household account became more generalized, reduced eventually to little more than a monotonous nondescriptive list of acquisitions, it began to swell to altogether new proportions as more and more acquisitions were made with ever-greater frequency. One has the impression that as people became greater consumers, accumulating a larger number of objects, they began to take their possessions for granted, thus losing something of that self-consciousness about their possessions we can perhaps read into the careful attention to detail with which their grandfathers in the fifteenth century accounted for the fewer things they bought.

A second feature of the procedure used to keep the account of household furnishings is that it is never closed. The account was not subject to periodic balancing: it remained open when the accountant transferred his accounts from a filled page to a new page and then from a filled ledger to a new ledger. Entries simply continued to accumulate. In other words, at any one moment in the lifetime of the Florentine consumer, he could know exactly how much he had spent up to that point for household furnishings simply by a glance at the account. If on his death bed, in his last living moment, he had the desire and lucidity, he could call for his ledger, open it to the household account, add up the total on the debit side, enter the balance on the credit side, and so, finally, with a stroke of the pen, close out this lifetime account to go on to a better life with the satisfaction that he had precise knowledge of just how much he had spent over his entire lifetime for all of his household furnishings—and, of course, had he a few more minutes to live and had he kept his older ledgers, as Florentines usually did (that is why so many survive), he would have had no difficulty whatsoever in drawing up a complete list of those acquisitions.

Although it may seem obvious that, at least in part, the function of such an accounting procedure was to facilitate an assessment of an estate for equitable division among heirs, the procedure continues unchanged into the period, beginning in the sixteenth century, when primogeniture replaced partible inheritance practices as a device to keep estates intact. Obviously, the procedure points up the importance of furnishings in a family patrimony. Yet, furnishings were not the only expenditure isolated on the accounting record; the same procedure was followed for all the accounts of personal consumption, so that a dying Florentine could draw up a complete and total accounting of his entire life as consumer—to find out, for example, how much he had spent for food, for dress, for his children, for real estate, as well as for household furnishings—and this is why we can learn so much more about the details of these men's lives than we can even of our own.

BY THE SIXTEENTH CENTURY, with goods accumulating all around them, first concentrated in the chamber and then scattered throughout the house, Florentines were experiencing the slow emergence of a new material culture, for accumulation did not mean just more goods: it was a dynamic process of change. Thus the transformation of the Renaissance world of goods enters a third phase, largely a sixteenth-century phenomenon, that can be described as corollaries to the process of accumulation: first, goods evolved into more complicated forms; and, second, this evolutionary process eventually led to a redefinition of the space being filled up by these goods.

The first corollary to the accumulation of goods was the evolution of household forms as they became subject to variation, elaboration, refinement, and innovation. In the fifteenth century furniture consisted mostly of highly generalized forms such as benches and chests or massive pieces such as beds. Bruni mentions only benches in his idealized description of the Florentine interior, cited above. Likewise, Giovanni Rucellai, in exalting the greatness of his own times toward the middle of the century by observing how houses were furnished better than ever, singles out only benches. Writing about his visit to the Medici palace in 1459, the eldest son of Francesco Sforza, Duke of Milan, was struck more by its architecture and interior decoration than by its furnishings, of which he mentions only tapestries and "chests of inestimable workmanship and value."[122] The aesthetic quality of this furniture would

122. Hatfield, "Some Unknown Descriptions," p. 232.

seem to have consisted of architectonic mass and the decorative modes of woodwork, not the variety of forms.

By the sixteenth century, however, furniture evolved into a wide variety of types. Storage pieces evolved into elaborate chests, cabinets, credenzas, and armoires; benches evolved into chairs, and these in turn evolved into a variety of types—a 1663 inventory of the Strozzi palace includes *seggiole a braccioli coperte di vacchetta, seggiole alla genovese, seggiole con fondo, seggiole con cuscine, seggiole basse coperte di vellutino, sgabellini, sgabelloncini, sgabelloni, sgabelli con spalliera*, and *sgabelli senza spalliera*.[123] The bed of the master of the house remained probably the single most imposing piece of furniture, but it also underwent a radical transformation, evolving from the elaborate wood structures already mentioned into something that can more correctly be described as a large frame for the mounting of an abundance of luxurious stuffs. Tooled and gilded leather and luxury stuffs, in fact, became permanent fixtures in the decorative ensemble as an essential part of furniture (such as the bed) and as wall coverings; and with the frescoing of walls and ceilings, the impulse for interior decoration sought to bring the entire space into its scheme. Other furnishings also proliferated and evolved into endless varieties: glass and ceramics; sculpture in terra cotta, wood, stone, and bronze; and, last but not least, painting.

The history of secular panel painting, in fact, encapsulates this evolution. In the fifteenth century painting appears as decoration applied to chests and beds and inserted into wainscoting; and as decoration subordinated to furniture forms, one had to look downward to floor level to see much of it. When painting finally appeared as an independent decorative object hung on a wall, the frame began its own evolution as a richly carved and gilded tondo or *cassetta* that could be made by artists as prominent as the painter himself and could cost almost as much as the picture.[124] Along with its evolution as a physical form, the picture, once it emerged in a domestic setting, became subject to the influence of the entire range of secular culture and took on greater variety in its content and a more highly charged cultural meaning.

With the accumulation of pictures through the sixteenth century, they came to constitute a decorative ensemble in their very quantity, and accordingly the frame receded in importance to a more modest item, often simply painted black or gilded in gold. By the beginning of the seventeenth century many Florentine patricians had dozens and

123. Richard A. Goldthwaite, "L'interno del palazzo e il consumo dei beni," in *Palazzo Strozzi metà millennio, 1489–1989* (Rome, 1991), p. 164.

124. Creighton Gilbert, "Peintres et menuisiers au début de la Renaissance en Italie," *Revue de l'art*, no. 37 (1977), 11, 16, 19, 20–21.

sometimes hundreds of pictures in their houses. A 1626 inventory of Piero Guicciardini lists a total of 230 paintings and 165 sculptures: two-thirds of all these items were collected together in only three rooms, which had little else in them, while the major living rooms had few of these kinds of art objects. The measure to which painting became an essential part of interior decoration everywhere in Italy (and not just in Florence) can be taken in the advice for the hanging and preserving of paintings Giulio Mancini included in his unpublished treatise on painting written in the early seventeenth century as a manual for consumers even of modest means entering the growing art market.

Given the cult status art has achieved in our own time, we would probably consider the painted picture the highest form any household object achieved in the evolution that accompanied the accumulation of objects. Other, more mundane objects, however, also underwent a complex evolution—for instance, pottery. In the age of Dante and Giotto, at the beginning of the fourteenth century, wealthy Florentines, like everyone else in Europe who could afford it, ate off pewter and perhaps on grander occasions used silver display pieces; and any pottery they used was of the simplest kind. By the sixteenth century, two hundred years later, maiolica, or tin-glazed ceramics, had become one of the glories of Italian craftsmanship. Its manufacture reached a technical and artistic proficiency that has probably never been excelled since: it was produced in a great number of centers all over Italy, each with its own characteristic qualities; and the production of any one of these centers is so profuse in forms and styles as to defy attempts by scholars to impose clear typologies on it. Italians not only changed the tableware they used, they needed much more of it to get through a meal. While other Europeans were still eating off pewter and wood and still shared common plates at table, the Italians built up complete services of dishes in the modern sense, so that each diner had his or her own place setting, with many dishes for specific uses; and dishes were changed frequently during a meal.

Along with this evolutionary process accompanying the proliferation of objects, the other corollary to the accumulation of furniture and furnishings and the elaboration of these things is the filling up of interior space and the specialization of room function—which is to say the spatial reorganization of domestic life. The history of how life evolved inside many early palaces can be written around the adaptation of the great generalized spaces of the original plan to the more particular needs the family developed as it adjusted to life inside with its expanding variety and function of goods.

The process by which the great Strozzi palace was adapted for use, and readapted with changes in fashion, can be described in great detail, thanks to the survival of the household accounts of subsequent generations down to the end of the line in this century, along with complete inventories at each juncture when the palace passed from one generation to the other. Its builder, Filippo Strozzi, one of the wealthiest merchant-bankers in fifteenth-century Florence, bought only a few expensive pieces of furniture during his lifetime, described in the 1501 inventory recording the division among his sons as simply beds, chests, tables, and benches, the most expensive items being a selection of "beautiful wood furnishings from the chamber of Filippo." When his widow moved into his great palace at this time, on its completion over a decade after Filippo's death, she must have lived in only a few rooms in this vast house, the largest built to date in Florence. A century after it was begun, the family still occupied principally only one floor, the *piano nobile*, which was, however, now filled up with furnishings, including many things that had not existed at the time the building was put up. The next inventory just a few years later, in 1611, reveals that the living space, in addition to being filled up with furnishings, was also more functionally specialized. There were now two chapels, one with a sacristy, whereas in the fifteenth century, town houses had not had any chapel at all. The principal bedroom, described as an alcove, consisted now mainly of the bed itself; and a series of small service rooms opened up from it, the entire ensemble being organized exclusively for sleeping and dressing—a far cry from the multifunctional chamber of the fifteenth century filled with the owner's personal treasury. At the end of the century there were separate rooms for sleeping, for eating, for receptions, for visitors, for games, for artworks, and—to our good fortune!—for the family archives.[125]

This story of the considerable modification of interior space over the sixteenth and seventeenth centuries is dramatized in the radical transformations that had to be made when an older Renaissance palace was remodeled in the seventeenth century for more modern living.[126] When the Riccardi bought the Medici palace, they found that what had been in its time the grandest palace in Florence, if not all of Italy, could no longer satisfy the needs of a rich family almost two centuries later. No sooner did the new owners take possession of it than they virtually gutted it, putting in two staircases in the new fashion—one a spiral, the other grandly sweeping through the height of the building; needing a

---

125. The Strozzi inventories are cited in Goldthwaite, "L'interno del palazzo," p. 165.

126. Frank Böttner, "Der Umbau des Palazzo Medici-Riccardi zu Florenz," *Mitteilungen des Kunsthistorischen Institutes in Florenz* 14 (1970), 393–414; and his contribution in *Il Palazzo Medici Riccardi di Firenze*, ed. G. Cherubini and G. Fanelli (Florence, 1990).

larger reception hall than any the house then had, they threw several of the larger older rooms together and raised the already high ceiling on the *piano nobile* well into the floor above; the loggias were enclosed to make galleries around the courtyard; an extension was added almost doubling the size of the house and including a grander hall, the famous library, and accommodations for stable and carriages; and, finally, no fewer than four chapels were opened, replacing the former Medici chapel, itself apparently an anomaly in fifteenth-century town houses. The remodeled and greatly enlarged Medici-Riccardi palace, filled with goods scattered throughout its many clearly defined and distinctly different spaces, stands in stark contrast to the house in which Cosimo de' Medici—of comparable economic status in his own day— grew up two centuries earlier, with its most valuable goods largely concentrated in a single chamber set amidst a welter of other, largely empty and multifunctional, rooms.

The transformation of interior domestic space has been recounted on the basis of the Florentine documentation because these records extend further back into the past and because they have been better studied. The Florentines may have been precocious in the development described here; and in fact, given the widespread fame of Cosimo de' Medici in his own time and long after for the splendor of his palace, both inside and out, Florentine taste in these matters may have become a model for other Italians. There is no reason to think, however, that rich Italians elsewhere did not undergo the same transformation as consumers. The earlier, fifteenth-century phase of this development is difficult to document for other places, although evidence from Venice and from some of the courts would indicate that in these places, too, luxury was highly concentrated in a chamber or a study, that other household goods were not numerous, and that these were scattered about in relatively vast and multifunctional spaces.[127] In any case, by the early seventeenth century inventories throughout Italy reveal a similar pattern of room functions and furnishings and a world of goods remarkably homogeneous in its forms, albeit with regional variation in styles.[128]

The evolution of the Italian world of goods marked something new

127. Molmetti's well-known survey of Venetian life in the Middle Ages has virtually nothing about furnishings; but things had changed by the sixteenth century: see Isabella Palumbo Fossati, "L'interno della casa dell'artigiano e dell'artista nella Venezia del Cinquecento," *Studi veneziani* 8 (1984), 1–45. The accumulation in Bologna is described by Ludovico Frati, *La vita privata di Bologna dal secolo XIII al XVII* (Bologna, 1900).

128. A survey of over five hundred Venetian inventories from the second half of the sixteenth century reveals that pictures had a "massive presence": Palumbo Fossati, "L'interno della casa dell'artigiano," pp. 1–45.

in the spending habits of the rich. In many respects Italians continued to spend money in the traditional ways. Clothing was still by far the largest category of expenditures; jewelry and plate became more conspicuous items with the passing of time; and expenses for servants, including feeding, clothing, and housing, mounted sharply with the enlargement of residences, the elaboration of furnishings, and (in the seventeenth century) the opening of stables to accommodate coach transport. In all this Italians followed a model the rich had always followed everywhere in Europe. In the course of the Renaissance, however, one distinct new area of material culture opened up—household furnishings; and its expansion included many new forms and a proliferation of varieties within traditional forms. By the beginning of the seventeenth century the house of the rich Italian was a far different place from what it had been three centuries earlier, in the age of Dante and Giotto and of the Bardi and Peruzzi. On the whole it was a much larger and more artistically conceived building, it certainly was filled with many more objects, and these furnishings defined the functions of space more precisely. Here we have the first manifestation of a new kind of consumption of durable goods in the economic history of the West.

WHAT KIND OF LIFE THE ITALIANS were defining for themselves as they filled up their domestic world with goods is not so clear. For all the fascination palace architecture has held for scholars, the literature addresses primarily the external presence of these great buildings; little is known about how these houses functioned as homes and how life inside may have been the occasion for establishing other identities for their owners and residents. F. W. Kent has recently begun to look at Florentine palaces as "centres of wider family and neighbourhood cooperation and sociability, magnets to attract clients of diverse social rank to the patronage networks run by their owners," but for the moment the evidence for this wider social and political life centering on the private residence is largely limited to the Medici palace, hardly a typical example. Nor is the sense of place at all clear in the rich picture of intimate family relations Christiane Klapisch is still engaged in drawing.[129] The great Renaissance palace, in short, remains a mysterious kind of house. On the one hand, recent studies pointing up the closer relations within the family, the sharpened sensitivity to infants, and the role of women might be cited to argue that the enlargement of the domestic world of

---

129. Kent, "Palaces, Politics, and Society"; many of Klapisch's studies have been collected in *Women, Family, and Ritual in Renaissance Italy* (Chicago, 1985) and *La famiglia e le donne nel Rinascimento a Firenze* (Bari, 1988).

goods was a corollary of the withdrawal of the family into the closed and more intimate bourgeois household—a place, incidentally, beyond the scope of sumptuary legislation, which was in the sixteenth century increasingly limited to clothing and jewelry in public. On the other hand, the physical ambience of family life in the Renaissance has always struck architectural historians as well as historians of furnishings, from antiquarians to the theorists and philosophers Siegfried Giedion and Mario Praz, for its cold formality and lack of comfort, at least as judged by modern standards; and indeed the pictorial arts do not document domestic life with that feeling of immediacy and intimacy found, for example, in seventeenth-century Dutch painting. The task remains for someone to pull all these approaches and materials together and breathe a little social life into the Renaissance palace.

Such a study will have to come to terms with the increased consumption of durable goods during these centuries destined for the private household. Burckhardt, in elaborating his thesis that the birth of modern man came with the Italians' discovery of the world and of man, emphasized their discovery of private life and the domestic world; but this theme, for all of its prominence among current historiographical fashions, has hardly been considered in its relation to material culture. Although recent scholarship has deepened our knowledge of the demography and structure of the family and penetrated into the psychological reality of family life, especially for women and children, it has paid little attention to the material conditions of the household. In any event, these studies have for the most part been limited to Florence and hardly extend beyond the classical period of the fifteenth century. Much useful material can be mined from studies of the private life of the upper classes in several centers over the "long" Renaissance by antiquarian historians writing a century ago, but the subject will have to be put in a larger chronological and geographical framework and recast in the mold of more modern social history before we can fully integrate the material world of the house into the culture of family life.

In whatever way Italians lived out their lives in their increasingly dense world of goods, there is little in their evolving consumption model to suggest that they were moving toward the expansive and expensive social life still very much in evidence among the rural nobility of northern Europe at the end of the sixteenth century. Italian elites never abandoned the city as their principal place of residence and as the place of burial. The "return to the land" that is so much a part of the endless discussions of the "refeudalization" of late Renaissance Italy refers only to investment strategies, not to spending habits. Hospitality on the grand scale was not such a social imperative for elites who lived in the city just down the street from one another and who in any case could never call forth the vast array of serfs, tenants, servants, clients, and other hangers-on who were so much a part of the household scene of a rural noble in the north.

Moreover, with all the documentation that exists for Quattrocento Florence, no one has brought forth any evidence that much social activity beyond the family took place in private palaces, as large as they were. It is not such an amazing fact, therefore, that despite the enormous size of the houses they were building, the richest Florentines, from Francesco Datini at the beginning of the century to Filippo Strozzi at the end, did not have many servants at all. A man as wealthy as Giovanni Rucellai at midcentury had only eight between his country house and his town palace, including stable hands and two female slaves; and hardly anyone in the city could round up any more servants than this for something as ceremonious as a funeral cortege.[130] In Florence slaves were preferred to servants because they were not subject to the high mobility of wage labor in an urban market, but few people had as many as two and hardly anyone had male household servants. No private household in Quattrocento Florence or, no doubt, in any other Italian city at the time had a staff as large as the twenty to thirty servants that was the norm in the contemporary household of an English noble of the relatively modest rank of knight or squire, not to mention the households of the upper nobility, which could easily reach well above a hundred servants.[131]

That life inside a great palace changed as it filled up with goods and became spatially redefined goes without saying. Once the private domestic world became the stage on which people played out their lives, social life within the home must have become more expansive if for no other reason than to create occasions for the assembling of an audience to view one's increasing possessions. This is not a subject we know much about, however. Pallavicino's chronicle (cited above), which has much to say about aristocratic life in late sixteenth-century Genoa, mentions banquets and balls in private homes with great frequency and

---

130. Strocchia, *Death and Ritual*, pp. 64–65.

131. On the mobility of servants in fifteenth-century Florence, see Richard A. Goldthwaite, *The Building of Renaissance Florence: An Economic and Social History* (Baltimore, 1980), pp. 106–8; Christiane Klapisch-Zuber, "Célibat et service féminins dans la Florence du XVe siècle," in *Annales de démographie historique: Démographie historique et condition féminine* (Paris, 1981), pp. 289–302. A mid-sixteenth-century survey of Florentine households includes number of servants: Archivio di Stato di Firenze, MSS, no. 179. Figures for England come from Chris Given-Wilson, *The Royal Household and the King's Affinity* (New Haven and London, 1986), p. 259; and Mertes, *English Noble Household*, pp. 18, 187, 218; Heal, *Hospitality*, pp. 46–47.

records the number of guests as varying from about two to four dozen. In the history of music the development of the madrigal and other forms involving amateur performance is closely tied to the increase of social activities by the upper class within the privacy of their homes. In the course of the sixteenth century more servants became necessary to accommodate this style of social life within the home and to tend to the greater burden of household chores occasioned by more furnishings and new practices such as the use of carriages and the keeping of horses; and by the seventeenth century a great household could have two or three dozen servants.[132] Yet, hospitality hardly entered the purview of the treatises on household management mentioned earlier. The staff of a rich urban dweller never became the vast horde of dependents and poor relatives that so characterized the household in the north, with its orders and ranks of servants organized into a precise hierarchy and regulated by its own rules.[133] Moryson correctly observed that since in Italy peasants worked for wages, they did not work as servants in their employer's household; and he noted how few menservants there were.[134] Montaigne found Venice "the city in the world where one lives most cheaply, as a train of valets is here of no use whatsoever . . . everybody going about by himself"; and in Padua he marveled that "it is not the custom here to ride about the town on horseback, and not many are followed by a lackey."

Moryson remarked how closed and small the Italian household was, so that although their palaces were "fit to receive a King with his Court for the stately building," they lacked the "capacity" to do so. He noted how little Italians were inclined to spend for entertainment and criticized the country for the "dearth of victuals," the "solitary tables," and the "wickedness of Hosts"—and these observations led him repeatedly to tirades, by way of contrast, against the good old ways in which the English were spending their money at the time.[135] It was precisely "the natural hospitality of England" that led Sir Henry Wotton, in 1624, to regard certain aspects of Italian palace design as unsuitable for imitation in England—namely, the small size of the service rooms and the fact that they were confined to the basement and therefore not "more visible."[136]

---

132. See the comment of Rinuccini, "Considerazioni," pp. 276–77; also Adam Mani-kowski, "Elitist Consumption Society: Lorenzo Strozzi's Aristocratic Enterprise in the Seventeenth Century" (typescript of English translation of book published in Warsaw, 1987); Pierre Hurtubise, *Une famille-témoin: Les Salviati* (Vatican City, 1985), p. 434 n.

133. Friedman, *House and Household*, pp. 41–46.

134. *Shakespeare's Europe*, pp. 150–51; also Thomas, *History of Italy*, p. 80.

135. *Itinerary*, 1:192–93; 3:492–93; 4:93–99, 172–74.

136. Quoted in Heal, *Hospitality*, p. 153.

THE RISE IN DEMAND FOR durable goods marked not only the difference between Italy in 1600 and Italy in 1300 but the difference between Italy and north Europe. The northern nobility spent lavishly for their households, often more lavishly than Italians, since the greatest nobles lived on a far grander scale appropriate to their elevated position in society. The range of goods they bought, however, was limited in the traditional way described at the outset of this discussion, with most of their spending directed to food, clothing, wall hangings and other stuffs, armor, jewelry, plate, and the appurtenances of the household chapel— all those things, in short, that made for a grand public appearance.[137] Gold, silver, and jewelry could be the most costly items in a fifteenth- or sixteenth-century inventory, but much of the "expenditures" for such things was really a form of conspicuous hoarding. So much silver was put into plate in the north at the end of the Middle Ages, much of it with a minimum of artistic elaboration, that the practice has been cited as a cause of serious bullion famines in that part of the world. Obviously, for Italians, such as the Venetian ambassadors who commented on the great quantities of plate they saw in England, this form of consumption made little economic sense.[138]

As for furniture, much of this had to be mobile, since well into the sixteenth century the household of the greater rural nobility in France and England remained itinerant. Furniture forms were therefore simple, probably similar to what they had been in Italy before the fifteenth century. There is little evidence that spending habits changed before the end of the sixteenth century.[139] When furnishings began to evolve in the north in the course of the sixteenth century, it was not so much that northerners imitated Italians as that the conditions that had generated change in Italy were beginning to obtain also in the north— that is, the adjustment of spending habits to urban living by a greater number of rich people. Still, at the end of the century, however, interiors were more notable for the lavish display of textiles than for furniture. With a weaker market and hence a less-developed artisan tradition, moreover, the unfolding of this domestic world of goods in the

---

137. K. B. McFarlane, *Nobility of Later Medieval England* (Oxford, 1973), pp. 96–98.

138. F. C. Lane and R. C. Mueller, *Money and Banking in Medieval and Renaissance Venice*, vol. 1: *Coins and Moneys of Account* (Baltimore, 1985), p. 67; John H. Munro, "Monetary Contraction and Industrial Change in the Late-Medieval Low Countries, 1335–1500," in *Coinage in the Low Countries (880–1500)*, ed. N. J. Mayhew (Oxford, 1979), pp. 102–3; Peter Spufford, *Money and Its Uses in Medieval Europe* (Cambridge, 1988), p. 346.

139. Christopher Dyer, *Standards of Living in the Later Middle Ages: Social Change in England, c.1200–1520* (Cambridge, 1989), ch. 3 ("The Aristocracy as Consumers").

north could be very rough indeed: Nikolaus Pevsner mused that the interior and furnishings of Hardwick Hall, one of the most sumptuous houses in Elizabethan England, would have been "a monstrous show in the eyes of a visitor from Fontainbleau [decorated mostly by imported Italians] or Florence, barbaric in the extreme."[140]

Northern travelers to Italy were struck by the distinctive world of goods they found there. In Venice Fynes Moryson commented on how much was spent on houses and furniture rather than on "diet and apparel"; and in general he was much impressed by the Italian passion for buildings, furnishings, and ornamental gardens: "they bestow their money in stable things," he says, "to serve their posteritie, where as [he adds, referring to the value the English put on feasting] our greatest expenses end in the casting out of excrements." Moryson criticizes the Italians because they "are so ravished with the beauty of their own Country . . . holding Italy for a Paradise" that they never travel abroad. "In truth," says Moryson's contemporary Giovanni Botero, "we Italians are too much friends to our own selves and too much involved admirers of our own things, when we prefer Italy and its cities to all the rest of the world."[141]

The Neapolitan cardinal Antonio de Beatis, who traveled through northern Europe in 1517–18, found much to praise enthusiastically in the cities, buildings, and art he observed there; but in the end nothing could compare with Italy. In the opinion of de Beatis, Lyon was the fairest city of all because the presence of so many Italians gave it something of the quality of Italy; and in praising the arca of Saint Augustine in Pavia as "one of the most beautiful things in Italy, or indeed anywhere," he immediately added, "There is no need to take the foreigners into account: what cannot be found in Italy will never be found anywhere."[142] No wonder that Vincenzo Scamozzi, on the moment of his reentry into Italy from France in 1600, for once broke the impersonal and objective tone of his journal to exclaim how much he had longed for the place, "both for the uniformity of customs and for belonging

---

140. On France: Diefendorf, *Paris City Councillors*, pp. 59–66; Neuschel, "Noble Households," pp. 595–622 (survey of three families of the upper provincial nobility just below ducal level). On England: William Harrison, *The Description of England [1577]* (Ithaca, N.Y., 1968), bk. 2, ch. 12; McFarlane, *Nobility*, pp. 96–98; Mertes, *English Noble Household*, pp. 102–20; Alan Simpson, *Wealth of the Gentry, 1540–1660* (Chicago, 1961), pp. 166–67. Pevsner's comment is taken from the entry in the Penguin guide to Derbyshire; cf. Eames, *Furniture*, pp. 236–39.

141. Moryson, *Itinerary*, 1:93; 4:82, 94; Botero, "Delle cause della grandezza e magnificenza delle città," bk. 2, ch. 12.

142. *Travel Journal of Antonio de Beatis*, pp. 139, 184.

to all of us together."[143] Material culture may have been what Italians mostly shared with one another for all the diversity of their political traditions.

## CONSUMPTION AND THE GENERATION OF CULTURE

With the construction and furnishing of interior space from the fifteenth to the seventeenth century Italians created a world in which they could develop a different style of life and in which a new culture came to be defined. This is why so much was spent on objects, why so many new kinds of objects came into existence, why the arts flourished now in the domestic world as they had earlier in the ecclesiastical world. Consumption was a creative force to construct a cultural identity. In inventing all kinds of new furnishings ranging from pottery to paintings, in elaborating their forms, in refining their production, and in organizing them into new spatial arrangements within their homes, Italians discovered new values and pleasures for themselves, reordered their lives with new standards of comportment, communicated something about themselves to others—in short, generated culture, and in the process created identities for themselves. In this cultural development there was a dynamic for change that resulted from the interaction between people and physical objects.

The cultural development that resulted from this interaction is most evident in the process by which these objects acquired the attributes of secular art. The painted picture was probably the highest form of any of the household objects that evolved in the Renaissance. Already in the fourteenth century some religious pictures were transformed into something rightfully called works of art. How the highly visual nature of their religious culture aroused the Italians' awareness of an aesthetic sensibility has been remarked elsewhere in this book; and that sensibility was further sharpened once religious pictures moved as permanent fixtures into the private, secular world of homes. Petrarch's comment in his will about the Giotto he owned—that it was beyond the appreciation of ignorant men—suggests that it was more than just the usual devotional object; and the same inference can be drawn from the presence of several religious representations in the same room as recorded in many fifteenth-century inventories. The five Madonnas, for instance, Luigi Martelli collected in one place—one in marble, one in copper, and three in wood (one of the latter a Flemish work)—cannot

143. Vincenzo Scamozzi, *Taccuino di viaggio da Parigi a Venezia*, ed. Franco Barbieri (Venice, 1959), p. 86.

in all probability be explained altogether by a special devotion to the cult of the Virgin.[144]

Moreover, once household furnishings came to be considered as a decorative ensemble, worthy of greater attention and resources, room was made also for yet another transformation of the picture into a secular object, thus opening up an outlet for the visual expression of the expanding secular interests of the times. That the subject matter of much of this secular painting was classical in its inspiration is of secondary importance—had the same development occurred in the north of Europe, painting might have been predominantly chivalric in its subject matter and still had a stylistic development as original and vigorous as it had in Italy. The material conditions of the demand for painting were different in Italy: painting, having already taken on a conscious aesthetic identity in its religious and civic forms, now took on yet another identity that was no less complex than the entire range of secular culture it represented. This happened in Italy partly because the religious tradition in art had both aroused demand by conditioning people to a richer visual culture and stimulated productive forces ready to meet the new demand that arose in the secular world. The reasons this new secular demand arose with greater force in Italy are to be found in the new arrangements for the interior decoration of residences, be they patrician or princely.

The picture, in short, evolved into different things that were not always altogether distinct—a religious object, a household furnishing, a work of art, and a cultural statement; and as its meanings thus became more complex, involving people more intimately with the object, it achieved a cult status. The zealous efforts of Isabella d'Este, in the early sixteenth century, to assemble pictures by specific artists on specific subjects for a specific place indicate that the picture as object had acquired multiple meanings that it had not possessed two centuries earlier. It had become a collectible thing sought for a variety of reasons, not the least of which was respect for the artist himself—as the best of contemporary artists (one of the principles of Isabella's commissions), as one of the great artists of the past (a status first achieved in the later sixteenth century by Raphael and Andrea del Sarto, among others, whose works were sought also in copies), as a member of a school (for example, the Flemish painters collected by the Gonzaga duke of Mantua), as a painter of his own portrait (collected by the Medici), and as a draftsman (collected by Vasari and later by the Medici). A picture there-

144. Archivio di Stato di Firenze: Carte strozziane, ser. 5, no. 1428 (accounts of estate), fol. 103.

fore came to be charged with a great variety of cultural meanings in the course of this evolution.

Painting was thus a physical object with which its owner established a special identity in the social world—hence, the social importance of patronage. Already in the early fifteenth century humanists—like Poggio, in his dialogue on nobility—cite the example of ancient patrons such as Lucullus and Alexander the Great to promote the patronage and possession of works of art as one way a person can lay a claim to fame. Vespasiano da Bisticci, a less learned man, took this for granted as a quality of the famous men whose biographies he wrote; and many princes were explicit about the matter. By the mid-sixteenth century the proposition had become so much part of the cultural baggage of Italians that Cosimo I could utilize it in order to establish his credentials as a new prince by creating an elaborate myth about the historical mission of the Medici as patrons going back a century to Cosimo il Vecchio and Lorenzo the Magnificent. This political role of art is essential to understand much patronage in later Renaissance Italy. Art became a matter of taste by which people could demonstrate something of their true worth, and it is not surprising to find the seventeenth-century Florentine Ferdinando Del Migliore asserting that art had in fact emerged in Florence out of the very nobility of Florentine society. In Italy the appreciation of painting seldom took on the high moral and civic flavor that characterized the "discovery" of painting in Georgian England, notwithstanding the efforts that arose in various cities to assert the validity of local schools of painting to challenge the claims Vasari made about the absolute preeminence of Florence.[145]

Pictures were obviously charged with a particular and highly articulated cultural meaning in refining aesthetic sensibilities. Other objects could be the occasion for refining also people's mode of comportment. The proliferation of dinnerware referred to above brought with it a profound change in the way Italians conducted themselves at table. Pontano included the quality of dining in his discussion of the five social virtues associated with the spending of money, since it is one of the most important activities people do together. He called this virtue "conviviality," and in defining it he went beyond the traditional medieval notion of expansive hospitality and extravagant feasting to emphasize the civility of being in the company of others at table. This civility, moreover, required things. Already in the fifteenth century the poet Il Pistoia remarked the urbanity of the new utensils: "Sundays I dine on a

145. Iain Pears, *The Discovery of Painting: The Growth of Interest in the Arts in England, 1680–1768* (New Haven, 1988), pp. 173–75.

plate with a fork like the city folk, never fishing with my hand in the bowl."[146] The diner confronted the full complement of knives, forks, and spoons made in silver and monogrammed with the family coat of arms; separate plates for each diner, with frequent change of plates in the course of a meal; and the napkin as the indispensable item at each place setting and the essential utensil in the liturgy of table ritual. Italians sought to impose rules on the entire organization of a meal, including the order of courses and the setting of the table, just as they rationalized the more studied consideration they gave to the preparation of food by relating it to the social virtues of elegance and good taste. All these concerns surfaced in the form of treatises Italians wrote on the entire range of subjects related to dining, from gourmet cooking to the folding of napkins at table.

Montaigne, Moryson, and other northern European travelers in Italy were impressed by the array of dishes, glasses, silverware, and napkins they found before them. Forks were particularly notable because more than anything else they marked a different standard of behavior at table. Montaigne deemed it worthy of comment that in Italy all diners at table had their own napkins and complete service of silverware, so that they did not touch their plates with their hands while eating. A few years later, the English tourist Fynes Moryson marveled that Italians touched "no meate with the hand, but with a forke of silver or other mattall, each man being served with his forke and spoone, and glasse to drinke"; and Thomas Coryat warned, talking about Italians and their forks, "[If anyone] should unadvisedly touch the dish of meate with his fingers from which all at the table doe cut, he will give occasion of offence unto the company, as having transgressed the lawes of good manners, in so much that for his error he shall be at the least browbeaten, if not reprehended in wordes." When back in England Coryat took up the habit of eating with a fork, his friends had much amusement at his expense. In a caricature of the affected manners at the French court, much fun is made of courtiers' attempt to use a fork rather than their fingers, since, for lack of skills in handling it, food was always falling off on their plates and on the ground. As accustomed as they were to eating without forks, they must have been somewhat used to biting their fingers occasionally when eating in haste—Montaigne admitted as much. One can imagine the perplexity, if not the embarrassment and even intimidation, felt by northern Europeans on being confronted with this Italian splendor at table, fearful about how to proceed

---

146. Cited by Andrew Ladis, *Italian Renaissance Maiolica from Southern Collections* (Athens, Ga., 1989), p. 17.

to eat lest they reveal their barbaric ways. These northerners might have agreed with the German preacher who found Italian forks positively suspicious as a "diabolic luxury." In short, the expanding production of tableware was the necessary material concomitant for a revolution in human behavior.[147]

Another consumption habit generated by the accumulation of goods was collecting. Medieval princes, with their passion for displaying wealth as a symbol of power, collected gold and silver objects, jewels, reliquaries, and other luxury goods; and wealthy Italians did the same. In the course of the fifteenth century, however, Italian collections took on a different cast than medieval treasury hoards as the collecting instinct became informed by cultural values other than the traditional ones of wealth and religious piety. The humanists' interest in Roman culture gave rise to a flourishing market in antiquitics, including everything from coins, medals, and cameos to major pieces of sculpture; and the scientific and philosophic interests aroused the instinct to collect all those objects that filled up the virtuoso cabinet of curiosities in the sixteenth century. Such collections represented the humanist ideal of the universal man, with interests ranging from nature to art.

This new passion for collecting was itself an active force for generating demand for many new kinds of things, ranging from medals in imitation of ancient models to porcelain in the search for understanding the secrets of nature; and it was also directed to some of the very objects that now came into production for the first time—such as pictures, for instance, and other so-called artworks. Collecting, in short, followed the same process as consumption in general: an enlargement of the range of objects, refinement and specialization, and finally the reorganization of space into cabinets, studies, and galleries to accommodate it. The passion for collecting that was aroused in the Renaissance was itself a product of a new consumer mentality: it represented not just the objectification of cultural values but the rationalization of possessiveness in an expanding world of goods.

These Italian habits of spending cannot be explained away as the conspicuous expression of wealth, for many of these objects, such as glass and ceramics (both mentioned by Pontano), were in fact relatively

147. Richard A. Goldthwaite, "The Economic and Social World of Italian Renaissance Maiolica," *Renaissance Quarterly* 42 (1989), 24–27; Thomas Coryat, *Coryat's Crudities* (Glasgow, 1905), 1:236–37; the caricature is cited in Jean-Louis Flandrin, "Distinction through Taste," in *A History of Private Life*, vol. 3, ed. Roger Chartier (London, 1989), p. 269. Few forks are found in French inventories before the seventeenth century: Françoise Lehoux, *Le cadre de vie des médecins parisiens aux XVIe et XVII siècles* (Paris, 1976), pp. 305–6.

inexpensive; and their value seldom consisted in their cost. With the price of maiolica ranging from the equivalent of only 75 grams of silver for a large plate to somewhat less than 200 grams for the entire service of eighty-four pieces purchased by the Medici wife of Filippo Strozzi the Younger, Italians got much more for their money with ceramics than if they had melted down this bullion into plate—a value to be measured by taste and also by the etiquette imposed by the product on the ritual of dining. Likewise, the subordination of precious stones to the craftsmanship of the goldsmith reduced the cost of jewelry but yielded a final product more valued for those intangible qualities of skill and taste, just as the fall in the value of the stuffs used for clothing was much greater than the increased labor cost of the tailoring needed to satisfy new fashions. Most domestic furnishings, including paintings, cost little more than the value of labor.

The Medici palace represented one of the most splendid residences in fifteenth-century Italy, and the famous inventory of its contents made on the death of Lorenzo il Magnifico in 1492 reflects something of the new spending habits. The forms of conspicuous wealth associated with the princely treasuries in the north are less in evidence: there is little silver plate, and liturgical utensils and vestments in the chapel fill up less than three folio sides. Arms and armor are concentrated in the chamber of Lorenzo's son Piero and in the munitions rooms; and little was in evidence in the rest of the house. Most of the gold jewelry falls into the range of only 15 to 30 florins, and the most precious jewels are assessed at no more than the ancient cameos. The extraordinary collection of Chinese porcelain had a relatively modest monetary value. The most valuable items are antiquities, such as cameos and objects made out of semiprecious stones. The splendor that emanated from the contents of Italy's most magnificent household at the time was not in the intrinsic value of rare materials or even in market values.[148]

In the overall picture of luxury expenditures, in short, consumption demonstrated taste more conspicuously than wealth. The more intimate relation with objects sharpened one's appreciation of them for their craftsmanship apart from the inherent value of materials and generated that self-conscious refinement of a sense of taste that is one of the highest expressions of culture developed in Italy during this period. Perhaps, as is often said, there is no accounting for taste; but it is another

148. Cf. Wolfgang Liebenwein, *Studiolo: Die Entstehung eines Raumtyps und seine Entwicklung bis um 1600* (Berlin, 1977), pp. 70–83, who sees the model of Lorenzo's study in the collection of Charles V of France, but contrast what he has to say on pp. 42–44. The Medici inventory has been published by Giovanna Gaetà Bertelà and Marco Spallanzani, eds., *Libro d'inventario dei beni di Lorenzo il Magnifico* (Florence, 1992).

matter when taste, whatever that taste may be, is extended to new kinds of objects. What is taste, after all, but one way of transforming physical objects into high culture, thereby rationalizing the feeling of possessiveness, the sense of attachment to physical objects? And it was with taste that one established social credentials. These objects incorporated values other than sheer wealth: for a product as mundane as a maiolica plate, these values ranged from standards of personal comportment at table to the literary erudition displayed by its painted decoration. These were social values through which people sought to say something about themselves and to communicate that to others, thereby establishing their credentials as a new elite, one of wealth, to be sure, but also one of taste and refinement. As Sabba da Castiglione wrote in his chapter on household ornaments, musical instruments, sculpture, antiquities, medals, engravings, pictures, wall hangings all testify to the intelligence, civility, and manners of the owner.[149]

Splendor is one word Italians repeatedly used in talking about this phenomenon. The humanist Matteo Palmieri exalts splendor as the quality sought in all those things needed to enhance one's life with beauty ("per bellezza di vita"), including the house, its furnishings, and other appurtenances for living in private splendor ("nello splendido vivere de' privati cittadini").[150] Machiavelli observes that Italians eat and even sleep with greater splendor than other Europeans; and Pontano criticizes the French because they eat only to satisfy their gluttony and not to endow their lives with splendor. Another one of the five virtues associated with the spending of money in Pontano's scheme was, in fact, splendor. It is the complement of magnificence, being the logical extension of magnificence into the private world. Whereas magnificence is manifest in public architecture, splendor expresses itself in the elegance and refinement with which one lives his life within buildings; it therefore consists of household furnishings, everyday utensils, and ornaments of personal adornment as things that go with town houses as well as in the gardens that go along with villas in the countryside. The objects Pontano refers to are all of the traditional kind; in fact, he points to the famous gem collection of the Duke de Berry to illustrate his point. Nevertheless, Pontano gives this medieval tradition of courtly splendor a new life by emphasizing the moral quality of possessiveness itself, tempered of course by the humanist virtues of moderation and appropriateness. These things give pleasure and excite admiration

---

149. Sabba da Castiglione, *Ricordi overo ammaestramenti* (Venice, 1555), ch. 109.

150. Matteo Palmieri, *Della vita civile*, ed. Felice Battaglia (Bologna, 1944), pp. 154, 164.

because of their beauty; and this beauty consists not in utility and inherent value of materials but in rarity, variety, and craftsmanship. Pontano, in other words, endows possessiveness with both ethical and aesthetic qualities; and he organized behavior, or manners, around these possessions.[151]

The first stirrings of a new attitude toward possessions can thus be detected in Renaissance Italy. It was then that people entered into a new world of goods as they became more self-conscious about taste and extended taste throughout the material world to appropriate traditional things such as the town house, the rural villa, and the garden as well as furnishings. Moreover, they pushed manners and taste well beyond the confines of traditional material culture to arouse demand for new objects that simply had not existed earlier, from secular pictures complete with picture frames on the walls inside the home to glazed pottery on the dining room table—and many of these things were thereby elevated to the status of art for the first time. The Renaissance represents much more than just a change in style: it marked the very discovery of art and the imperial expansion of the realm of art into new worlds.

Consumption was thus a dynamic cultural process. The Italians' material world cannot be understood as just the embodiment of culture according to the dichotomous and static scheme of traditional anthropological analysis, which too often posits a culture "out there" apart from its material embodiment and ignores the dynamic and creative nature of changes in the things themselves. "Thick description" of the world of goods, patterned according to social or cultural structures, is not enough. For culture is, by its very nature, a process of emergence, development, and change in the search for, and the definition of, values; and consumption can be a vital part of this process. The consumption habits we have observed in Italy were, in fact, a dynamic for the generation of culture, a culture derived from material goods in an ongoing interactive process. It is in this sense that we can talk about a culture of an incipient consumption, about consumption as the supreme consummative act, or, even, about consumerism.[152]

RECENTLY, IN THE EFFORT TO GET AT THE ROOTS of one of the most characteristic features of our own times, much scholarship has been expended on pushing the history of consumerism back into the eighteenth century in France, England, and America and well into the sev-

151. Tateo, *Umanesimo etico*, pp. 171–77.

152. For a general critique of the study of consumption and a large-scale discussion of the theoretical issues, which contributed much to my views in this section, see Daniel Miller, *Material Culture and Mass Consumption* (Oxford, 1987).

enteenth century in Holland. The emerging picture of this early history reveals that the market for durable goods expanded as people from farther down the social scale bought more and cheaper goods; and the course of evolution in their spending habits curiously follows the same patterns uncovered in this general view of Italy from the fifteenth to the seventeenth century—a "great rebuilding" of the housing stock followed by the growth of demand for consumer durables and semidurables, especially in household furnishings and tableware. With the release of one of the most characteristic dynamics of the economic growth of the modern world, Italy appears to have anticipated—in yet another respect—general European developments.

The consumer-driven sector of the Italian economy during this period, however, did not take off as it later did in the north once demand began to well up from the lower ranks of society. In Italy the lower classes did not enter the market for household furnishings to the same extent as they later did in the north, although this subject has yet to be investigated. Inasmuch as many of these new consumer goods cost much less than traditional luxury objects, some of these things, such as painted pictures, found buyers correspondingly farther down in the social hierarchy. Inventories of more ordinary people from the fifteenth century onward document how their houses, too, slowly filled up with all kinds of durable goods. A writer of a book on practical household management published in mid-seventeenth-century Rome recognized that in fact there was a wider market for his services: in directing his discussion beyond princes and the rich to include artisans, he proffers them advice about furnishings and utensils, observing that all these things can be found in the secondhand market and at pawn banks and shops, where they cost much less.[153] Demand as it has been described here, however, was largely limited to luxury objects and too confined within a social structure where the enormous wealth of Italy was not widely enough distributed to permit expansion of the mass market for durable goods that began to open up in the eighteenth century.

The growth of consumerism in early modern Europe is not simply a matter of market expansion as measured on a quantitative scale. A veritable consumer culture also emerged in the conscious awareness of the economic potential of expanding consumer markets that surfaced both in government policies and in producer strategies. In Italy, however, such a culture was still inchoate. In the later sixteenth century the grand dukes of Tuscany anticipated mercantilist policy in their efforts to turn the Uffizi into a vast arts-and-crafts center for the production of

---

153. Antonio Adami, *Il novitiato del Maestro di casa* (Rome, 1657).

everything from sculpture and painting to pottery and scientific instruments with the objective of capturing the market for such luxury goods, but otherwise Italian governments seem not to have recognized the possibility of exploiting growing consumer demand to promote economic development. They did not anticipate the well-articulated economic policies developed by the northern European states in the course of the seventeenth century. The French monarchy took one approach in its effort to capture a new market for itself by establishing monopoly enterprises for production of luxury goods and at the same time promoting the court at Versailles as a consumer model for its products; and in the end it succeeded in setting high fashion throughout Europe. England instead went the other way in pursuing a policy to free markets by abandoning sumptuary legislation and monopoly privileges, encouraging new industries, and promoting international trade in consumer goods; and in the end it built up nothing less than a worldwide empire.[154]

Italian artisans, of course, were not blind to the development of new market strategies. In engendering a proliferation of objects and an increase of their variety—indeed, redefining the very concept of luxury—the new dynamic that came into play in the Italian marketplace opened up incomparable opportunities for producers—from painters, sculptors, and architects to modest potters; and they took the initiative with new ideas to shape taste and so arouse demand yet further, thereby getting a certain control over demand. This is part of the dynamic behind the expanded production that created the Renaissance world of goods. Vasari incorporated these new market conditions in his concept of artistic progress, which he saw as arising out of the artist's struggle for a livelihood, the competition among artists, and the consequent sharpening of their critical faculties. The rise of the status of the artist and the extraordinary vitality of stylistic developments are marks of the success some producers had in seizing the initiative in the market for consumer goods to generate demand. Nevertheless, these strategies were confined to the luxury market. It is perhaps significant that Mancini's manual for the dilettante consumer of paintings (written at the beginning of the seventeenth century) never found a publisher. Likewise, the genre of practical manuals directed to guide consumers who wanted to build their own house through the market maze of artisans and prices, of the kind that began to proliferate in France at the end of the seventeenth century, never flourished in Italy.[155]

154. Joan Thirsk, *Economic Policy and Projects: The Development of a Consumer Society in Early Modern England* (Oxford, 1978).

155. For France, see Richard Cleary, "Romancing the Tome; or an Academician's Pursuit of a Popular Audience in Eighteenth-Century France," *Journal of the Society of*

The "consumer revolution" came, finally, in the eighteenth century when producers themselves—like Wedgwood in England—seized the initiative to take more control of mass demand: the new merchandizing and advertising techniques they developed to pull more people into the market aroused the insatiable appetite for goods that is the dynamic behind modern economic growth. Intellectuals, too, were stimulated by a more conscious awareness of the phenomenon of consumerism than ever surfaced in Italy. In England the spectacle of the expanding world of goods at first alarmed moralists, who feared the threat to social and political order posed by the arousal of what seemed to be a universal desire for luxury. Economic arguments, however, anticipated by Mandeville and Defoe eventually won out: luxury was defended on the grounds that it encouraged trade, redistributed wealth, and in the end strengthened the nation.

With an optimism characteristic of the age, some of these thinkers went beyond economic arguments to suggest something of the social and moral implications of the new relation between people and things, thus defining—finally—the culture of consumption. For David Hume the appreciation of craftsmanship apart from inherent value of materials heightens the gratification of the senses and hence leads to refinement in taste and in the arts generally; and likewise for Adam Smith, increasing the variety of commodities expands the range of people's sensibilities and opens up new possibilities for their development. These thinkers regarded consumption as the engine for the advancement of civilization, not the nemesis today's social critics like to make of it.[156]

Today the consumer instinct is taken for granted: the challenge to producers is to introduce new products, reduce prices, and change fashion, while governments trying to regulate consumer-oriented economies direct policy to control how much wealth is to be released for private spending to maintain market activity at the desired level. The result is a world of goods constantly in flux, whose very materiality is threatened by a restless drive toward what Schumpeter called "cre-

*Architectural Historians* 48 (1989), 139–49. Adami's *Novitiato* is a book on practical household management written for princes and private persons including even artisans.

156. On the consumer revolution, see Thirsk, *Economic Policy and Projects*; Neil McKendrick et al., *The Birth of a Consumer Society: The Commercialization of Eighteenth-Century England* (London, 1982); Daniel Roche, *La culture des apparences: Une histoire du vêtement, XVIIe–XVIIIe siècle* (Paris, 1989); and, for a more tentative comment on Venice, Fritz Schmidt, "Zur Genese kapitalistischer Konsumformen im Venedig der frühen Neuzeit," in *Stadtgeschichte als Zivilisationsgeschichte: Beiträge zum Wandel städtischer Wirtschafts-, Lebens- und Wahrnehmungsweisen*, ed. Jürgen Reulecke (Essen, 1990), pp. 23–40. On the concern with luxury in England, see John Sekora, *Luxury: The Concept in Western Thought, Eden to Smollett* (Baltimore, 1977).

ative destruction." If, on the one hand, we decry what this consumerism has developed into in our own times, with its commodity culture of planned obsolescence, throwaway goods, and fashion-ridden boutiques, on the other hand we have enshrined its very spirit in our great museums. These veritable temples to the consumption habits of the past, where we worship as art one of the dynamics that gives life to the economic system of the West, mark the supreme achievement of capitalism.

THE DEVELOPMENT OF A SENSE OF CIVILITY and a consciousness of manners has been a prominent theme in the history of early modern Europe; but, except for Werner Sombart's generally neglected study of luxury, little attention has been paid to the material embodiment of these new cultural values. Apart from comment on the elaboration of furnishings and refinement of interior space that have been related to a keener desire for privacy, the history of European manners and taste, from the precocious work of Norbert Elias to the recent collaborative effort organized by Philippe Ariès, has been seen, curiously, as behavior completely disembodied from material culture.[157] Moreover, these histories have largely left Italy out of the picture altogether, even though from at least as far back as Burckhardt Italy has generally been regarded as the first step in the history of this civilizing process. Elias opens his study with Erasmus's well-known treatise on the behavior of children and then jumps to the seventeenth century, giving special prominence to the formation of a hierarchical social order centering on the court of Louis XIV; and the French school makes only passing reference to translation of the more obvious Italian treatises. Perhaps because of their northern European perspective and hence their focus on the post-Renaissance period, these scholars take Baroque luxury and the expanding world of goods for granted. In any case, as Fernand Braudel observed, writing about "Italy outside of Italy" in the early modern period, a history of the diffusion of Italian culture abroad has yet to be written.[158] Such a history will have to deal with the Renaissance world of goods as at once something a good deal more and something somewhat less than the high art that won over the rest of Europe and has ever since monopolized the attention of historians of culture.

157. See the collection of articles, with comments by Ariès and Roger Chartier, in *A History of Private Life*, vol. 3, especially those by Jacques Revel on civility and Jean-Louis Flandrin on taste (only the contribution by Orest Ranum, on intimacy, takes cognizance of the material world). Chartier comments on manners in his *Culture Uses of Print in Early Modern France* (Princeton, 1987), ch. 3.

158. In *Storia d'Italia*, vol. 2, pt. 2 (1974), p. 2145.

In this perspective we can, in Burckhardtian fashion, locate yet another beginning of the modern world in Renaissance Italy. To whatever extent the Renaissance was or was not a period of "rebirth," the new demand signaled a sharp break with past consumer behavior and heralded the advent of one of the most characteristic features of modern life—the culture of consumerism. The ongoing, interactive process of the generation of culture through consumption quickened its pace perceptibly. The relatively stagnant medieval world of goods was stirred up and transformed by a new dynamic for expansion and change, for invention and refinement; and new ideas, values, attitudes, habits of behavior, and taste worked themselves out in the material world. This new culture was not just inextricably tied up with things: it was generated by things. The new spending habits thus brought the consumer into a dynamic and creative relation with things. People entered a realm where possessions become an objectification of self for the first time—a step that was to have enormous implications for the subsequent history of the West.

It has always somewhat puzzled scholars that, ironically, the one subject Burckhardt—a founder of the history of Italian Renaissance art and a historian with an anthropological bent of mind—did not include in his sweeping survey of the civilization of the Renaissance in Italy is, in fact, art. When finally he wrote his history of Italian art, the subject remained totally disembodied from the context he had so comprehensively laid out in his earlier book. Had he pursued his own argument to its logical conclusion, however, pushing on from the Italians' discovery of the world and the discovery of man to consider also their discovery of things, he might have found at least one way to formulate an economics and sociology of Italian art and so bring art into his scheme. If, as Burckhardt would have it, the Renaissance saw the development of the individual and the discovery of what he called "the full, whole nature of man," this happened largely because man attached himself in a dynamic and creative way to things, to material possessions; and with the discovery of things modern civilization was born, for man embarked on the adventure of creating that dynamic world of goods in which he has found his characteristic identity. In this enterprise his highest quest has been the elevation of things into a spiritual realm, and we celebrate his success—and the very essence of our civilization—in today's temples of art.

# Index

Abisola, 24

Adami, Antonio, 251, 253n

Aethelbert, king of Kent, 152

Alberti, Leon Battista: on architecture, 133–34, 190, 198, 215, 219, 220, 222, 223; on cities, 183, 184, 185; on furnishings, 224, 225, 230; on households, 228; on painting, 145, 146; on villas, 217; on wealth, 206, 208, 210–11

Alberti chapel, 122

Albi, order of, 88

Alghensi Canons, 93

Altarpiece. See Panel painting, religious

Altars, 133–34; private, 121–22. See also Panel painting, religious

America, and beginnings of consumerism, 250

Amsterdam, 17, 60, 63

Ancona, 41

Andrea del Sarto, 229, 244

Angelico, Fra, 230

Angevins, in Naples, 29

Anonymo d'Utopia, 25

Antonino, Saint, 128

Aragonese, in Naples, 29–30

Architecture: and cities, 178–92, 219–20; and Italian consumption model, 213–24. See also under Church

Arezzo, 37

Ariès, Philippe, 254

Aristocracy, See Elites of Italy

Aristotle, 75, 206, 207, 208, 219

Armenini, G. B., 143

Arms: and feudal consumption model, 153; and Italian consumption model, 162–63

Art. See also Architecture; Liturgical apparatus; Mural painting; Painting in Italy; Panel painting

—Christian: cost of, 61; demand for, 70–71; and imagery, 76–81; and material culture, 70, 71

—in Italy: civic, 178–92; definition of, 1–2, 5–6, 26, 145–46, 181, 245, 252; demand for, 1–2; markets for, 6, 42, 43; as material culture, 1–2, 6; social context of, 6

Artists in Italy, status of, 145–46. See also Producers

Arundel and Surrey, Earl of, 35

Assisi, 114, 135

Augsburg, 47, 192

Augustinian (Austin) Canons, 88, 93

Augustinian (Austin) Friars, 89, 92–93, 102

Avignon, 19, 30, 50

Bacchiacca, 229

Baptisteries, 73, 179

Barbadori family, 51, 123

Barbarigo, Andrea, 51

Barbieri, Gino, 210

Barcelona, 29

Bardi chapel, 122

Barnabites, 96

Baron, Hans, 206

Bartolini, Leonardo, 124

Bassano family, 44, 142

Beatis, Antonio de, 164, 203, 242

Bellini, Giovanni, 129

Benedetto da Maiano, 229

Benedictines, 90

Bentivoglio, Giovanni II, 223

Berengo, Marino, 193

# Index

# Index

Martin V, 221
Massa Marittima, 180
*masserizia,* 210–11, 230
Masses, commemorative, 108–9, 121–22
Material culture: and art, 1–3; of the
church, 1–2, 7, 70, 72, 129–40. *See also*
Consumption model; Liturgical apparatus
Medici family: building by, 222; chapel
of, 122; and coat of arms, 168, 169;
collections of, 244; company of, 34,
64; Cosimo, 216, 221, 236; Cosimo I,
186–87, 245; court of, 172, 175, 197;
and court crafts, 251; Giovanni di Bicci, 51, 225; government by, 48, 56, 57,
170, 191; inventories of, 162, 225–26,
248; Lorenzo, 36, 163, 188, 222, 223,
230, 248; palace of, 58, 62, 124, 169,
216, 224, 232, 235–36, 237; Piero, 138,
248
Mendicant orders, 121; and art, 77–78;
and confraternities, 115–16; and institutional proliferation, 88–91; and institutional reform, 91–93. *See also names
of specific orders*
Michelangelo, 145, 148, 217, 230
Milan: churches of, 133, 137; and civic
art, 183; economy of, 18, 35, 39, 41;
and Italian economic system, 21, 23;
princely building in, 184; and religious
institutions, 89, 117; Spanish domination of, 31, 56, 175, 198; and urbanization, 100. *See also* Lombardy
Miller, Daniel, 3
Minims of San Francesco di Paolo, 92, 94
Monasticism: and cities, 90; institutional
proliferation, 87–88, 93. *See also names
of specific orders*
Montaigne, Michel de, 163, 166, 240,
246
Monti di Pietà, 38, 39, 53, 121
Mora, Domenico, 167
Morelli, Giovanni, 144, 205; Lorenzo,
230
Moryson, Fynes, 166, 174, 198, 240, 242,
246
Mural painting, 77–78, 139–40;
religious, 80, 114, 141; secular, 171,
216
Music, social aspects of, 168, 198, 240

Naples: as art market, 43, 106, 218;
churches of, 132; court at, 175, 197;
economy of, 39, 66; growth of, 101;
invasions of, 29; and Italian economic
system, 17, 21, 23–24, 51, 67; nobility
of, 195, 198, 218; private wealth in, 36,
49, 55; Spanish domination of, 31, 52,
56
Narni, 135
Near East, and Italian economic system,
13–20 passim, 27, 63. *See also* Ottoman Empire
Neri di Bicci, 47, 82
Nicholas V, 185, 220
Nobility, ideas about, 177, 192–204. *See
also* Elites of Italy
Norcia, 118
Nosadella (G. F. Bizzi), 143
Nunneries. *See* Women
Nuremberg, 47, 133

Observant movement, 91–95, 102
Olivetans, 90, 93
Oratorians of Saint Philip Neri, 96
Orders, military, 88
Orphanages, as deposit institutions, 38
Orvieto, 216
Ottoman Empire, and Italian economic
system, 15, 17, 18, 19, 20, 30, 33
Ottonian Emperors, 29

Paatze, W. and E., 104
Padua, 41, 170, 198, 240
Painting in Italy: communal, 141–42;
market potential of, 138–39; and pictorial culture, 140–48, 244; religious,
140–41, 147–48; schools of, 19, 42. *See
also* Art; Mural painting; Panel painting
Palaces: chapels in, 124–25; and consumption model, 213; cost of, 61–62;
life within, 237–40; private, 190–92,
216–17, 218; spatial reorganization of,
234–36. *See also* Architecture; Household
Paleotti, Bishop, 147
Palermo, 39
Palladio, 44, 125
Pallavicino, Gianlodovico, 187
Pallavicino, Giulio, 59, 165, 239

# Index